Think tanks across nations

MANCHESTER
UNIVERSITY PRESS

Think tanks across nations

A comparative approach

edited by
**Diane Stone, Andrew Denham
and Mark Garnett**

Manchester University Press
Manchester and New York
distributed exclusively in the USA by St. Martin's Press

Published by Manchester University Press
Oxford Road, Manchester M13 9NR, UK
and Room 400, 175 Fifth Avenue, New York, NY 10010, USA

Distributed exclusively in the USA by
St. Martin's Press, Inc., 175 Fifth Avenue, New York,
NY 10010, USA

Distributed exclusively in Canada by
UBC Press, University of British Columbia, 6344 Memorial Road,
Vancouver, BC, Canada V6T 1Z2

British Library Cataloguing-in-Publication Data
A catalogue record for this book is available from the British Library

Library of Congress Cataloging-in-Publication Data applied for

ISBN 0 7190 5054 5 *hardback*

First published 1998

05 04 03 02 01 00 99 98   10 9 8 7 6 5 4 3 2 1

Typeset in Sabon with News Gothic
by Northern Phototypesetting Co. Ltd, Bolton
Printed in Great Britain
by Bookcraft (Bath) Ltd, Midsomer Norton

Contents

List of figures and tables   *page* vii

List of contributors   viii

Acknowledgements   xi

List of abbreviations   xii

Introduction: think tanks, policy advice and governance   1
Diane Stone and Mark Garnett

1 Think tanks, British politics and the 'climate of opinion'   21
Andrew Denham and Mark Garnett

2 French think tanks in comparative perspective   42
Catherine Fieschi and John Gaffney

3 Think tanks, advocacy coalitions and policy change: the Italian case   59
Claudio M. Radaelli and Alberto P. Martini

4 Think tanks in Germany   82
Winand Gellner

5 Think tanks in the United States   107
Donald E. Abelson

6 A quarter century of Canadian think tanks: evolving institutions, conditions and strategies   127
Evert A. Lindquist

7 The development and discourse of Australian think tanks   145
Diane Stone

8 **Think tanks and intellectual participation in Malaysian
   discourses of development**   166
   Su-ming Khoo

9 **Think tanks in Japan: towards a more democratic society**   188
   Makiko Ueno

10 **Russian think tanks, 1956–1996**   202
   Mark Sandle

   Conclusion: ideas and influence   223
   William Wallace

   Index   231

Figures and tables

Figures

4.1	Preferred sources for research	page 96
4.2	Importance of German think tanks	97
4.3	To what extent do the publications of and contact with the following institutes influence your parliamentary work?	99

Tables

1.1	British think tanks	page 22
2.1	Select sample of French think tanks	54
3.1	Italian think tanks	66
4.1	Personnel and revenues of German think tanks in 1992 (1991)	87
4.2	Research institutes: year of foundation, location and legal status	90
4.3	Preferred sources of information according to the parliamentarians' main fields of activity	101
4.4	Significance of individual research institutes for advocacy coalitions (means)	103
5.1	A selected profile of American think tanks	116
6.1	Selected Canadian policy think tanks	131
7.1	Australian think tanks	149
8.1	Malaysian think tanks	169
9.1	Japanese think tanks reference guide	197
10.1	Selected profile of Russian think tanks	217

Contributors

Donald E. Abelson is an Assistant Professor in the Department of Political Science, University of Western Ontario, where he teaches courses on American domestic and foreign policy. He has published in the *Canadian Review of American Studies* and with Christine M. Carberry in the *Presidential Studies Quarterly*. He is also the author of *American Think Tanks and their Role in U.S. Foreign Policy* (Macmillan and St Martin's Press, 1996). He is currently examining the influence of policy experts serving on policy taskforces during, and transition teams following, American presidential elections.

Andrew Denham is Lecturer in Politics, University of Nottingham. He is the author of *Think-Tanks of the New Right* (Dartmouth, 1996), for which he received the Walter Bagehot Prize for 'Best Thesis in Government and Public Administration' from the (UK) Political Studies Association in 1994, and articles and papers on aspects of contemporary British Conservatism. His second book, *British Think Tanks and the Climate of Opinion* (with Mark Garnett), will be published by UCL Press in 1998.

Catherine Fieschi is a Lecturer in European Politics in the School of European Studies at Aston University and is currently completing her doctoral thesis in political science for McGill University, Canada. Her research is in the field of comparative politics and more particularly on the evolution of extreme right ideologies and patterns of mobilization and change in France and Italy.

John Gaffney is Professor of French and European Politics at Keele University. He is the author or editor of a dozen books, most recently *Political Parties and the European Union* (Routledge, 1997) and *French Presidentialism and the Election of 1995* (co-ed. Lorna Milne, Ashgate, 1997). He is currently writing a book on political leadership.

Mark Garnett is a political researcher. He has taught politics at the Universities of Durham, Bristol and Exeter. He is the author of *Principles and Politics in Contemporary Britain* (Longman, 1996) and co-author (with

Ian Gilmour) of *Whatever Happened to the Tories?* (Fourth Estate, 1997). With Andrew Denham, he is the co-author of several articles on think tanks and of the book *British Think-Tanks and the Climate of Opinion* (UCL Press, forthcoming, 1998).

Winand Gellner has worked at the University of Trier and is now Professor in the Department of Political Science, University of Passau and Lecturer, University of Miami, Dolibois European Centre, Luxembourg. He has published in *Presidential Studies Quarterly* and *Zeitschrift fur Parlaments-fragen* and two books: *Ideenagenturen fur Politik und Offentlichkeit: Think Tanks in den USA und in Deutschland* (Westdeutscher Verlag, 1995) and *Umbruch und Wandel in westeuropaischen Parteiensystemen* (M. Lang, 1995 with Hans-Joachim Veen). His research interests also include political communication, interest groups, the Internet and democracy.

Su-ming Khoo is a Lecturer in the Department of Sociology, University College Cork. She has also taught in the Department of Sociology and Social Policy, Queen's University, Belfast, where she is completing a doctoral dissertation on intellectual participation and the discourse of development in Malaysia. Her research interests also include NGOs, democratization, nationalism and Islamic revival.

Evert A. Lindquist is an Associate Professor in the Department of Political Science, University of Toronto. He is currently Chair of the Research Committee of the Institute of Public Administration in Canada. He has published numerous chapters in edited anthologies including 'Confronting Globalization and Governance Challenges: The Canadian Think Tanks and the Asia-Pacific Region' in John W. Langford and Lorne Brownsey, *Think Tanks and Governance in the Asia-Pacific Region* (Institute for Research on Public Policy, 1991) and 'Balancing Relevance and Integrity: Think Tanks and Canada's Asia-Pacific Policy Community' in Stephen Brooks and Alain-G. Gagnon, *The Political Influence of Ideas: Policy Communities and the Social Sciences* (Praeger, 1994), as well as in journals such as *Canadian Public Administration*. Additional research and publication has focused on the Canadian budgetary process and on transition teams and government succession.

Alberto P. Martini is a Senior Research Fellow at the Urban Institute in Washington DC where he has done research on social policy and evaluation. Recently, he has published in the *Policy Studies Journal* and in *Statistics in Transition*.

Claudio M. Radaelli is a Lecturer in Comparative Public Policy in the Department of European Studies, University of Bradford. He has published on aspects of European public policy and theoretical policy analysis in *Comparative Political Studies*, the *Journal of European Public Policy* and the *Journal of Public Policy and Evaluation*, while his book *The Politics of Corporate Taxation in the European Union: Knowledge and Inter-*

national Policy Agendas was published by Routledge in 1997. He is completing a book on *Technocracy in the European Union Policy Process* (Longman, 1998).

Mark Sandle is a Senior Lecturer in Russian and Soviet History, De Montfort University. He conducts research into the intelligentsia and ideology in the post-Stalin era. His publications include articles in *Europe Asia Studies* and with Georgii Shakhnazarov in *Studies in East European Thought*. His book *A Short History of Soviet Socialism* will be published by UCL Press in 1998.

Diane Stone is an Economic and Social Research Council Fellow and Lecturer, Department of Politics and International Studies, University of Warwick. She has published articles in *West European Politics* and *Policy and Politics*, and a book *Capturing the Political Imagination: Think Tanks and the Policy Process* (Frank Cass, 1996). She is currently working on a book on *Ideas, Interests and Identity: Think Tanks in Southeast Asia*. Additional research interests focus on higher education policy, globalization and policy studies, and non-state actors.

Makiko Ueno received her engineering degree from the University of Tokyo. Currently, she is a Research Fellow at a leading American think tank, the Urban Institute in Washington DC. Her research has specialized in housing policy, the US non-profit sector and think tanks. One recent publication, co-edited with Jeffrey Telgarsky, is *Think Tanks in a Democratic Society: An Alternative Voice* (Urban Institute, 1996).

William Wallace (Lord Wallace of Saltaire) is a Reader in International Relations at the London School of Economics and Political Science. In the House of Lords he speaks for the Liberal Democrats on foreign affairs and defence questions. From 1978 to 1990, he was Director of Studies at the Royal Institute of International Affairs in London. His current research interests include the transformation of European order after 1989, the implications of the enlargement to Eastern Europe for European Union and NATO, the impact of integration on the European nation-state, and US–European relations in the 1980s and 1990s. Books include *Regional Integration: The West European Experience* (Brookings, 1994) and *Policy-making in the European Union* (Oxford University Press, 1996, with Helen Wallace and others).

Acknowledgements

Several chapters in this volume were first presented to the 1995, 1996 and 1997 annual conferences of the Political Studies Association (PSA) at the Universities of York, Glasgow and Ulster respectively. We are very grateful to those who participated in the panels on 'Think Tanks in Comparative Perspective' on each occasion. In addition, we wish to acknowledge the support of the British Academy Conference Fund for the award of a travel grant to bring Donald Abelson and Evert Lindquist to the Glasgow PSA Conference in 1996; the British Academy for the award of a Social Sciences Research Award on 'Think Tanks and British Politics' to Andrew Denham; and the Economic and Social Research Council (ESRC) for providing assistance to Diane Stone in the form of a research fellowship (ref: H52427008094).

Among the many individuals who have assisted us in this enterprise, we should like to thank Richard Purslow for his early enthusiasm for the project and contracting the book to MUP, Nicola Viinikka for her advice and support and Rachel Armstrong, Rebecca Crum, Gemma Marren and Pippa Kenyon for their assistance and cheerfulness throughout. Anne Hegerty has been a careful and diligent proofreader. William Wallace was strongly supportive from the outset, provided sound advice at critical moments and agreed to write the conclusion among the many other demands on his time. Erik Jones provided invaluable assistance with IT, without which further delays in completion and delivery of the manuscript would have been inevitable. Finally, we wish to thank the members of our respective families to whom this book is affectionately dedicated.

DS, AD, MG

Abbreviations

ABIM	Angkatan Belia Islam Malaysia
ADELS	Association pour la Démocratie et l'Education Locale et Sociale (France)
ADIPA	Association for Development Research and Training Institutes for the Asia-Pacific
AEI	American Enterprise Institute (USA)
AIIA	Australian Institute of International Affairs
AILES	Autogestion Initiative Locale et Economie Sociale (France)
AIPP	Australian Institute of Public Policy
ALP	Australian Labor Party
AREL	Agenzia di Ricerche e Legislazione (Italy)
ARES	Action pour le Renouveau Socialiste (France)
ASEAN	Association of Southeast Asian Nations
ASI	Adam Smith Institute (Britain)
BN	Barisan Nasional (Malaysia)
CC	Central Committee (Russia)
CCF	Chicago Civic Federation (USA)
CCSD	Canadian Council on Social Development
CDU	Christlich Demokratische Union (Germany)
CED	Committee for Economic Development (USA)
CEDA	Committee for the Economic Development of Australia
CEPR	Centre for Economic Policy Research (Britain)
CER	Centro Europa Ricerche (Italy)
CFDT	Confédération Française Démocratique du Travail (France)
CFR	Council on Foreign Relations (USA)
CIDA	Canadian International Development Agency
CIEP	Canadian Institute for Economic Policy
CIS	Centre for Independent Studies (Australia)
CM	Cabinets Ministériels (France)
CNRS	Centre National de la Recherche Scientifique (France)

COHA	Council on Hemispheric Affairs (USA)
CPD	Committee on the Present Danger
CPR	Centre for Policy Research (Malaysia)
CPRN	Canadian Policy Research Networks
CPRS	Central Policy Review Staff (Britain)
CPS	Centre for Policy Studies (Britain)
CPSU	Communist Party of the Soviet Union (Russia)
CSA	Conseil Scientifique de l'Audio-visuel (France)
CSCAP	Council for Security Co-operation in Asia-Pacific
CSIS	Centre for Strategic and International Studies (USA)
CSSP	Centre for Studies in Social Policy (Britain)
CSU	Christlich Soziale Union (Germany)
CTF	Canadian Tax Foundation
CWF	Canada West Foundation
DEA	Department of Economic Affairs (Britain)
DFG	Deutsche Forschungsgemeinschaft (Germany)
DGAP	Deutsche Gesellschaft für Auswärtige Politik (Germany)
DIW	Deutsches Institut für Wirtschaftsforschung (Germany)
EAC	Economic Advisory Council (Britain)
EAEC	East Asian Economic Caucus
EAEG	East Asian Economic Grouping
ECC	Economic Council of Canada
EKO	Institute of Economics and Industrial Organization (Russia)
ENA	Ecole Normale d'Administration (France)
EPAC	Economic Planning Advisory Council (Australia)
EU	European Union
FDP	Freie Democratische Partei Deutschlands (Germany)
FES	Friedrich Ebert Stiftung (Germany)
FNS	Friedrich Naumann Stiftung (Germany)
GRECE	Groupe de Recherche et d'Etude pour la Civilisation Européene (France)
HWWA	Hamburgisches Weld-Wirtschafts-Archiv (Germany)
IAC	Industries Assistance Commission (Australia)
ICARE	Initiatives de Citoyenneté Active en Réseaux (France)
IDS	Institute of Development Studies (Malaysia)
IEA	Institute of Economic Affairs (Britain)
IEEP	Institute for European Environment Policy
IFO	Information und Forschung (Germany)
IFS	Institute for Fiscal Studies (Britain)
IW	Institut für Weltwirtschaft (Germany)
IIE	Institute for International Economics (USA)
IISS	International Institute for Strategic Studies (Britain)
IKD	Institut Kajian Dasar (Malaysia)

IKIM	Institut Kefahaman Islam Malaysia
IMEMO	Institute of the World Economy and International Relations (Russia)
IMF	International Monetary Fund
INMIND	Institute of Mind Analysis (Malaysia)
INSAP	Institute of Strategic Analysis and Planning (Malaysia)
INSEE	Institut National de Statistiques et d'Études Économiques (France)
IPA	Institute of Public Affairs (Australia)
IPPR	Institute for Public Policy Research (Britain)
IRPP	Insitute for Research on Public Policy (Canada)
IRS	Instituto per la Ricerca Sociale (Italy)
ISEAS	Institute for Southeast Asian Studies (Singapore)
ISIS	Institute of Strategic and International Studies (Malaysia)
ISKAN	Institute for the Study of the USA and Canada (Russia)
ISS	Institute of Sociological Studies (Russia)
IW	Institut der Deutschen Wirtschaft (Germany)
IWG	Institut für Wirtschaft und Gesellschaft (Germany)
IWH	Institut für empirische Wirtschaftsforschung Halle (Germany)
KAS	Konrad Adenauer Stiftung (Germany)
LPA	Liberal Party of Australia
LUTH	Lembaga Urusan Tabung Haji (Malaysia)
MCA	Malaysian Chinese Association
MIC	Malayan Indian Congress
MIER	Malaysian Institute of Economic Research
MOE	Ministry of Education (Japan)
MRI	Mitsubishi Research Institute (Japan)
MSRC	Malaysian Strategic Research Centre
NBER	National Bureau of Economic Research (USA)
NCF	National Civic Federation (USA)
NECC	National Economic Consultative Committee (Malaysia)
NEDC	National Economic Development Council (Britain)
NEP	New Economic Policy (Malaysia)
NIESR	National Institute of Economic and Social Research (Britain)
NIRA	National Institute for Research Advancement (Japan)
NGO	non-governmental organization
OECD	Organization for Economic Cooperation and Development
PAS	Parti Islam Se-Malaysia
PBS	Parti Bersatu Sabah (Malaysia)
PEP	Political and Economic Planning (Britain)
PPI	Progressive Policy Institute (USA)

PSI	Policy Studies Institute (Britain)
PSU	Parti Socialiste Unitié (France)
RAU	Russian-American University (Corporation) (Russia)
RFF	Resources For the Future (USA)
RIIA	Royal Institute of International Affairs (Britain)
RPR	Rassemblement pour la Republique (France)
RWI	Rheinisch-Westfälisches Institut für Wirtschaftsforschung (Germany)
SAU	Social Affairs Unit (Britain)
SDI	Strategic Defense Initiative (USA); Sarawak Development Institute (Malaysia)
SDP	Social Democratic Party (Britain)
SMF	Social Market Foundation (Britain)
SOVNA-PECC	National Committee for Economic Cooperation on the Asia-Pacific (Russia)
SPD	Sozialdemokratische Partei Deutschland (Germany)
SWP	Stiftung Wissenschaft und Politik (Germany)
TIER	Taiwan Institute of Economic Research
UDF	Union pour la Démocratie Française (France)
UMNO	United Malays Nationalist Organization
VtsIOM	All-Russian Centre for Public Opinion Research
WETtank	Women's Economic Think Tank (Australia)
WRI	World Resources Institute (USA)
WSI	Wirtschafts- und Sozialwissenschaftliches Institut (Germany)
WZB	Wissenschaftszentrum Berlin (Germany)

Think tanks, policy advice and governance

Think tanks are increasingly prominent actors in the policy processes of many countries. Until recently, policy research institutes of this kind have been accorded little scholarly investigation. One possible reason for this neglect is the difficulty of defining and categorizing such bodies (see below). Although a few book-length studies have appeared (for example, Cockett, 1994; Denham, 1996; Ricci, 1993; Smith, 1991; Weiss, 1992) the field is dominated by popular or journalistic accounts of the largest and best-known institutes. As in other areas of political science, most of the literature is American, and these discussions tend only to discuss developments in the USA. Comparative analysis of these bodies, by contrast, has been very limited in scope (Stone, 1996). This volume is intended as a corrective to the predominant focus on Anglo-American think tanks by bringing to attention the extent of think tank development in countries as diverse as Malaysia, Russia, Japan and Italy, amongst others. The approach is to explore the think tank phenomenon in several countries and enhance our knowledge of both think tanks and the extent of their involvement in the policy process.

Each chapter begins with an empirical and historical analysis of developments of the range of think tanks within a country in order to gain insight into their diverse forms and behaviours. Different institutional and cultural environments affect think tank modes of operation and their capacity or opportunity for policy input and influence. With generous foundation and corporate support, as well as government contract research opportunities, the proliferation of think tanks has been especially noticeable in the USA where the constitutional architecture and weak party system are said to provide a peculiarly conducive environment for think tanks to emerge and interact with government. Over 1,200 think tanks have emerged in the USA since 1945 (Hellebust, 1997), while they are relatively few in number in European countries. American analysts often argue that the US system is more open, pluralistic and permeable than European political systems. They often assume (see, for example, Polsby, 1983; Weaver, 1989) that there are fewer

opportunities for think tanks to enter the policy fray in Europe and elsewhere due to factors such as stronger party systems, corporatist modes of
decision-making, strong and relatively closed bureaucracies, or weak philanthropic sectors. Such assumptions about the 'exceptionalism' of American
political structures and institutions should not be taken entirely at face value.
Many of the German foundations, for instance, have been established by
political parties or have strong ties to the *Länder*, but other bodies have also
been established as politically independent, non-profit research organizations. Some of the German institutes have grown to such a large size as to
rival some of the major American institutes. In short, there are interesting
questions to ask, which this volume addresses, about the extent of think tank
activity in one country compared to another, why they have developed dif-
ferently, and the relative status or credibility of these organizations in different countries.

Studying think tanks cross-nationally may shed light on how government
institutions and political actors interpret and respond to political problems.
It is possible to explore the extent to which political parties, bureaucracies
and interest groups in different systems have established formal and informal ties with think tanks, not only because they are a source of policy ideas
and innovation, but also because think tanks are symbolic of intellectual
authority that can be used to legitimize and bolster prior policy positions.
Apart from specific trends in different countries, the activities of think tanks
can also help to identify general trends in world politics: for example, is
think tank growth indicative of a need for more information, analysis and
advice as economies and societies become more complex? Does the greater
attention that think tanks attract reflect a politicization of knowledge? Is the
international spread of think tanks and development of think tank networks
symptomatic of globalization and the presence of a transnational community
of intellectuals and experts? Or do think tanks emerge in response to pressures for democratization?

Defining 'think tank'

Think tanks are a remarkably diverse groups of organizations. They vary
considerably in size, structure, policy area and political significance. Some
organizations at least aspire to function on a 'non-partisan' or 'non-ideological' basis and claim to adopt a 'scientific' or technical approach to social and
economic problems. Other organizations discussed in this volume are
overtly partisan or ideologically motivated (although these are more prominent in English speaking countries than in Italy, Malaysia or Japan). Some
think tanks are 'academic' in style, focused on research, geared to university
interests and to building the knowledge base of society; others are more rou-

tinely engaged in advocacy and the marketing of ideas whether in simplified policy-relevant form or in soundbites for the media. Specialization is another characteristic of think tanks in a number of countries. There are environmental think tanks (World Resources Institute (WRI) in the USA), regionally focused operations (such as the Institute for Southeast Asian Studies (ISEAS) in Singapore) as well as economic policy think tanks (for example, the Institute for International Economics (IIE) in Washington DC). Additionally, there are numerous foreign policy institutes worldwide (Wallace, 1994) and, in fewer numbers, think tanks addressing the concerns of specific groups in society, such as the feminist WETtank in Australia.

As a consequence of the diversity of style, activity and focus of these organizations, alongside cultural variations in comprehending the role of these organizations, there are considerable difficulties in defining 'think tank' (see Denham and Garnett, 1996). As the chapters on France, Italy and Britain indicate, significant dilemmas are created by adopting a North American definition of think tank. In particular, the notion that a think tank requires independence or autonomy from the state in order to be 'free-thinking' is a peculiarly Anglo-American notion that does not travel well into other cultures. As discussed in the chapter on France, the line between policy intellectuals and the state is blurred to such an extent that to talk of independence as a defining characteristic of think tanks makes little sense in the French cultural context; the same is true in other countries.

'Think tank' is a slippery term which is applied in a haphazard fashion to organizations undertaking policy-related, technical or scientific research and analysis. Such organizations may operate within government (this is evident in the case of most Russian think tanks), or be independent non-profit organizations, or be attached to a profit-making corporate entity (as is often the case in Japan). Most of the organizations discussed here are of a specific kind. They are relatively autonomous organizations engaged in the analysis of policy issues independently of government, political parties and pressure groups. We say 'relatively autonomous' as think tanks are often in resource-dependent relationships with these organizations. Funding may come from government sources but these institutes attempt to maintain their research freedom and at least claim not to be beholden to any specific interest. They attempt to influence or inform policy through intellectual argument and analysis rather than direct lobbying. They are engaged in the intellectual analysis of policy issues and are concerned with the ideas and concepts which underpin policy. Toward this end, think tanks collect, synthesize and create a range of information products, often directed towards a political or bureaucratic audience, but also for the benefit of the media, interest groups, business and the general public. Sometimes, they can also be conceived as public-spirited civil society organizations that aspire to assist those engaged in policy thinking and debate, and to educate or inform the wider community.

There is a considerable degree of overlap between think tanks and other organizations in society. Accordingly, it is frequently difficult to establish a precise, clear-cut boundary between think tanks and other organizations. For example, some observers regard think tanks as more intellectual variants of pressure groups (Grant, 1995). This is because institutes in many countries advocate policy positions that favour specific sectors of society or the economy, and many pressure groups now base their arguments on relatively sophisticated research. It would be convenient to treat think tanks as pressure groups, but it is not a satisfactory categorization. There are important differences between think tank and pressure group activity – for example, think tanks do not engage in public demonstrations. Think tanks tend to address multiple policy areas (notwithstanding specialization) rather than focus on a single issue as do many pressure groups. Think tanks have common features with other organizations but differ sufficiently to justify separate categorization. Some think tanks have been described as 'universities without students' (Weaver, 1989: 564). Activities undertaken by most think tanks – research and analysis, seminars and workshops, conferences and scholarly exchange, publications – are also conducted in universities and colleges. The difference is that think tanks are not normally degree-granting institutions (there are a few exceptions, notably RAND in the USA). Moreover, many institutes retain close relationships with universities. For example, both the Hoover Institution in California and ISEAS in Singapore are located on university campuses. Additionally, some of the more scholarly think tanks often contribute to disciplinary developments, whether through establishing specialist libraries or publishing books or journals of high academic repute.

A few institutes share some common territory with foundations. Foundations tend to be grant-giving organizations that fund research rather than undertake it. Yet, the Russell Sage Foundation, for example, is a foundation which provides grants but which also houses academic researchers who spend a year or so at the Foundation headquarters in New York. The Carnegie Endowment, with its endowment of over US$90 million, would rank alongside some of the larger American foundations except that it also operates as a scholarly kind of think tank that draws in researchers to investigate foreign policy and defence issues. In Italy, the Fondazione Giovanni Agnelli is also an 'operating foundation', producing policy-relevant research.

Given that think tanks are usually established as private organizations, they could be said to be functioning in the same way as consultancy firms, financial institutions or legal offices which provide advice and analysis. However, while a number of think tanks provide advice or analysis on a fee-for-service basis, such services often represent a minor part of their overall activities, whereas for a consultancy it is the main operation. Banks and law firms are primarily engaged in other, considerably more profitable activities than policy research.

The way in which think tanks operate can also be compared to government research bureaux. Such bureaux are often engaged in technical analysis assessing the implications of new or possible future policy developments. A sizeable proportion of think tanks also have a strong technical orientation. For example, the Institute of Fiscal Studies (IFS) in London engages in sophisticated statistical studies of monetary and fiscal policy in the UK as does the Conference Board of Canada and the National Bureau of Economic Research (NBER) in the USA. The respectable reputation of IFS is indicated by the fact that the British media often treats its findings as an 'objective counterweight to government figures, as well as its credibility within European Union (EU) regulatory circles (Radaelli, 1995). Similarly, a major project of a think tank may appear to be similar to a commission of inquiry or a significant policy report equivalent to a government green paper. The significant differences are that think tanks are outside government, the policy reviews they undertake are not officially sanctioned (although they may be privately encouraged) and the recommendations that result may be completely ignored by government. Think tanks do not enjoy the automatic bureaucratic route to decision-makers which is available to most official bodies.

Think tanks need to have some kind of engagement with government if they are to succeed in influencing policy. However, their desire to preserve intellectual autonomy means that most think tanks try to strike a delicate balance between dependence on government and total isolation from it. In fact, the precise nature of think tank 'independence' is an awkard problem which must be treated with flexibility. While the majority of institutes discussed in this volume are established as private non-profit organizations, the degree of independence of these organizations varies across a number of dimensions. Some of the organizations may be said to have resigned their autonomy to government, a political party or a corporation. For example, in Malaysia the Institute for Strategic and International Studies (ISIS) was established at the instigation of the Malaysian Cabinet (although it has since acquired formal independence). A number of think tanks are dependent on a single funding source (whether governmental or private). Accordingly, *financial independence* could be construed as developing an endowment or having numerous sponsors and a diverse funding base, so that the organization is not dependent on any *one* benefactor. *Scholarly independence* is a different concept, and reliant upon certain practices within an institute: for example, the processes of peer review and a commitment to open inquiry rather than directed research. As the following chapters show, the degree of think tank autonomy and the extent of interest in policy and political issues vary not only from country to country but from one institute to another.

The worldwide proliferation of think tanks

Think tanks are spreading around the world. Initially present only in the developed industrialized nations of North America and Europe, the think tank form has spread extensively into Central and Latin America (see Rubio, 1996), East Asia (Whang and Kim, 1991) and, since the collapse of the Soviet Union, into Eastern and Central Europe. Despite the assumption that think tanks are unique to the USA (or at least that they originated in that country), a comparative perspective suggests that this impression has arisen only because of the unparalleled expansion in think tank numbers (and size) in the USA since World War Two. Unfortunately, quantitative data on think tanks is only just emerging. Directories of think tanks are frequently out of date by the time of publication, or incomplete (but see Hellebust, 1997; Day, 1993). It is even more difficult to acquire up-to-date and accurate financial information, particularly when some institutes do not make such data publicly available. Nevertheless, the tables in each chapter provide a basic quantitative dimension, indicating the degree of diversity or similarity between think tanks within a country. The tables are representative only, but also provide the reader with a quick comparison between countries. Yet, this information can only provide a snap-shot of think tank development. Accordingly, historical analysis and institutional explanation is necessary to put flesh onto the data.

There are a number of possible hypotheses regarding think tank proliferation. Factors such as constitutional changes and government reform, the intensity of political debate and opposition, the attitudes of political leaders and the political culture of a society, levels of literacy and press freedom, the development of a domestically based intellectual elite, a history of philanthropy, independent organization and voluntarism within the civil society, are all relevant factors in explaining the emergence of think tanks within a particular country. There are, however, significant differences in the organizational characteristics and number of think tanks between countries.

We have already noted several factors which account for the greater number of think tanks in the USA. These bodies benefit from a tradition of corporate giving that is not as apparent elsewhere. The American tax structure encourages the formation of foundations and individual giving, creating a massive source of funding for think tanks and other non-profit organizations (O'Connell, 1983). As a consequence, there are a significant number of institutes operating with large budgets. Even so, the majority of American think tanks have very small budgets and only a handful of staff. In Australia and Canada, the foundation sector is less developed and corporate funding of think tanks is paltry compared to the USA. In some countries, think tanks are recognized as engaging in charitable and educational activities and accordingly they often benefit from financially significant tax exemptions. This factor is one reason why the extensiveness of think tanks varies from country to country. Stone and Ueno, in their discussions of Australia and Japan respectively, indicate that restrictive tax laws in these countries, and the absence of a philanthropic tradition, have constrained think tank development.

The federal structure of government has also aided the proliferation of US think tanks (Moore, 1988). Federal systems supposedly provide more fora into which think tanks can target their activities. However, while this may be true of Germany and to a lesser extent Malaysia, it evidently cannot explain the situation in Australia or Canada where think tanks are less numerous than in a unitary system such as the UK. The USA has a presidential system whereas Britain, Canada and Australia are parliamentary systems of a 'party government' type (Weaver and Rockman, 1993: 20). It is often claimed that the checks-and-balances system of the USA provides interstices through which think tanks can emerge. By contrast, parliamentary systems involve greater centralization of legislative power and accountability, supposedly allowing for greater control over policy and exclusion of external policy actors. Furthermore, political parties in parliamentary systems tend to be more cohesive and disciplined. In the USA, individual legislators have considerable autonomy and face little pressure from their party to conform to policy positions. Consequently, it would seem more likely they would benefit from contacts with think tanks, experts and interest group activists. These factors would appear to make the USA a more congenial home for think tanks than France, for instance, where the central bureaucracy is more powerful. Notwithstanding the differences, there appear to be some common political dynamics evident in all countries encouraging the growth of these institutes.

A frequent proposition regarding think tank growth concerns government 'overload' and the increasing complexity of decision-making processes. In this view, think tank growth is indicative of a need for more information, analysis and advice as economies and societies become more complex. Big government, globalization and the flood of information from interest groups, industry and new government programmes mean that think tanks become one source of expertise able to explain the nature, causes and likely remedies of problems. Similarly, they have become useful translators of the abstract modelling and dense theoretical concepts characteristic of contemporary social science. Theoretically, think tanks can help to create a more 'rational' policy process by augmenting in-house research capacities, circumventing time and institutional constraints and alerting elites to changing global circumstances (Dror, 1984).

Rather than promoting 'rationality', think tank development could be indicative of the politicization of knowledge. Think tanks can be used instrumentally by individuals. In a few countries think tanks are a means of career advancement or a stepping stone for the politically ambitious. The 'revolving-door' of individuals moving between executive appointment and think tanks, law firms or universities is a well-known phenomenon in the USA. In Britain, the Conservative MP David Willetts has won media prominence and, presumably, faster promotion because of his connection with both the Centre for Policy Studies (CPS) and the Social Market Foundation (SMF). Su-ming Khoo reveals that a handful of Malaysian think tanks are a means of promoting the political ambitions of a few politicians. In particular, ISIS is associated with Prime Minister Mahathir. Furthermore, political parties and/or interest groups in different systems have established formal and informal ties with think tanks, not only because they are a source of policy ideas and innovation, but also because think tanks have intellectual authority that can be used to give established policy positions additional credibility. This theme is developed in the chapter on German think tanks. Similarly, in a number of countries, the media has developed an enormous appetite for think tank services. Mutually beneficial relationships develop whereby think tanks represent an 'expert' source of information and commentary for journalists who, in turn, play a key role in amplifying or broadcasting think tank analyses (Abelson, 1992; Cornford, 1990).

A related (economic) explanation for the emergence of think tanks is that their growth is symptomatic of failure in the policy advice market. For example, the Tasman Institute in Australia claims that the worldwide growth of think tanks reflects a market response to the failures and limitations of other institutions – political parties, bureaucracies, universities, trade unions and business interests – in providing effective and diverse policy ideas (Tasman Institute, 1995). The massive growth in think tank numbers worldwide, it is argued, arises from the 'inability of traditional bureaucracies and interest groups to put aside sectorally narrow, self-serving policies and develop innovative and integrative solutions to policy problems' (Langford and Brownsey, 1991: 2). The private provision of policy advice thus represents a form of market correction. Similarly, some non-profit sector advocates argue that non-profit organizations provide goods and services needed by the public that are not produced by either the state or the market (Ware, 1990). On this reading, non-profit think tanks emerge as an alternative source of research, analysis or policy thinking to that provided by both state and market.

A political factor promoting the growth of think tanks is the dissatisfaction of political leaders or parties with existing sources of policy advice. The establishment of ISIS was a means for Prime Minister Mahathir to circumvent the Malaysian bureaucracy, while think tanks such as the Institute of Economic Affairs (IEA), the CPS and the Adam Smith Institute (ASI) were used by Margaret Thatcher and some of her cabinet colleagues for additional ideas and information. Bureaucratic structures and styles differ markedly among all countries. Government appointees are more apparent in presidential systems. By contrast, in Japan, Britain, Canada and Australia, permanent civil services dominate as a source of policy advice. The use of special advisors from universities, business, think tanks and elsewhere is not extensive in these countries. Yet, since the 1970s there seems to have been a tendency towards drawing upon external sources of advice, possibly in response to what is seen as the 'rubber stamp' role of parliaments, or a reaction against the civil service view or *pensée unique*. Thus, the 'closed' nature of these sysems can be overstated. Although Japan is an exception here, it is not unknown for think tank representatives to appear before commissions of inquiry, to speak at parliamentary committees or be incorporated into bureaucractic taskforces. Nevertheless, the circumstances in these countries do contrast with the USA where administrative permeability of the executive is commonplace.

It is not clear from the following chapters whether think tanks are more likely to develop further within multi-party systems contributing to coalition government (as in Germany) or in strong two-party systems which alternate in office (as in Britain and Australia). In the dominant party system of Malaysia, where party competition is circumscribed, think tanks have boomed in number. The link with political parties is clearly central to understanding the role of think tanks in Germany. In other countries, such as Italy, the ties to political parties are less formal and substantial.

Another thesis which might explain the recent spread of think tanks is that a long-term process of learning and convergence has taken place. That is, the creation of (quasi-) independent policy research institutes is indicative of national intellectual and decision-making elites copying Western bodies (particularly those of the USA). There is some evidence to support this explanation for think tank dispersion. Some individuals trained in Western educational systems or who have acquired fellowships in think tanks have gained familiarity with the think tank form and occasionally a desire to replicate them in their countries of origin. For example, an innovative enterprise is currently underway to export the US think tank model to Japan (see Struyk, Ueno and Suzuki, 1993). The Ford Foundation played an important role in the establishment of organizations such as the International Institute for Strategic Studies (IISS) in London. The Atlas Foundation and the Mont Pelerin Society (both mentioned in a number of chapters) have been an important funding organization and intellectual society respectively that have supported libertarian and free market institutes around the world. Another dynamic for convergence is old imperial ties. For example, the Royal Institute for International Affairs (RIIA) spawned a number of similar organizations throughout the Commonwealth.

While the convergence argument has considerable appeal, it does not explain the development of all institutes outside the Anglo-American world.

Many bodies emerge as the result of initiatives and dynamics within, rather than outside, the host country. Furthermore, rather than mimicry, a range of organizational forms, styles and practices have emerged. The think tank form is adapted and mediated by national political cultures and institutional arrangements.

Another thesis which may partially explain the development of think tanks emphasizes the spread of democracy, often in tandem with economic development. Think tanks seem to be more prevalent in industrially advanced democratic polities. This could easily lead to the inference that think tanks are symptomatic of democratization and national prosperity. A diversity of organizations – none of which has a monopoly on policy advice – strengthens the democratic functioning of society by educating the populace and providing another forum for political debate and participation. This theme is developed in the chapter on Japan. A comparative examination, however, suggests that there is no simple correlation. Given the long-standing democratic traditions and institutions in Australia and its high degree of economic prosperity over the century, one would infer from the above proposition a much greater number of think tanks than currently exist in Australia. Yet, the chapter on Australia suggests that think tank discourse is exclusive rather than inclusionary. Similarly, as the chapter on Malaysia reveals, think tanks are associated with political elites rather than the wider citizenry in a political system with the trappings if not the substance of democracy. Think tanks can duplicate a closed and secretive environment, and instead of presenting opportunities for participation, their prestige can act as a barrier to policy input from more democratic sources.

As outlined in the majority of chapters, there appear to be 'waves of think tank development' within the countries considered here. For example, Lindquist refers to first and second waves of Canadian think tank development from the 1970s onwards. Similarly, in Australia, the first (albeit sporadic) wave of think tank development occurred from the 1920s until the 1970s; the second wave from the 1970s to mid-1980s; and a third wave since. Abelson refers to four generations of think tank development in the USA, as do Denham and Garnett in their chapter on Britain. Such waves of development will vary from country to country but may provide some guide to patterns of international growth. For example, foreign policy think tanks emerged in large numbers after World War One, security studies institutes during the Cold War, and peace institutes in the context of nuclear proliferation and post-Vietnam. New Right think tanks proliferated around the world from the 1970s. Similarly, whether as a cause or a consequence of the rise of environmental considerations, environmental policy institutes have burgeoned since the 1970s. Yet, the think tanks in the two Asian countries – Japan and Malaysia – exhibit a different evolutionary pattern from that in the West. Their proliferation has occurred much later. Additionally, there are relatively few think tanks in other Asian countries such as Indonesia, Singapore and Thailand where they have appeared only since the 1970s (see Langford and Brownsey, 1991). As would be expected, independent think tanks in Russia appeared only after 1989.

In many instances, the heightened activity of think tanks appears to be related to periods of economic and political instability. The rise of some of the so-called 'New Right' think tanks illustrates this point as their emergence coincided with a crisis in the Keynesian paradigm in policy-making. This theme is explored in the chapter on Great Britain. This suggests that the 'waves of think tank development' in a particular country do not occur in an even linear fashion. There are fluctuations within the industry as a whole. Indeed, think tank numbers could dip at certain points in time such as during recession, war or periods of authoritarian government. Similar questions apply to individual organizations. Some think tanks experience decline or periodic crises, a number are disestablished or alternatively have developed into different kinds of organization. Funding sources can dry up, an organization can suffer from a lack of leadership or poor management, or fail to adapt to a changing world.

In some countries, patterns of think tank organizational behaviour are changing fast. Radaelli and Martini consider that while Italian think tanks are becoming less academic in character, they are not being politicized. By contrast, Abelson, Denham and Garnett, and Stone all note how later generations of American, British and Australian think tanks are more advocacy-oriented, partisan or ideological. Furthermore, at a round table meeting of think tank executives from around the world convened by the Urban Institute during 1991, participants remarked upon how their mode of information dissemination was changing rapidly.

> One pattern is the shift from written products to meetings of various kinds to increase the impact of research findings on policy formulation. This shift appears to be driven by several factors: the brief period over which some policy deliberations take place and therefore the need to communicate very quickly; the greater impact which face-to-face, often informal discussions can have when compared with written reports; and the huge volume of written policy products, which makes it difficult for any single product to catch the attention of the client. (Struyk, 1993: 49)

There was a general perception among North American and European executives that think tank activity was more about informal interaction with decision-makers as competition between think tanks (and other policy related bodies) intensified, and as those in government suffered from both time constraints and information overload.

A final common feature of think tank activity in a number of countries is the increasing density of links with counterpart organizations around the world. The above quote emerged from an early Global ThinkNet meeting which has now transformed into a regular international meeting for senior think tank executives. Khoo writes of the Association of Southeast Asian Nations (ASEAN)–Institutes of Strategic and International Studies which is a regional network of leading think tanks collaborating on strategic and foreign policy issues. Whilst not discussed in this volume, there appears to be increased think tank networking at the EU level. For example, the Institutes for European Environmental Policy based in the UK, France, the Netherlands, Germany and Belgium represent a formal network. More informally, 'libertarian' institutes maintain worldwide lines of communication and occasionally engage in research or conference collaboration on an *ad hoc* basis. This kind of interaction and collaboration varies in intensity and degree from one institute to another but is more common with greater ease in international travel and developments in communications technology.

Think tanks and the issue of influence

One of the most common questions associated with the study of think tanks is how to identify their influence. However, attempts to measure this influence or relevance are plagued with methodological problems. As a result there are wild fluctuations in assessments of think tank influence; their impact on policy thinking is often exaggerated while other commentators refuse to acknowledge that they can have any genuine input at all. In particular, foreign observers of American think tanks sometimes have an exaggerated conception of their power. In November 1985, Gorbachev 'lambasted' the Heritage Foundation as the 'ideological headquarters' of the Reagan Administration (Reilly, 1986). Similarly, 'America Watchers' in the People's Republic of China have argued that the American Enterprise Institute (AEI), Hoover Institution, Heritage Foundation and Center for Strategic and International Affairs (CSIS) have a direct impact on policy, thus furthering the ambitions of their corporate funders (Shambaugh, 1991: 194–9).

The media is particularly important here – one might even claim that 'think tanks are important because the media believes they are important and the media believes in this importance because think tanks tell them they are' (Hames and Feasey, 1994: 233). In those political systems where there is a high degree of media freedom, think tanks can influence policy-makers both indirectly (by disseminating their ideas to the wider public) and directly (by convincing decision-makers that they are worth consulting). The Canadian Parliamentary Channel and C-Span in the USA, for example, provide ample opportunity for think tanks to broadcast their views. In countries such as Malaysia, however, there are significant constraints on the media, while in France the media currently gives think tanks scant attention.

'Influence' is a word that is itself open to a variety of interpretations. For scholars, the problem is complicated by the fact that think tanks often need to convince members, their donors and benefactors, their media contacts and decision-makers of their influence, relevance or importance. As a result, think tanks often claim an influence over policy which proves to be unrealistic, and even careful observers can over-react to this tendency by downplaying the role of policy institutes. The politics and policy process in any country is invariably complicated, and it is certainly rare to find examples of a one-to-one correspondence between a think tank report and a policy subsequently adopted by government. The problem of gauging or measuring the impact of think tanks cross-nationally is also fraught with difficulties. For example, the attraction of foundation funding is one potential indicator of think tank success. However, a large foundation grant to an Australian institute is more noteworthy than a similar grant to an American think tank simply because of the greater difficulty experienced by Australian think tanks in winning such funding. Similarly, the NBER may be subject to regular attention from the American media but less so outside the USA, while ISIS in Malaysia attracts a high level of interest throughout Southeast Asia and beyond. These differences highlight the incommensurability of indicators across borders. However, these methodological dilemmas do not mean that the question of influence cannot be meaningfully explored.

Early studies of think tanks tended to adopt a macro-level focus of explanation. Many of these studies adopted power approaches to the role of think tanks in decision-making. Elite studies of institutes such as the Brookings Institution (Critchlow, 1985; Dye, 1978) have emphasized how think tanks are key components of the 'power elite' where decision-making is concentrated in the hands of a few groups and individuals. The problem with such studies is that analysis is directed towards well-known policy institutions with links to political parties or the corporate sector, neglecting the role of smaller, lesser-known institutes which exist in much larger numbers than the 'elite' think tanks. Neo-marxists have argued that establishment think tanks are a means of maintaining hegemonic control (Desai, 1994) or are consensus-building organizations for the 'power elite' whereby think tanks develop the ideology and long-range plans that convert problems of political economy into manageable objects of public policy. Furthermore, as the common economic interests and social cohesion among the power elite are insufficient to produce consensus on policies, agreement on such matters requires 'research, consultation and deliberation' to form a coherent sense of long-term class interests (Domhoff, 1983: 82). These institutes mobilize elites to re-define the terms of debate in order to translate class interests into state action (Peschek, 1987). Similar to elite theorists, scholars in this tradition have given most attention to those policy institutes whose activities and/or high profile confirm their assumption that capitalist problems lead to statist solutions. Following this logic, it is difficult to account for the growth of business-funded think tanks promoting 'anti-statist' policies. Nor do structuralist theories of a passive capitalist class and relatively autonomous state help to explain why corporations fund and support non-profit organizations challenging government positions. Instrumentalist approaches assume, however, that capital will attempt hegemonic projects. In common with elite theorists, they perceive capitalists as cohesive and active in sustaining privilege. While instrumentalists identify think tanks as a central component in the political mobilization of business, the approach has not been used to explain the growing numbers, their increasingly specialized character or their more partisan and ideological stances (Himmelstein, 1990: 159). Instead, neopluralist and structuralist arguments that capital is divided and uncoordinated potentially provide better explanations for the diversity of think tanks and their fluctuating fortunes.

In contrast to elite and marxist approaches, pluralist studies of think tanks have emphasized the competition between think tanks for access to the political system and how the market-place of ideas is open and pluralistic. Those with a normative position have argued that think tanks help create a more open, participative and educated populace and represent a counter to the influence of powerful techno-bureaucratic, corporate and media interests on the policy agenda. Similarly, advocates of policy analysis have suggested that a more informed, knowledge-based policy process – a role that experts based in think tanks can help fulfil – could enlighten decision-making (Weiss, 1990). The problem with such studies is that all groups do not have equal access to the political system and the policy agenda is distorted by the muscle of groups with structural power.

Whilst some of these organizations have links into the policy formation processes and have some kind of presence in the broader social–political system, their power or influence is limited and dependent. For example, rather than think tanks exerting influence over government, governments can use think tanks in an instrumental fashion. Thus, it may be less the case that think tanks have an impact on government and more the case that governments employ these organizations as tools to pursue their own interests. This can be achieved through a variety of formal and informal strategies. Political or bureaucratic leaders may encourage a certain think tank to pursue a particular avenue of research. In a more direct fashion, governments may commission studies to be undertaken by institutes (as discussed in the chapters on Britain and Malaysia). Whilst government patronage – such as the links which existed between Thatcher and the CPS, President Clinton and the Progressive Policy Institute (PPI), or President Reagan with Heritage and Hoover – provides greater access to information and the corridors of power, there are also dilemmas. Changes in political leadership may spell marginalization for some think tanks.

Think tanks appear to be useful in periods of critical transition in a number of chapters. Such transitions may occur with electoral change whereby an in-coming party requires transition thinking in the form of policy ideas and blueprints. This is clearly evident in the USA where Abelson identifies the role of the Heritage Foundation in providing advice for the incoming Reagan administrations. In the disarray of conservative political forces in Australia, after the collapse of United Australia Party, a think tank – the Institute of Public Affairs (IPA) – helped provide the impetus and re-fashioned ideological foundations for the establishment of a new political party. 'Paradigm shift' represents another form of transition (Hall, 1990). Indeed, many of the Russian 'instituteniki' were constitutive of changing policy orthodoxies that led to 'glasnost' and perestroika' in the Soviet Union.

Some of the authors in this volume suggest that fluctuating think tank influence has more to do with the way in which think tanks successfully interact in policy networks. Policy network is a generic term for a variety of different conceptual models including 'policy communities' or 'epistemic communities', 'advocacy coalitions' and 'discourse coalitions'. A policy network is a mode of governance that incorporates actors from both inside and outside government to facilitate decision-making and implementation. Through networks, think tanks can be integrated into the policy-making process. Pluralists usually stress the openness and informal participation in decision-making offered by networks. Yet it has also been recognized that policy networks can prevent the emergence of challenges to the dominant values or interests in society suppressing or thwarting demands for change in the existing allocation of benefit and privilege. Networks undermine 'political responsibility by shutting out the public' (Rhodes and Marsh, 1992: 200). Institutional procedures entail that the system responds better to the well-organized, wealthy, skilled and knowledgeable than to disorga-nized, poorly financed, unskilled pressure groups. Non-decision-making is the likely consequence. Thus the network literature can accommodate elite views that networks are closed and dominated by a small number of key actors as well as marxist perspectives that networks are dominated by inter-ests representing capital (see Smith, 1993).

Within policy communities, think tanks (or their scholars) are likely to acquire 'insider' status if they share the prevailing values and attitudes of the policy community. The advocacy coalition approach places greater empha-sis on the view that analysis has a long-term enlightenment function in alter-ing policy orthodoxies, and highlights the role of beliefs, values and ideas as a neglected dimension of policy-making (Sabatier, 1987). This approach is employed by Radaelli and Martini, and by Gellner in chapters on Italian and German think tanks respectively. Discourse coalition comes from the 'argu-mentative turn' in policy studies and emphasizes language and political sym-bolism (Fischer, 1993; Pal, 1990). The focus is on how a policy problem is defined and the discourse through which the problem is understood. The epistemic community concept (Haas, 1992; and also Adler, 1992 in relation to RAND) concentrates on the specific role of knowledge or experts in the policy process and is a theme developed in the chapter on France.

All these network concepts include a mix of interest group leaders, politicians, bureaucrats, and business representatives, but also give consideration to the potential role of academic analysts, think tanks, senior journalists, intellectuals and other actors. Rather than concentrating on formal decision-making procedures, the policy milieu is assumed to include non-formal actors. The policy network literature can be used to illuminate how think tanks seek to influence political agendas and the manner in which networks involve think tanks as 'policy entrepreneurs'. Within networks, think tanks contribute policy-aware advocates, researchers and other specialists who analyse problems and propose solutions. In short, they provide intellectual resources. The scholars and executives of think tanks act as policy entrepreneurs, first, by promoting ideas and pushing them higher on the public agenda; and, second, by 'softening-up' actors in the political and policy system to new ideas so that when an opportunity arises (for example, elections or a policy crisis) an entrepreneur's ideas meet a receptive audience (Kingdon, 1984).

Think tanks are often conceived as a bridge between academia and decision-makers and having a strategic role of interpreting and communicating the pure and applied research of their colleagues to the wider world. Think tanks bring social science research into the public domain by seeking appointment to government commissions or industry delegations and by giving evidence to congressional or parliamentary committees. Seminars, lectures, lunch meetings and conferences are other means to spread ideas. In this context, the ability of think tank members to establish links with the media, trade unions, pressure groups, political parties, bureaucrats and departments is essential to their networking and coalition building. The links – often informal – create a route of access to decision-makers in order to promote ideas and soften up public opinion. Additionally, the influence of think tanks – that is, their agenda-setting abilities and powers to manipulate social myths, language and symbols – can be assessed in terms of power over meaning, drawing attention to 'constructivist' theories of social problems or the 'argumentative turn' in policy studies (Fischer, 1993). In the chapter on Malaysia, for example, Khoo emphasizes the discourse of 'development' created and reinforced by elite think tanks.

Networking is also an organizational mode of operation for some think tanks (Portes, 1996). Instead of functioning with an in-house research staff, these think tanks draw upon a network of scholars based in universities, bureaucracies and elsewhere to generate research or analysis. At the same time, think tanks can still be a physical intersection of ideas and people through conferences, study groups, seminars and other forms of outreach. Within such networks think tanks draw together people from diverse backgrounds in government, law, universities, the military, international agencies and elsewhere, with the purpose of establishing lines of communication among disparate actors with common objectives or interests. Institutes build an infrastructure to maintain contact and keep actors in policy networks abreast of current activities and research. Networking helps promote solidarity, loyalty, trust and reciprocity. In itself, such networking does not equate with political influence, but it aids the effectiveness of think tanks in promoting policy ideas.

Networking and policy entrepeneurship to capture political agendas are manifestations of the way in which knowledge has become politicized by think tanks. The ways in which interest groups, government and political parties draw upon think tank work is another manifestation. Their formal and informal ties with think tanks have become increasingly beneficial not only because think tanks are a source of policy ideas and innovation, but also because they are symbolic of intellectual authority that can be used to support entrenched policy prejudices. In democratic states, such reputed intellectual authority might not win elections directly, but the impression that a political party has strong think tank support can be very useful in convincing commentators that their views coincide with the 'climate of opinion'. For example, in the UK during the 1980s, the notion that the Conservative Party had won the 'battle of ideas' owed much to the perceived support of New Right think tanks (see Denham and Garnett below).

Despite its utility, the network literature has its limitations. It is tempting for the observer to equate successful networking with influence. Yet, the informal access that networking might afford does not mean that decision-makers pay attention to what think tanks write or advocate. Networks may generate intense activity that does not necessarily translate into policy input. Careful analysis is required to distinguish instances where think tanks are providing real input into policy deliberation from those (more frequent) occurrences when they do not. In the last instance, think tanks operate on their own. They are in competition with other think tanks and policy advice organizations to attract political and media attention as well as foundation, corporate and individual support. Consequently, think tanks advance themselves by successfully championing issues and placing themselves towards the centre of debate on key issues. Notwithstanding the difficulty of determining influence, it is evident that in so many countries today think tanks do have an audience in government and media circles. In the future, this audience is likely to grow rather than diminish, and academic studies will at last accord them greater recognition.

References

Abelson, Donald. E. (1992) 'A New Channel of Influence: American Think Tanks and the News Media', *Queens Quarterly*, 99(4): 849–72.

Adler, Emanuel (1992) 'The Emergence of Cooperation: National Epistemic Communities and the International Evolution of the Idea of Arms Control', *International Organization*, 46(1): 101–45.

Cockett, Richard (1994) *Thinking the Unthinkable: Think Tanks and the Economic Counter-Revolution, 1931–1983*, London, HarperCollins.

Coleman, David A. (1991) 'Policy Research – Who Needs It?', *Governance: An International Journal of Policy and Administration*, 4(4): 420–55.

Commission on Social Justice (1994) *Social Justice: Strategies for National Renewal*, London, Vintage.

Cornford, James (1990) 'Performing Fleas: Reflections from a Think Tank', *Policy Studies*, 11(4): 22–30.

Critchlow, D. T. (1985) *The Brookings Institution, 1916–52: Expertise and the Public Interest in A Democratic Society*, Dekalb, Northern Illinois Press.

Day, Alan (1993) *Think Tanks: An International Directory*, Harlow, Longman Group.

Denham, Andrew (1996) *Think Tanks of the New Right*, Aldershot, Dartmouth.

Denham, Andrew and Garnett, Mark (1996) 'The Nature and Impact of "Think Tanks" in Contemporary Britain', *Contemporary British History*, 10(1): 43–61.

Desai, Rhadika (1994) 'Second-hand Dealers in Ideas: Think Tanks and Thatcherite Hegemony', *New Left Review*, 203: 27–64.

Domhoff, William. G. (1983) *Who Rules America Now? A View for the '80s*, Englewood Cliffs, NJ, Prentice Hall.

Dror, Y. (1984) 'Required Breakthroughs in Think Tanks', *Policy Sciences*, 16: 199–225.

Dye, Thomas R. (1978) 'Oligarchic Tendencies in National Policy Making: The Role of Private Planning Organizations', *Journal of Politics*, 40 (May): 309–31.

Fischer, Frank (1991) 'American Think Tanks: Policy Elites and the Politicization of Expertise', *Governance*, 4(3): 332–53.

Fischer, Frank (1993) 'Policy Discourse and the Politics of Washington Think Tanks', in F. Fischer and J. Forester (eds), *The Argumentative Turn in Policy Analysis and Planning*, London, UCL Press.

Grant, Wyn (1995) *Pressure Groups, Politics and Democracy in Britain*, Hemel Hempstead, Harvester Wheatsheaf.

Haas, Peter (1992) 'Introduction: Epistemic Communities and International Policy Coordination', *International Organization*, 46(1): 1–35.

Hall, Peter A. (1990) 'Policy Paradigms, Experts, and the State: The Case of Macroeconomic Policy-Making in Britain', in S. Brooks and A.-G. Gagnon (eds), *Social Scientists, Policy and the State*, New York, Praeger.

Hames, T. and Feasey, R. (1994) 'Anglo-American Think Tanks under Reagan and Thatcher', in A. Adonis and T. Hames (eds), *A Conservative Revolution? The Thatcher–Reagan Decade in Perspective*, Manchester, Manchester University Press.

Heclo, Hugh (1980) 'Issue Networks and the Executive Establishment', in A. King (ed.) *The New American Political System*, Washington DC, American Enterprise

Institute.

Hellebust, L. (ed.) (1997) *Think Tank Directory: A Guide to Nonprofit Public Policy Research Organizations*, Topeka, KS, Government Research Service.

Himmelstein, Jerome. L. (1990) *To the Right: The Transformation of American Conservatism*, Berkeley, University of California Press.

Kingdon, J. (1984) *Agendas, Alternatives and Public Policies*, Boston, Little, Brown and Co.

Langford, John W. and Brownsey, K. Lorne (1991) 'Introduction: Think Tanks and Modern Governance', in John W. Langford and K. Lorne Brownsey (eds), *Think Tanks and Governance in the Asia-Pacific Region*, Halifax, Nova Scotia, Institute for Research on Public Policy.

Lindquist, Evert A. (1989) 'Behind the Myth of Think Tanks: The Organization and Relevance of Canadian Policy Institutes', unpublished doctoral thesis, Berkeley, University of California.

Lindquist, Evert A. (1993) 'Think Tanks or Clubs? Assessing the Influence and Roles of Canadian Policy Institutes', *Canadian Public Administration*, 36(4): 547–79.

Moore, W. John (1988) 'Local Right Thinkers', *National Journal*, 1 October: 2455–9.

O'Connell, Brian (ed.) (1983) *America's Voluntary Spirit*, New York, The Foundation Center.

Pal, Leslie A. (1990) 'Knowledge, Power, and Policy: Reflections on Foucault', in S. Brooks and A.-G. Gagnon (eds), *Social Scientists, Policy and the State*, New York, Praeger.

Peschek, J. S. (1987) *Policy Planning Organizations: Elite Agendas and America's Rightward Turn*, Philadelphia, Temple University Press.

Polsby, N. (1983) 'Tanks But No Tanks', *Public Opinion*, April–May (14–16): 58–9.

Portes, Richard (1996) 'The Centre for Economic Policy Research: A "Think Net" Model', in Jeffrey Telgarsky and Makiko Ueno (eds), *Think Tanks in a Democratic Society: An Alternative Voice*, Washington DC, Urban Institute.

Radaelli, Claudio (1995) 'Corporate Direct Taxation in the European Union: Explaining the Policy Process', *Journal of Public Policy*, 15(2): 153–81.

Reilly, A. (1986) 'Heritage Ascendant', *Fortune*, 31 March.

Rhodes, R. A. W. and Marsh, David (1992) 'New Directions in the Study of Policy Networks', *European Journal of Political Research*, 21: 181–205.

Ricci, David (1993) *The Transformation of American Politics: The New Washington and the Rise of American Politics*, New Haven, CT, Yale University Press.

Rubio, Luis (1996) 'Think Tanks and One Case in Mexico', in Jeffrey Telgarsky and Makiko Ueno (eds), *Think Tanks in a Democratic Society: An Alternative Voice*, Washington DC, Urban Institute.

Sabatier, Paul A. (1987) 'Knowledge, Policy Oriented Learning, and Policy Change: An Advocacy Coalition Framework', *Knowledge: Creation, Diffusion, Utilization*, 8(4): 649–92.

Shambaugh, David (1991) *Beautiful Imperialist: China Perceives America, 1972–1990*, Princeton, NJ, Princeton University Press.

Smith, James A. (1991) *The Idea Brokers: Think Tanks and the Rise of the New Policy Elite*, New York, Free Press.

Smith, Martin (1993) *Pressure, Power and Policy: State Autonomy and Policy Networks in Britain and the United States*, Hemel Hempstead, Harvester Wheatsheaf.

Stone, Diane (1996) *Capturing the Political Imagination: Think Tanks and the Policy Process*, London, Frank Cass.

Struyk, Raymond J. (1993) 'Learning from the US and European Experience', in Raymond J. Struyk, Makiko Ueno and Takahiro Suzuki (eds), *A Japanese Think Tank: Exploring Alternative Models*, Washington DC, Urban Institute.

Struyk, Raymond J., Ueno, Makiko and Suzuki, Takahiro (eds) (1993) *A Japanese Think Tank: Exploring Alternative Models*, Washington DC, Urban Institute.

Tasman Institute (1995) *Annual Review*, November, Melbourne, Tasman Institute.

Wallace, William (1994) 'Between Two Worlds: Think Tanks and Foreign Policy', in C. Hill and P. Beshoff (eds), *Two Worlds of International Relations: Academics, Practitioners and the Trade in Ideas*, London, Routledge and London School of Economics.

Ware, Alan (1990) *Between Profit and the State: Intermediate Organizations in Britain and the United States*, Princeton, NJ, Princeton University Press.

Weaver, R. K. (1989) 'The Changing World of Think Tanks', *PS: Political Science and Politics*, September: 563–78.

Weaver, R. K. and Rockman, B. A. (1993) 'Assessing the Effects of Institutions', in R. K. Weaver and B. A. Rockman (eds), *Do Institutions Matter? Government Capabilities in the United States and Abroad*, Washington DC, Brookings Institution.

Weiss, Carol (1990) 'The Uneasy Partnership Endures: Social Science and Government', in S. Brooks and A.-G. Gagnon (eds), *Social Scientists, Policy and the State*, New York, Praeger.

Weiss, Carol (ed.) (1992) *Organizations for Policy Advice: Helping Government Think*, London, Sage.

Whang, In-Joung and Kim, Dong-Kyun (1991) 'Role of Policy Research Institutes in the Economic Policy-Making Process: The Korea Development Institute', in John W. Langford. and K. Lorne Brownsey (eds), *Think Tanks and Governance in the Asia-Pacific Region*, Halifax, Nova Scotia, Institute for Research on Public Policy.

Think tanks, British politics and the 'climate of opinion'

Introduction

As the Introduction to the present volume has shown, it is frequently assumed (particularly in the American literature) that 'think tanks' are unique to the US political system. The American historian James Smith, for instance, has described think tanks as *'quintessentially American* planning and advisory institutions' operating on the margins of that country's formal political processes (Smith, 1991: xiii; our emphasis). The *scale* of think tank development in the US is certainly 'unique' (James, 1993: 492). It has been estimated that more than 1,000 private, non-profit research institutes now exist in the USA, approximately 100 of which are based in and around Washington DC (Smith, 1991). Most other Western democracies, including Britain, have relatively few such groups, even if (as we shall see later in this chapter) several new London-based think tanks have been established in recent years. Table 1.1 lists the best-known British think tanks by date of origin and provides basic information about each institute.

As a comparison of Table 1.1 with Table 5.1 shows, British think tanks are (generally speaking) smaller and poorer than their US counterparts, several of which employ considerable numbers of permanent, full-time research staff and boast multi-million dollar budgets. Yet far from being unique to the US, what is also evident is that think tanks have a long history in Britain (see later). Indeed, given the early foundation of the Fabian Society (1884), even the claim that think tanks were originally a US 'invention' (Dror, 1980) is difficult to sustain; depending on how the term is defined (see later), it could be said that 'think tanks' are a peculiarly British – or even, as one intellectual historian has recently claimed, 'very English' – phenomenon (Bradley, 1981; Harrison, 1993: 73).

Explanations for the unique scale of think tank development in the USA frequently point to the 'exceptional' characteristics of the American political system. Think tanks, it is argued, 'bloom according to the political compost in which they grow' (Hennessy and Coates, 1991: 5). Their presence on the unique scale found in the US is said to reflect such 'elemental political realities' as America's constitutional separation of powers, a genuinely bicameral legislature, a party system historically grounded in electoral–political ambitions rather than ideology and 'a civil service tradition that gives leeway to numerous political appointees' (Smith, 1991: xv). In a seminal article published in the late 1980s, Weaver (1989: 570) has described think tanks as 'policy entrepreneurs' operating in a distinct political system characterized by the 'division of powers between President and Congress, weak and relatively non-ideological parties and [the] permeability of administrative elites'. A final component of American 'exceptionalism' is the peculiarly robust private philanthropic sector which has traditionally existed in the USA. As Weiss (1992: 8) has pointed out, in no other country have the resources on which all think tanks ultimately depend been so richly available.

Table 1.1 *British think tanks*

Organization	Date established	Staff	Budget (£ million)
Fabian Society	1884	7	0.25
RIIA	1920	84	3.5
PSI (formerly PEP)	1931	54	4.2
NIESR	1938	43	1.8
IEA	1955	19	1.5
CPS	1974	4	0.5
ASI	1977	7	0.33
IPPR	1988	35	1.5
SMF	1989	7	0.5
Demos	1993	10	0.4

Note: The above figures are based on annual reports and private information and relate to the most recent calendar year for which information was available at the time of going to press (September 1997). Where an organization employs both full- and part-time staff, the overall figure has been adjusted accordingly.

All of these factors, it is alleged, provide US think tanks with uniquely favourable opportunities not only to emerge, but also to gain access to decision-makers and so exert political influence (Weiss, 1992: 6–8). Conversely, however, it is possible to argue that American think tanks find it more difficult than is sometimes assumed to make much headway, precisely because the US political system is so competitive. As Weiss (1992: 7) also notes, the number of players in the policy game in the USA is legion. Hence, American think tanks have to compete not only among themselves, but also with a huge number of other lobbyists in order to persuade policy-makers in both the executive and legislative branches of government to adopt a particular policy or, more ambitiously still, embrace an entire agenda for policy. British think tanks, by contrast, are far fewer in number and have as their target audience a relatively small and easily identifiable set of political actors located, like the think tanks themselves, in the two to three square miles that contain Westminster, Whitehall, the City and 'Fleet Street'. In short, the 'extreme centralization' of British political and public life means that access to key decision-makers is potentially well within the reach of these few, well-located institutions (Desai, 1994: 31). Arguably, then, these characteristics of the British political system compensate, to some degree at least, for the fact that UK think tanks lack the human and financial resources available to several of their US counterparts; many of their contributors (especially academics) are also willing to provide their services for minimal reward. In sum, it is worth exploring the hypothesis that British think tanks have never grown to the size of US institutes at least partly because there has never been a need for such expansion.

What is a think tank?

The false assumption that think tanks are unique to the American political system is one reason for the shortfall in analysis of these bodies outside the US and helps explain the relative lack of comparative investigation (for exceptions, see Gaffney, 1991; Hames and Feasey, 1994; Wallace, 1994; Stone, 1996). Even in the USA, however, political scientists have only recently begun to document and analyse the importance of think tanks (an early exception is Dickson, 1971). During the 1970s and 1980s, for instance, the major American political science journals published only one article dealing with leading think tanks (Dye, 1978). The second important contribution appeared (in one of the discipline's lesser-rated journals) more than a decade later (Weaver, 1989). As Ricci (1993: 2) has noted, while think tanks are active in Washington's political affairs, their presence there is barely mentioned in standard textbooks on American politics. Political scientists, he argues, have not yet portrayed Washington think tanks and their recent growth as a 'new, important and institutional force in American life and the nation's capital'.

A likely reason for the lack of systematic scholarly work on think tanks to date is the difficulty of establishing an agreed definition. Borrowed from World War Two military jargon for a secure room where plans and strategies could be discussed, the term 'think tank' was first used in a political sense during the 1950s to denote the 'contract research organizations' (see later), such as the RAND Corporation, which were set up by the US government

after the war (Dickson, 1971; Smith, 1991). By the 1960s, 'think tank' had
entered popular, as well as political, discourse in the United States. Even at
this stage its meaning was imprecise. Hames and Feasey (1994: 216) have
suggested that a broad definition of the term would be 'a non-profit public
policy research institution with substantial organizational autonomy', but
concede that this 'hardly reveals much about the character and nature of
these entities'. The sheer number and diversity of private research institutions found in the US has made an exact definition problematic, and perhaps
ultimately elusive (Denham and Garnett, 1995; 1996). American scholars
have responded to this difficulty by identifying and distinguishing between
three categories of think tank: 'universities without students', 'contract
research organizations', and 'advocacy tanks' (Weaver, 1989).

The first category consists of large institutions whose staff work mainly on
book-length studies. These institutes differ from universities in at least two
important respects. First, staff are not required to teach students in the same
way that (most) full-time academics are. Second, the subject areas investigated tend to have a stronger policy focus than the research and analysis
undertaken in university departments, which is (usually) 'more academic,
theoretical and less palatable for general consumption' (Stone, 1991: 201).
Think tanks in this category have long-term horizons, target the 'climate' of
intellectual and political opinion and secure most of their core funding from
a multiplicity of donors in order to reduce the risk of client backlash over
particular research results (Ricci, 1993: 20). US think tanks which fit this
model include the Brookings Institution and the American Enterprise Institute (AEI); British examples of this type of think tank would arguably
include the Royal Institute of International Affairs (RIIA), the National Institute of Economic and Social Research (NIESR) and the International Institute for Strategic Studies (IISS).

A second type of think tank described in the American literature is the
'contract research organization'. These institutes, as the name suggests, serve
government agencies and private sponsors on a contractual basis by execut-
ing research solicited in a variety of fields. Contract researchers cannot claim
to be entirely 'objective' in their areas of study, because if their conclusions
are too much at odds with a client's interests, future research contracts may
be awarded to their competitors. The emphasis here, then, is on 'excellence'
defined by contract success, rather than by the kind of 'peer group recognition offered within research communities such as academic disciplines'
(Ricci, 1993: 20). As Ricci notes, there are many think tanks in Washington,
such as the Mitre Foundation, that undertake one piece of contract research
after another. More famous US think tanks that fit this model include the
RAND Corporation (operating mainly in defence-related fields) and the
Urban Institute (covering mostly domestic policy issues). British think tanks
that undertake at least some contract research for government agencies

include the Policy Studies Institute (PSI) and the Institute for Fiscal Studies (IFS).

The third category of think tanks identified in the American literature has only emerged since the 1970s. These bodies, collectively labelled 'advocacy tanks', combine a strong policy, partisan or ideological outlook with aggressive sales techniques in a deliberate effort to influence the course of current policy debates. Advocacy tanks synthesize and put a distinctive 'spin' on existing research, rather than conduct enquiries on their own account. The format chosen for their studies is, typically, the short pamphlet or paper, rather than books or monographs. As Weaver (1989: 567) has argued, what their publications may be thought to lack in terms of genuine scholarship is made up for by their accessibility to policy-makers. Just as think tanks in the 'universities without students' category bear some resemblance to academic institutions, advocacy tanks are frequently difficult to distinguish from 'pressure groups', in that both are 'essentially interested in political lobbying' (Hames and Feasey, 1994: 217). Some pressure groups, indeed, conduct more primary research than advocacy tanks in order to provide 'scientific' backing for their causes. An important difference between the two, however, is that the latter tend to operate across a broad range of policy areas, whereas the former normally organize their campaigning activities around issues that relate to one particular field. As the number and variety of bodies claiming the status of 'think tanks' has increased, however, even this distinction can be pushed too far (Denham and Garnett, 1996: 45–6). US think tanks which fit this model include the Heritage Foundation and the Institute for Policy Studies; British examples include 'New Right' organizations such as the Adam Smith Institute (ASI), the Centre for Policy Studies (CPS) and the Social Affairs Unit (SAU) (Denham, 1996: see later).

While typologies of this sort have some use and validity for explanational purposes, they should not be interpreted too literally. As Stone (1991: 201) has argued, models like this do not always allow a perfect 'fit' and 'grey areas' persist. While the three categories outlined above are analytically distinct, the reality is more complicated. In practice, the aims and activities of *individual* think tanks are frequently diverse and subject to change over time. Hames and Feasey (1994: 217) note that the AEI, for instance, has at various times undertaken research of a kind that would fit all three of Weaver's categories, while the Heritage Foundation (normally considered an advocacy tank) has also published some bulky research of a flavour consistent with the 'universities without students' model. In short, think tanks do not have a generic form in the same sense as (say) families, armies, churches or industrial corporations. Instead, the term is used to refer to institutions 'whose aims may vary across time and whose researchers may associate with one another only temporarily and for personal convenience' (Ricci, 1993: 21).

Moreover, as Dickson has argued, a further problem has to do with the fact that while most groups that are (in his view) 'think tanks' dislike (and in some cases disavow) the term, 'pretentious little research groups' frequently invoke it for reasons of self-aggrandizement. Genuine think tanks, he argues, consider the term 'think tank' limiting, confusing and even demeaning; it sounds too passive, connotes non-accomplishment (a place where thinking is an end in itself, irrespective of the impact of such thinking on policy and events) and produces confusion as to the goals of these organizations (Dickson, 1971: 28). As Rivlin (1992: 22) has recalled, staff at the Brookings Institution used to disdain the 'faintly pejorative' appellation 'think tank', even if they now use it as freely as everyone else. In conducting the research for this chapter, we have uncovered evidence of this in the British context also – notably when the director of one institution insisted that her organization is not a 'think tank' but an 'independent public policy research institute'. At the other end of the spectrum, meanwhile, we have argued elsewhere that the term 'think tank' carries an unmistakable prestige which is sometimes undeserved and that political commentators should be more careful when bestowing such accolades (Denham and Garnett, 1995: 326). Interestingly, Margaret Thatcher, in her second volume of memoirs, suggests that the CPS, a body which she helped to found in the mid-1970s, 'could not properly be called a think tank, for it had none of the corporate grandeur of the prestigious American foundations which that term evokes' (Thatcher, 1995: 252).

The role of think tanks

While an exact definition of the term 'think tank' is problematic, their role (what think tanks do, or at least attempt to do) appears more straightforward. As Ricci (1993: 1) notes, think tanks of every magnitude and persuasion organize seminars and conferences, publish books, pamphlets, reports and journals, and they encourage their fellows to write topical articles or co-opted commentaries on a broad range of public affairs. Especially during the 1980s, the advocacy tanks were a godsend to the editors of Britain's Sunday broadsheets, always ready to fill up spare column inches with their musings. As the range of British political ideas narrowed in the post-Thatcher era, the partisan think tanks were still providing much-needed copy – only the articles were increasingly about the think tanks themselves, and not their ideas (for one example of many, see Caulkin, 1997).

Specifically, there seem to be two main objectives that all think tanks endeavour to achieve. The first is to conduct research to produce findings which inform decision-making on discrete policy issues; the second is to influence the 'climate' of elite opinion within which, it is assumed, political actors are bound to operate (see, for example, Keynes, 1936; Hayek, 1967).

To date, however, the academic literature on think tanks has failed, for the most part, to address systematically the question of how far these objectives have been achieved. In Britain, this task has become more urgent because of the claims made by (or on behalf of) 'New Right' think tanks in recent years (Denham and Garnett, 1995; 1996).

The problem here, of course, is that precision in such matters is extremely difficult, if not impossible, to attain. This is because think tanks deal in ideas, whose circulation and impact cannot be measured satisfactorily (Ricci, 1993: 208–9). The late Lord Rothschild, the first head of the Central Policy Review Staff (CPRS) (see later), once defined a 'policy' as 'what is left, if anything is left, of a plan after the politicians have worked it over' (quoted in Colville, 1977: 97); tracing the effect of particular ideas on opinion (whether within elite circles or among the wider public) is, if anything, even more difficult than establishing the nature and extent of any connection that may exist between think tank output and policy outcomes. In what follows, we review those bodies which have attempted to fulfil the role of a think tank in Britain and provide a necessarily qualified assessment of their effectiveness.

The British think tank tradition

Relatively organized groups concerned either to bring about specific policy changes or to effect a more general change in the prevailing intellectual climate have a long history in Britain (Bradley, 1981; Harrison, 1993). In the early nineteenth century the 'Philosophic Radicals' identified closely with the ideas of Jeremy Bentham; apart from efficient campaigners such as Francis Place and the dynamic civil servant Edwin Chadwick they also boasted supporters in the House of Commons, including Joseph Hume and Sir William Molesworth. They compensated for their lack of numbers with their vigorous researches and relentless campaigning through their journal *The Westminster Review*. According to Dicey, liberalism of a Benthamite kind 'was not only dominant during what may be termed the era of reform, but betrayed, in parliament at least, little sign of weakening authority till the nineteenth century had run more than half its course' (Dicey, 1905: 181; cf. Finer, 1972). This view may be somewhat overstated (see later), but the influence of the Philosophic Radicals is apparent in much of the social and political legislation of the period, and their perceived effect on the 'climate of opinion' certainly worried their opponents, such as Benjamin Disraeli (*A Vindication of the English Constitution*) and Charles Dickens (*Hard Times*), even if their fate was 'never to command the people's confidence or affection' (Dicey, 1905: 181).

The impulses behind the activities of the Philosophic Radicals are clear;

their most notable work was done when the Industrial Revolution was producing new social pressures and the prestige of 'science' reached new
heights. Later in the century the roots of the Fabian Society (1884) are discernible in the years of economic 'depression' which succeeded the mid-Vic-
torian boom. As in the early years of the century, this was a period when
settled ideas were being challenged and when the electoral franchise was
being reformed to embrace the (male) working class (McBriar, 1966: 6–7;
MacKenzie and MacKenzie, 1977: 15–16). In many respects the early Fabians resembled the Philosophic Radicals: they backed their arguments with
exhaustive statistical evidence, and once their conclusions were reached it
was almost impossible to shake them. Like the Radicals, they were more
interested in 'permeating' the political establishment than in seeking election
to parliament (Harrison, 1993).

Fabians such as Bernard Shaw and Beatrice Webb were skilled self-publi-
cists and some historians have sought to debunk many of their claims (Hobsbawm, 1964; Thompson, 1967). Even so, this reaction can be taken too far;
if not directly responsible for laying the foundations of the welfare state, the
Webbs arguably provided at least some of the bricks and mortar (McBriar,
1966; 1987) and the establishment of the London School of Economics and
Political Science (LSE) was, above all, Sidney Webb's historic achievement
(Dahrendorf, 1995 – but see later). Although membership has remained
respectable (currently over 4,500) and the Society is still an active publisher,
its impact is widely believed to have diminished in the post-World War Two
period; whereas 'Fabianism' has been far from irrelevant in the conduct of
British politics since 1945 (Banting, 1979), the Fabian *Society* (as distinct
from powerful *individual* 'Fabians' within the party hierarchy) was not, for
the most part, a significant source of Labour Party policy formulation
(Callaghan, 1996). Whether or not its fortunes will improve under 'New'
Labour remains to be seen; with the Society's traditional 'collectivist' ethos
currently unfashionable with the party leadership, it may find that continued
prominence will have to be bought at the expense of its distinct identity.

A second 'wave' of British think tanks emerged in the inter-war period. The
British Institute of International Affairs (1920) was set up after the Versailles
peace conference. It acquired Chatham House in 1923, and received its royal
charter in 1926. Membership grew throughout the inter-war years and its
financial strength enabled it to establish its very influential journal (*International Affairs*), appoint a Director of Studies (Arnold Toynbee) and set up a
library (Higgott and Stone, 1994: 18). During the 1930s, the re-named *Royal*
Institute of International Affairs sponsored a range of studies including investigations of nationalism, monetary policy and international investment (Wallace, 1994: 141). Other activities during the 1930s included the publication
of a bulky annual *Survey of International Affairs* (which was quick to warn of
the growing Nazi menace) and a parallel series of *Documents*.

The RIIA emerged against a background of international crisis; it soon became the model for similar foreign policy think tanks in other countries. The inter-war period was also distinguished by severe economic disruption. In response, the 1930s saw the establishment of Political and Economic Planning (PEP) and the NIESR. In February 1931, a new periodical, *The Weekend Review*, published a pioneering article by its Assistant Editor, Max Nicholson, which outlined *A National Plan for Great Britain*. The article appeared at a time when a number of active spirits were disillusioned with the major political parties; only the Liberals under Lloyd George were ready to contemplate radical measures to tackle the economic crisis and there was little hope that they could form a government, at least in the foreseeable future. So much interest was aroused by Nicholson's article that the decision was taken to set up a research organization to advance the principles of 'planning', although the British tradition of piecemeal political change was so strong that even the enthusiasts who had relished Nicholson's article were divided on the advisability of using it (Pinder, 1981a). Like the Fabians before them, the founders of PEP aimed to collect information and 'permeate' the British political establishment with their ideas. In its first decade the organization produced reports on specific industries, and on housing and health services. Whatever the precise extent of PEP's influence in the 1930s, it has been credited with helping to prepare elite opinion for the changes of the 1940s, to which the cataclysmic events of World War Two added considerable impetus (Marwick, 1964; Addison, 1977; Barker, 1996).

During the period of post-war 'consensus' PEP's ideas found a more favourable reception in government (Goodman, 1981). It has been claimed, for instance, that in the decade leading up to the merger of PEP with the Centre for Studies in Social Policy (CSSP) to form the PSI in 1978, PEP's work had a significant impact in half a dozen main sectors of policy and made a notable contribution to public debate 'across the wide range of its economic, social and political research' (Pinder, 1981b: 155–7). While these judgements are those of insiders, Budd (1978: 86) has argued that PEP's report on *Growth in the British Economy* (1960) closely anticipated the approach of the National Economic Development Council (NEDC) set up in the following year, and the later Department of Economic Affairs (DEA). Its report on *Racial Discrimination* (1967) also appears to have had a direct and immediate impact on the decision by the then Home Secretary, Roy (now Lord) Jenkins, to proceed with a second Race Relations Act (Pinder, 1981b: 140–3; Rose *et al.*, 1969). PSI continues to produce thoroughly researched publications on a range of subjects; a measure of its proficiency is the fact that it continued to receive commissions from government throughout the 1980s and beyond, when the ethos in Downing Street was far removed from the relatively moderate and non-partisan approach which has always characterized the Institute (although claims that it has no ideological bias at all must be treated with great scepticism – cf. Daniel, 1989).

The decision to set up the NIESR was taken at the end of 1937, following a first initiative by Sir Josiah (later Lord) Stamp in the early 1930s. The motive, according to an early press release, was to counteract the perceived inadequacy of the facilities available for research in the social sciences compared to those in the natural sciences and to establish a national organization dedicated to the pursuit of 'independent' economic research. Stamp (among his numerous roles) had been appointed by Ramsay MacDonald to the Labour government's Economic Advisory Council (EAC) in 1931 (Howson and Winch, 1977); the subsequent obstruction of that group by the Treasury must have been a factor in convincing him of the need for a more independent source of expert economic advice. Stamp was present at a meeting as early as February 1933 at the home of the eccentric Conservative backbencher (but later Prime Minister) Harold Macmillan; the purpose of the meeting was 'to discuss the question of founding an Economic Institute on the lines of similar American Institutions (Brookings etc.)' in Britain (Thomas Jones, quoted in Marwick, 1964: 287). While these ambitions have not quite been fulfilled, the NIESR has undoubtedly influenced economic policy in Britain since the war, at least on those rare occasions when governments have been open-minded enough to listen to 'objective' advice, rather than distorting the economy for political gain. Apart from publishing regular economic forecasts for Britain and the world as a whole, an insider has claimed that the NIESR has also played an important educative role and has influenced the way economics is taught in British universities. In addition, the Institute has received extensive media coverage, both for its *Economic Review* (first issued in 1959) and for longer-term studies (Jones, 1988).

In short, there is ample evidence to show that policy bodies that belong to the first and second 'waves' have fulfilled the model of think tank functions outlined above. If they have not in many cases actually directed the policymaker's hand, they have at least jogged his elbow; attention of this kind was hardly unexpected given that these groups addressed themselves to the perceived problems facing British governments at various times, but the quality of their advice also ensured that they would continue to win a hearing once the immediate 'crises' were over. Although their publications may not have seriously affected 'public opinion' (broadly conceived) they have attracted informed support outside narrow parliamentary cliques. In sum, it is reasonable to conclude that a continuous and healthy British think tank tradition can be traced well into the nineteenth century.

The third wave: New Right think tanks

The prominence of New Right think tanks during the 1970s and 1980s has prompted the misleading assertion that the appearance of think tanks in Britain is 'only a recent phenomenon' (James, 1993: 492). As our brief discussion shows, the British think tank tradition is well established and British institutes, like those found in the USA, now range from quasi-academic bodies, at one end of the spectrum, to ideologically partisan groups, at the other. A further parallel is that the more partisan think tanks in both countries have been established, for the most part, since the 1970s (Weaver, 1989; Stone, 1991). The impression that British think tanks are a recent development owes much to the fact that the term was first used widely here only after Edward Heath set up the CPRS under Lord Rothschild in 1970–1. Even after its abolition by Margaret Thatcher following the 1983 General Election the CPRS continued to be known as *'the* Think Tank' (Hennessy *et al.*, 1985; James, 1986; Blackstone and Plowden, 1988). Heath intended the CPRS to symbolize his new, long-term approach to government, as opposed to what he saw as the empty gimmicks of Harold Wilson's period in office. The prestige invested in the CPRS has carried over to the benefit of the groups which outlasted it – bodies which might share something of the former's concern for longer-term policy work, but which in many cases have had their 'research' findings dictated to them by ideological pre-suppositions (Denham and Garnett, 1994; 1995; 1996).

Most commentators would accept that, with the partial exception of the (more academically inclined and earlier-founded) Institute of Economic Affairs (IEA), the New Right groups that first came to prominence in the late 1970s are best described as 'advocacy tanks' in the sense outlined earlier. As Wallace (1994: 149) notes, the new think tanks that sprang up alongside the IEA in the 1970s were (and remain) 'small, passionately committed and concerned only with providing arguments for those already half-persuaded'. Staff at the CPS, for instance, were 'already committed to the new economics of the market and monetarism' from the outset and sought merely to 'change other people's minds' (Cockett, 1994: 239). Indeed, however much the IEA may *aspire* to be (and to perceive itself as) a 'university without students' (Hames and Feasey, 1994: 216), it is important to recall that the Institute was 'formed by people who were safe in the knowledge that they had already discovered the Holy Grail – the free market' (Cockett, 1994: 326). In short, it can be argued that *none* of the New Right groups associated (in the minds of some journalists at least) with the 'Thatcherite' project has fulfilled a key function of traditional Anglo-American think tanks, namely that of *searching for* policies and ideas; instead, their primary task has been (and remains) to 'evangelize' for the causes of economic liberalism and 'liberal-Conservatism' (Cockett, 1994: 139; Harris, 1996).

Like the other 'waves' of think tanks discussed earlier, the third 'wave' of (predominantly) New Right groups appeared in response to a perceived 'crisis'. The IEA gestated over several years; its founders were followers of Friedrich Hayek, who like him were concerned that Britain (along with the whole Western world) was proceeding rapidly down the road to economic and political 'serfdom' (Hayek, 1944). The Conservative governments of Churchill and Eden were no more receptive to right-wing economic thought than the opposition Labour and Liberal Parties; the obvious answer was to proselytize outside of the main parties, in the hope that one or all of them would one day perceive and act upon the 'fundamental economic truths' rehearsed in the Institute's numerous publications (Seldon, 1981). Thus the IEA (rather like PEP before it) had party-political independence forced on it by circumstances.

The later New Right think tanks, the CPS (1974) and the ASI (1977) belong in the same 'wave' as the IEA because they were responding to the same problem: the alleged failure of the 'Keynesian' approach in arresting and reversing Britain's (relative) economic decline. The main difference is that the CPS and the ASI were established after the 1973–4 oil shock – a crisis in the Western world which provoked the search for policy alternatives of a kind that the IEA had looked for in vain over so many years. Unlike the IEA, the CPS has always enjoyed very intimate links with the Conservative Party – a former director has emphasized its role in speech-writing – and therefore its donors cannot claim tax relief through charitable status (Shearmur, 1995; Desai, 1994). One of the ASI's founders, and later its President, Madsen Pirie, has described its members as 'policy engineers', who seek to provide workable ideas for ministers, in contrast to the more abstract fare offered by the IEA (Pirie, 1988; Denham, 1996). To support this claim to a market niche, the ASI has been conspicuously more aggressive than other New Right think tanks in boasting of its direct influence over policy, as opposed to mere 'opinion forming'.

The question of how far the New Right think tanks have fulfilled their aims of influencing either policy-making or the 'climate of opinion' is particularly difficult to answer with any confidence. An avowedly ideological Prime Minister was a new phenomenon in British politics, and anyone who shared Mrs Thatcher's general outlook was bound to win publicity from the media whether she listened to them or not. Even the cheer-leaders of the think tanks are deeply confused on the subject of real influence. In his interesting full-length study based on privileged access to people and papers, Richard Cockett claims that the free-market groups 'did as much intellectually to convert a generation of "opinion-formers" and politicians to a new set of ideas as the Fabians had done with a former generation at the turn of the century' (Cockett, 1994: 5; unlike many recent historians (see earlier) Cockett seems to accept the self-proclaimed influence of the Fabians at face value). Yet Cockett himself allows that the ideas peddled by the New Right 'never captured the hearts, let alone the minds, of more than a small minority of Conservative MPs, even during the heyday of Thatcherism in the mid-1980s' (Cockett, 1994: 325). Nor, for that matter, does the free-market message appear to have impressed a stubbornly 'non-Thatcherite' electorate (Crewe, 1988). Seen in this perspective, Cockett inadvertently portrays the 'success' of New Right ideas in Britain as something like a *coup d'état* – a radical, even revolutionary, 'blueprint' imposed on (millions of) people who manifestly disagreed with it (Barry, 1989: 53). As we have seen, Dicey admitted that the Philosophic Radicals were equally unsuccessful in capturing hearts and minds, but they at least operated in a pre-democratic era.

To the extent that an agenda which broadly coincided with the ideology of the third-wave think tanks really has been imposed on Britain since the late 1970s, can the think tanks take any credit (or blame) for this? It would be an ironic conclusion that a right-wing movement which set out to convince the intellectual community as a whole 'succeeded' because the British constitution concentrates so much power in the hands of the Prime Minister. Even when the Cabinet papers for the period are released it seems unlikely that any direct influence will be proved; indeed, case studies of key 'Thatcherite' innovations like the Community Charge or 'Poll Tax' already suggest that the 'policy engineers' have exaggerated their role (Crick and Van Klaveren, 1991; Butler *et al.*, 1994; see also Jordan and Ashford, 1993). Certainly if Mrs Thatcher had not been elected in the special circumstances of 1979 the course of British history for the following 18 years (at least) would have been different, but this is not to say that there would have been no 'Thatcher experiment' had the IEA, the CPS and the ASI not existed. The most important MP who accepted right-wing ideas – Mrs Thatcher herself – clearly absorbed the basis of her 'thinking' from her father. She read Hayek and visited the IEA before becoming leader of the Conservative Party, but Hayek's work – like that of all extreme ideologues – is only convincing to those who are already predisposed to believe it. The best-known exception to this general rule was Sir Keith Joseph, whose intellectual acceptance of right-wing policies was at odds with an over-developed social conscience; significantly, Joseph was a hapless minister as a result (cf. Oliver, 1996: 81–2).

If the right-wing think tanks failed to influence the wider 'climate of opinion', and cannot prove that they directly shaped policy during the 1980s, what is left for them to claim? Are commentators merely guilty of an 'intellectualist fallacy' – attributing influence to intellectuals because, as intellectuals themselves, they have a vested interest in doing so? Just as the British think tank tradition is well-established, so too is the argument, furnished with impressive historical research and documentary evidence, that the role of ideas and intellectuals in British politics (and the extent to which either can be said to account for political change) was always a more modest one than writers such as Dicey (1905) and Halevy (1928), in the case of 'Benthamism' in the nineteenth century, or (more recently) Cockett, in the case of 'Fabianism' in the twentieth, have assumed (MacDonagh, 1958; Roberts, 1959; Thomas, 1979; Gamble, 1996; Green, 1997). As Dahrendorf (1995: 40) has shrewdly observed:

> [P]erhaps the most complicated reason for the Fabian hype has to do with the fact that many of the things which they said actually happened. In some cases they happened because they made them happen; Sidney Webb (though not *the* Fabians') actually wanted LSE and made it possible. In other cases, including the huge project of the welfare state, the connection is more tenuous. Keith Middlemas's *Politics in Industrial Society* gives a sobering account of the disjunctions between radical projects and practical actions; the two [world] wars stimulated more social reforms in this century than all [the] Labour governments put together, though Labour [politicians] and even Fabians prepared the ground. But we do not like the complexity of real history. The authors of ideas prefer to think that they are directly responsible for realities which correspond to their speeches or writings, and the rest love simple causal explanations, not to say conspiracy theories. The fallacy which logicians call *post hoc ergo propter hoc* is almost irresistible. The Webbs recommended universal insurance in their Minority Report for the Poor Law Commission. Its implementation many years later must then be their achievement. This is how myths are born which, if repeated often enough, sound almost like history.

There remain two respects – closely related, but distinct – in which think tanks really do seem to have played a role in contemporary British politics. Instead of the vague term 'climate of opinion' we should examine the concept of *ideological fellowship*. Even if few people accepted the arguments of the think tanks, the institutional setting which they provided for like-minded individualists undoubtedly helped to convince Mrs Thatcher that her views were supported by enthusiastic and well-informed people outside Whitehall. Although she regularly appealed to the 'common sense' of the British public, she could not have consulted this very deeply because opinion polls would have told her that she was out of touch from an early stage in her premiership; but with sympathetic think tankers in attendance, any evidence of dissent which reached her could be overlooked. It might be argued that in providing the Prime Minister with a kind of surrogate for real public opinion the think tanks were inadvertently harming their cause; the greatest policy failures of the 1980s generally arose when Mrs Thatcher and her ministers felt confident enough to dispense with even token consultations (Marsh and Rhodes, 1992). In view of this it is only fair to the think tanks to conclude that their advice even in these celebrated instances formed only part of the background from which half-baked policies emerged; in most cases they *responded* to a policy agenda which they knew already existed, rather than shaping it for themselves.

The second respect in which the think tanks can claim some influence is through *recruitment*. With the increasing 'professionalization' of politics, a background in think tanks has become a useful platform to a career in parliament. Alternatively, for a new MP to write a pamphlet for a think tank in the 1980s was a promising means to the establishment of a reputation for expertise in a specific area – whether or not senior figures within the Conservative Party did more than glance at the title page of the publication. John Redwood and David Willetts are only the most prominent examples of Conservative politicians whose careers have been advanced in this way, and the 1997 General Election brought to parliament new Labour MPs such as Stephen Twigg and Patricia Hewitt who had won prominence or patronage through work in think tanks.

The fourth wave: beyond the New Right?

Whether or not the New Right bodies made much difference to politics in the 1980s the public profile of the third-wave groups under Margaret Thatcher created a spirit of emulation in people who dissented from the rigid free-market model. The Institute for Public Policy Research (IPPR, 1988) was set up as a left-wing rival to the IEA, CPS and ASI (Ruben, 1996). With hindsight the main cause for surprise is that this did not happen earlier; certainly the opposition to Mrs Thatcher would have received a publicity bonus had a think tank been established to show that there really was an alternative to the right-wing agenda. In practice the IPPR has represented something of a mid-way point between second-wave think tanks like PSI and the Thatcherite bodies; it has a much more partisan edge than the former groups, but lacks the ideological certainties of the latter. It is fair to say that this identity has been forced upon it because the British left has been rethinking its politics since before 1988.

Demos (1993) could be described as the first post-modern think tank; instead of rehearsing a long-established ideological line it has emerged from the breakdown of belief. Its staff are young and, while its founder Geoff Mulgan is close to senior figures in 'New' Labour, Demos has sought to attract support for its ideas across the political spectrum rather than from any one political party (Bale, 1996). Like the ASI, it has dealt very effectively with the media; paradoxically, although it often urges more meaningful political participation from the electorate its message might not prosper if genuine enthusiasm for the British political process revives.

The Social Market Foundation (SMF, 1989) is a rather different case. Founded by the biographer of Lord Keynes, Robert Skidelsky, and Lord Kilmarnock, the SMF was originally associated with the Social Democratic

Party (SDP) but became independent when that party lost its separate existence (Baston, 1996: 63). At the time of its foundation the term 'social market' could mean almost anything; in continental usage it implied a fostering of community spirit by an active state, but after Sir Keith Joseph had hijacked the term in Britain it could be equated with the idea that community was a handicap to the free operation of the market. In practice, this latter meaning has predominated, but after the defeat of the Conservatives in 1997 the SMF is well placed to move towards the former if it chooses. It was founded too late to influence the Conservatives during the period of ideological excess, but with close links to influential party figures such as Danny Finkelstein and David Willetts it will be able to take the winning side once the Tory faction fights have been settled.

Conclusion: the future of British think tanks

This rapid survey of think tanks in Britain suggests that they have formed part of the policy environment for over a century. The name, at least, has become a part of the political vocabulary (at the time of writing, BBC Television is running a discussion programme called *Think Tank*, as if to re-emphasize the point that their main purpose is to provide media-friendly soundbites). On the basis of available evidence their impact has ranged from the important to the trivial, and it is by no means true that those which advertise their claims the loudest should be credited with the greatest influence. During the 1990s the term 'think tank' has been used in connection with a bewildering array of organizations, some of which seem to consist of little more than a secretary and a word-processor. Politicians who wish to be taken seriously as intellectuals can now win free publicity by 'setting up their private think tank' (best described as a 'vanity tank'), even if this never researches (or even publishes) anything at all. Although scholars might produce tighter definitions to exclude such bodies, the media will continue to call them think tanks. To the extent that these pseudo-think tanks might bring independent policy groups into disrepute, the future looks gloomy. Another consideration leading to the same conclusion is the new vitality of single-issue politics, which is sure to win new resources for pressure groups, many of which already enjoy impressive research capabilities.

At the time of writing (September 1997) the most likely short-term development is at least partial eclipse for the New Right bodies. Roughly since the fall of Mrs Thatcher there has been a tendency for the media to claim that the IEA *et al.* have 'run out of ideas'. Since they only really had one 'idea' in the first place – that market solutions are (almost) always best – presumably the New Right would only be stumped for new suggestions if Britain had really been transformed into a golden kingdom of *laissez-faire* equipped with a minimal framework of laws and a central bank which automatically keeps the money supply under control. Since this right-wing fantasy will never happen there will always be a market for the neo-liberals to exploit, and businesspeople to finance their operations. The New Right is as full of its idea as it ever was, even if the media is no longer quite so interested. The newspapers have decided to write articles about the 'climate of opinion' having shifted to the left – not because the Labour Party has more interesting ideas, but because it is more popular than the Conservatives. Nothing would help the New Right think tanks more than a period of genuine left-wing government, but since Tony Blair is unlikely to oblige them, full recovery looks a distant prospect. The ASI has led the way in courting a 'New' Labour government which has swallowed much of the Thatcherite agenda, but it must be doubted whether these flirtations will lead to a lasting affair (Denham and Garnett, 1998).

This would suggest that the future lies (appropriately enough) with the fourth wave of think tanks, whose light ideological baggage suits the tone of current Westminster politics. In order to consolidate their position, these groups need to rid themselves of the vices characteristic of the New Right – the tendency to publish under-researched pamphlets on subjects of current media interest. Despite the 'Thatcherite' storm, this problem has never affected the older-established think tanks, particularly the PSI and NIESR, even if they have seen the importance of providing concise summaries of their findings for the press. They continue to win media coverage not because their reports are 'sensational' but because their conclusions are based on solid research. A laudable development during the 1997 General Election campaign which confirms the new trend was the prominence accorded to another think tank which follows in this honourable tradition – the IFS. If the importance of think tanks should be measured in terms of truly lasting influence, recent experience has demonstrated that instead of 'thinking the unthinkable' (whatever that might mean), thinking on the basis of evidence is the true key to success.

References

The authors are indebted to Andrew Gamble, Jeremy Shearmur, William Wallace and Mark Wickham-Jones for comments on earlier drafts. In addition, we wish to acknowledge the financial support of the Research Committee, University of Nottingham and the British Academy (Social Sciences Research Award for 'Think Tanks and British Politics' to Andrew Denham).

Addison, Paul (1977) *The Road to 1945: British Politics and the Second World War*, London, Quartet Books.

Bale, Tim (1996) 'Demos: Populism, Eclecticism and Equidistance in the Post-modern World', *Contemporary British History*, 10(2): 22–34.

Banting, Keith (1979) *Poverty, Politics and Policy: Britain in the 1960s*, London, Macmillan.

Barker, Rodney (1996) 'Political Ideas since 1945, Or How Long was the Twentieth Century?', *Contemporary British History*, 10(1): 2–19.

Barry, Norman (1989) 'Ideas and Interests: The Problem Reconsidered', in Andrew Gamble, Mancur Olson, Norman Barry, Arthur Seldon, Max Hartwell and Andrew Melnyk, *Ideas, Interests and Consequences*, London, IEA.

Baston, Lewis (1996) 'The Social Market Foundation', *Contemporary British History*, 10(1): 62–72.

Blackstone, Tessa and Plowden, William (1988) *Inside the Think-Tank: Advising the Cabinet 1971–1983*, London, Heinemann.

Bradley, Ian (1981) 'Intellectual Influences in Britain: Past and Present', in Arthur Seldon (ed.), *The Emerging Consensus ...?*, London, IEA.

Budd, Alan (1978) *The Politics of Economic Planning*, London, Fontana.

Butler, David, Adonis, Andrew and Travers, Tony (1994), *Failure in British Government: The Politics of the Poll Tax*, Oxford, Oxford University Press.

Callaghan, John (1996) 'The Fabian Society since 1945', *Contemporary British History*, 10(2): 35–50.

Caulkin, Simon (1997) 'I Think Therefore I Am: Capital Brainboxes Who Set the Agenda', *Observer*, 16 February.

Cockett, Richard (1994) *Thinking the Unthinkable: Think-Tanks and the Economic Counter-Revolution 1931–1983*, London, HarperCollins.

Colville, John (1977) *The New Elizabethans 1952–1977*, London, Collins.

Crewe, Ivor (1988) 'Has the Electorate become Thatcherite?', in Robert Skidelsky (ed.), *Thatcherism*, London, Chatto and Windus.

Crick, Michael and Van Klaveren, Adria (1991) 'Mrs Thatcher's Greatest Blunder', *Contemporary Record*, 5(3): 397–416.

Dahrendorf, Ralf (1995) *LSE: A History of the London School of Economics and Political Science, 1895–1995*, Oxford, Oxford University Press.

Daniel, William (1989) 'PSI: A Centre for Strategic Research', *Policy Studies*, 9(4):24–33.

Denham, Andrew (1996) *Think-Tanks of the New Right*, Aldershot, Dartmouth.

Denham, Andrew and Garnett, Mark (1994) 'The Idea Brokers: A Reply to Simon James', *Public Administration*, 72(3): 482–5.

Denham, Andrew and Garnett, Mark (1995) 'Rethinking Think Tanks: A British Perspective', in Joni Lovenduski and Jeffrey Stanyer (eds), *Contemporary Political Studies 1995, Volume One*, Exeter, Political Studies Association.

Denham, Andrew and Garnett, Mark (1996) 'The Nature and Impact of Think Tanks in Contemporary Britain', *Contemporary British History*, 10(1): 43–61.

Denham, Andrew and Garnett, Mark (1988) *British Think Tanks and the Climate of Opinion*, London, UCL Press.

Desai, Radikha (1994) 'Second-hand Dealers in Ideas: Think Tanks and Thatcherite Hegemony', *New Left Review*, 203: 27–64.

Dicey, Albert Venn (1905) *Lectures on the Relation between Law and Public Opinion in England during the Nineteenth Century*, London, Macmillan.

Dickson, Paul (1971) *Think Tanks*, New York, Ballantine Books.

Dror, Yehezkel (1980) 'Think Tanks: A New Invention in Government', in Carol H. Weiss and Alan H. Barton (eds), *Making Bureaucracies Work*, Beverly Hills, Sage.

Dye, Thomas R. (1978) 'Oligarchic Tendencies in National Policy Making: The Role of Private Planning Organisations', *Journal of Politics*, 40 (May): 309–31.

Finer, Samuel E, (1972) 'The Transmission of Berthanite Ideas 1820–50', in Gillian Sutherland (ed.), *Studies in the Growth of Nineteenth-Century Government*, London, Routledge and Kegan Paul.

Gaffney, John (1991) 'Political Think Tanks in the UK and Ministerial Cabinets in France', *West European Politics*, 14(1): 1–17.

Gamble, Andrew (1996) 'Ideas and Interests in British Economic Policy', *Contemporary British History*, 10(2): 1–21.

Goodman, Raymond (1981) 'The First Post-war Decade', in John Pinder (ed.), *Fifty Years of Political and Economic Planning: Looking Forward 1931–1981*, London, Heinemann.

Green, E. H. (1997) 'Review of Richard Cockett, *Thinking the Unthinkable*', *Twentieth Century British History*, 8(1): 107–14.

Halévy, Elie (1928) *The Growth of Philosophic Radicalism*, trans. Mary Morris, London, Faber and Faber.

Hames, Tim and Feasey, Richard (1994) 'Anglo-American Think Tanks under Reagan and Thatcher', in Andrew Adonis and Tim Hames (eds), *A Conservative Revolution? The Thatcher–Reagan Decade in Perspective*, Manchester, Manchester University Press.

Harris, Michael (1996) 'The Centre for Policy Studies: the Paradoxes of Power', *Contemporary British History*, 10(2): 51–64.

Harrison, Royden (1993) 'The Fabians: Aspects of a Very English Socialism', in Iain Hampsher-Monk (ed.), *Defending Politics: Bernard Crick and Pluralism*, London, British Academic Press.

Hayek, Friedrich (1944) *The Road to Serfdom*, London, Routledge and Kegan Paul.

Hayek, Friedrich (1967) *Studies in Philosophy, Politics and Economics*, London, Routledge and Kegan Paul.

Hennessy, Peter and Coates, Simon (1991) 'Little Grey Cells: Think-tanks, Governments and Policy-making', *Strathclyde Analysis Papers*, No. 6, Department of Government, University of Strathclyde, Glasgow.

Hennessy, Peter, Morrison, Susan and Townsend, Richard (1985) 'Routine Punctuated by Orgies: The Central Policy Review Staff 1970–1983', *Strathclyde Papers on Government and Politics*, No. 31, Department of Government, University of Strathclyde, Glasgow.

Higgott, Richard and Stone, Diane (1994) 'The Limits of Influence: Foreign Policy Think Tanks in Great Britain and the USA', *Review of International Studies*, 20(1): 15–34.

Hobsbawm, Eric (1964) *Labouring Men: Studies in the History of Labour*, London, Weidenfeld and Nicholson.

Howson, Susan and Winch, Donald (1977) *The Economic Advisory Council 1930–1939: A Study in Economic Advice during Depression and Recovery*, Cambridge, Cambridge University Press.

James, Simon (1986) 'The Central Policy Review Staff 1970–1983', *Political Studies*,

34(3): 423–40.

James, Simon (1993) 'The Idea Brokers: The Impact of Think Tanks on British Government', *Public Administration*, 71(4): 491–506.

Jones, Kit (1988) 'Fifty Years of Economic Research: A Brief History of the National Institute of Economic and Social Research', *National Institute Economic Review*, May: 36–59.

Jordan, Grant and Ashford, Nigel (eds) (1993) *Public Policy and the Impact of the New Right*, London, Pinter.

Keynes, John Maynard (1936) *The General Theory of Employment, Interest and Money*, London, Macmillan.

MacDonagh, Oliver (1958) 'The Nineteenth-Century Revolution in Government: A Reappraisal', *Historical Journal*, 1(1): 52–67.

MacKenzie, Norman and MacKenzie, Jeanne (1977) *The First Fabians*, London, Weidenfeld and Nicolson.

Marsh, David and Rhodes, R. A. W. (eds) (1992) *Implementing Thatcherite Policies: Audit of an Era*, Buckingham, Open University Press.

Marwick, Arthur (1964) 'Middle Opinion in the Thirties: Planning, Progress and Political Agreement', *English Historical Review*, 79 (April): 285–98.

McBriar, Alan (1966) *Fabian Socialism and English Politics 1884–1918*, Cambridge, Cambridge University Press.

McBriar, Alan (1987) *An Edwardian Mixed Doubles: The Bosanquets versus the Webbs*, Oxford, Oxford University Press.

Oliver, Michael (1996) 'A Response to Denham and Garnett's "The Nature and Impact of Think Tanks in Contemporary Britain"', *Contemporary British History*, 10(2): 80–6.

Pinder, John (ed.) (1981a) *Fifty Years of Political and Economic Planning: Looking Forward 1931–1981*, London, Heinemann.

Pinder, John (1981b) '1964–1980: From PEP to PSI', in J. Pinder (ed.), *Fifty Years of Political and Economic Planning: Looking Forward 1931–1981*, London, Heinemann.

Pirie, Madsen (1988) *Micropolitics: The Creation of Successful Policy*, Aldershot, Wildwood House.

Ricci, David (1993) *The Transformation of American Politics:The New Washington and the Rise of Think Tanks*, New Haven, CT, Yale University Press.

Rivlin, Alice M. (1992) 'Policy Analysis at the Brookings Institution', in Carol Weiss (ed.), *Organizations for Policy Advice: Helping Government Think*, London, Sage.

Roberts, David (1959) 'Jeremy Bentham and the Victorian Administrative State', *Victorian Studies*, 2(3): 193–210.

Rose, E. J. B., Deakin, N., Abrams, M., Jackson, V., Peston, M., Vanags, A. H., Cohen, B., Gaitskell, J. and Ward, P. (1969) *Colour and Citizenship*, London, Oxford University Press for the Institute of Race Relations.

Ruben, Peter (1996) 'The Institute for Public Policy Research: Policy and Politics', *Contemporary British History*, 10(2): 65–79.

Seldon, Arthur (1981) 'Preamble: The Essence of the IEA', in Arthur Seldon (ed.), *The Emerging Consensus …?*, London, IEA.

Shearmur, Jeremy (1995) 'The Centre for Policy Studies', unpublished paper.

Smith, James A. (1991) *The Idea Brokers: Think Tanks and the Rise of the New Policy*

Elite, New York, Free Press.

Stone, Diane (1991) 'Old Guard versus New Partisans: Think Tanks in Transition', *Australian Journal of Political Science*, 26(2): 197–215.

Stone, Diane (1996) *Capturing the Political Imagination: Think Tanks and the Policy Process*, London, Frank Cass.

Thatcher, Margaret (1995) *The Path to Power*, London, HarperCollins.

Thomas, William (1979) *The Philosophic Radicals: Nine Studies in Theory and Practice 1817–1841*, Oxford, Clarendon Press.

Thompson, Paul (1967) *Socialists, Liberals and Labour: The Struggle for London, 1885–1914*, London, Routledge and Kegan Paul.

Wallace, William (1994) 'Between Two Worlds: Think Tanks and Foreign Policy', in C. Hill and P. Beshoff (eds), *Two Worlds of International Relations: Academics, Practitioners and the Trade in Ideas*, London, Routledge and the London School of Economics.

Weaver, Kent (1989) 'The Changing World of Think Tanks', *PS: Political Science and Politics*, September: 563–78.

Weiss, Carol (1992) 'Introduction: Helping Government Think: Functions and Consequences of Policy Analysis Organizations', in Carol Weiss (ed.), *Organizations for Policy Advice: Helping Government Think*, London, Sage.

French think tanks in comparative perspective

Introduction

A central theoretical preoccupation in social science is the problem of definition. The present volume (rightly, in our view) is no exception. In practical terms, however, there is no precise French definitional equivalent of the English term 'think tank'. 'Boîte à penser' is an anglicism which signifies nothing in the French political landscape, and has barely any currency at all. Significantly, the various librarians and information specialists we approached in undertaking the initial research for this chapter could not point us to any relevant headings in card catalogues or databases. This has afforded us the dubious luxury of elaborating our own definition (see below).

Several questions arise when defining a think tank. Which grouping or type(s) of grouping shall we take as constituting a 'think tank' in the French context? What is its relationship to established political parties? What is the capacity (and desire) of those involved to influence politics – and, more particularly, policy processes and outcomes? To these questions one needs to add that French think tanks (as we define them) have often had a greater impact on the wider *political* process than on the *policy* process. The fact that many French think tanks have relatively weak links (or none at all) to the latter means that they are more difficult to assess in terms of their aims and effectiveness; policy impact is difficult enough to measure when it is obvious, but even more so when it is incremental, a mere 'by-product' of think tank activity.

After definition and an analysis of some of the specific formative characteristics of the French context in section one, we shall examine, in section two, the ministerial *cabinets*. Section three deals with the political clubs, the reasons for their emergence, their subsequent personalization and their pivotal role in the French political system. Section four analyses groups which more closely resemble Anglo-Saxon think tanks: the national research insti-

tutes, the independent policy research groups and the intellectual think
tanks of the French New Right. Finally, in section five, we will draw some
conclusions about political think tanks in the Fifth Republic.

Definition and context

Our definition of think tanks involves a compromise between a classificatory
and generalizable definition, and the recognition that France presents par-
ticularities which modify generalization. An observer of American think
tanks, Nelson Polsby (1983), makes a distinction between think tanks and
policy research institutes on the basis that the main task, indeed the function,
of the latter is to make a policy impact whereas the think tank is engaged in
purely intellectual enterprise. Polsby's definition is rooted in an American
distinction between the intellectual and the policy sphere. Such a definition
is unhelpful for the French case. It does, however, throw into relief the difficulty in defining think tanks, namely the relationship between think tanks
and the state/policy sphere. This is particularly relevant in the French case
where the line between intellectual, or at least a particular type of intellectual, and politician is blurred (Gaffney, 1991). A useful concept in a definition of think tanks applied to the French context is that of the 'epistemic
community'. Indeed, merging Haas's (1992) and Stone's (1996: 87) concepts of an epistemic community to our own treatment of the distinction
delineated by Polsby offers a working definition and basic classification of
French think tanks.

Epistemic communities are 'politically motivated intellectuals seeking to
inform limited areas of policy on the basis of their expertise' (Stone, 1996:
36). This allows for a broad range of think tanks to be taken into account,
while placing the necessary emphasis on the ideological and/or scientific
coherence and policy interest of the institution. The emphasis on shared
norms and beliefs allows for think tanks to be both independent and ideologically committed. In this respect, think tanks are a fascinating emanation
of conviction and expertise and of the manner in which these organizations
interact with policy-making at a time when knowledge and information are
increasingly bound up with areas of expertise inaccessible to the politician.
In this way, think tanks become one means by which ideological commitment and scientific expertise inform policy-making. This applies to think
tanks everywhere, but in the French case ideological positioning is structured in a forceful and influential way by the political culture. If think tanks
are the means by which policy and intellectual convictions inform one
another, then the French case is particularly interesting given the specific
nature of these ties. Before giving our definition, let us briefly mention three
contextual factors which structure the definition itself.

A first factor is that a non-profit attitude to research and a degree of financial independence from vested government and corporate interests further the think tanks' claim to produce scientifically sound, rational research. We can draw, here, a distinction between France and Germany. In Germany, direct or indirect state support is proof of independence – both of the think tank and in some measure of the state. In France, this is not the case. The nature of the state, and its relationship to political parties in France, is such that think tanks could not benefit from state support while maintaining their independence.

Alongside the question of independence from the state, think tanks are also normally considered as needing to be independent from the pressures exerted by the private sector. In the USA, think tanks benefit from extensive corporate support. The scientific quality of the research produced is not necessarily diminished by the use industry or private vested interests make of it, even if they have actively contributed to its undertaking. This view, however valid, is an Anglo-Saxon one and reflects different understandings of the relationship between state and civil society. In British and American political thought, civil society rests upon a liberal ethos, placing at its core the role of the market. Civil society is often conceived of as a market-place of ideas. The French conception of civil society virtually excludes the private sector, hinging on a direct relationship between the state and the individual, a relationship constructed on the basis of the notion of the Republic (mediated only grudgingly by political parties). Intrusion by the corporate sector, in the form of funding for research institutes or think tanks, is invariably perceived as a fundamental affront to the values of the republic.

French think tanks also differ from Anglo-Saxon and German think tanks in that while these seek substantial funds, French think tanks do not appear to exhibit the same degree of financial need. In essence, French think tanks are smaller than their British, American, Canadian or German counterparts (see chapters in this volume). France offers a sharp contrast (excluding the state-funded and affiliated national research institutes which we shall examine below), with think tanks generally working with a maximum of three full-time staff and a budget often well under $0.5 million.

Second, the geographical concentration of the myriad of political think tanks in Paris is also not without significance and demonstrates how these organizations, often designed to call into question the centralization of the state, imitate these very structures. In terms of personnel, moreover, graduates from the prestigious Ecole Normale d'Administration (ENA) and the Institut des Etudes Politiques dominate. The corollary of this is that members of Parisian political think tanks will be not only geographically close, but socially, even personally so, too. Many, fragile, Parisian, elitist, and historically aware, the French think tanks are *very French* and bear out, in this domain at least, the continuing phenomenon of the 'French exception'.

A helpful way of looking at French think tanks is to view them from two perspectives. The first is that of their relationship to France's political institutions and formal political structures. There is a spectrum of interaction with formal structures depending upon the type of think tank involved, its ideological affinity with a political party, or with a government or government ministry. When assessing interaction, moreover, it is not only the nature of the relationships between think tanks and formal politics which is of theoretical and empirical interest, but that of formal structures to one another – the state apparatus to the political party, the education system to the bureaucracy, the political elites to the wider electorate, and so on – which arguably call into existence and sustain the French think tank. The second perspective concerns their enacted relationship to the wider political culture. The think tanks' scope and influence are discernible, in part, in terms of how they are perceived, what assumptions are made about them and what their role purports and is perceived to be. It is the case that assumptions – for example those of a group of intellectuals 'rethinking socialism' – will themselves have a range of real political effects, irrespective of the actual effects the think tank may have been designed to have (upon, say, the policy of a political party or the re-evaluation of socialism).

A defining characteristic of political think tanks, therefore, is their relationship to the state and the state's apparatuses within the framework of the wider culture, that is to say, the *interrelationship* of the two perspectives mentioned. In theory, the French state has no interlocutors – parties, associations, think tanks, interest groups – between it and the people. The French notion of popular sovereignty upon which republicanism is built posits no mediation. In practice, the nation-state teems with mediating institutions, and exercises a systematic – and indeed systemic – relationship with interest groups and pressure groups of various kinds in its policy elaboration and legislation.

The seedbed of these pressure groups is not only professional and other interest groups, but also the estimated half a million (and rising) active 'associations' in France (mainly sporting and cultural groups, sometimes no less politically significant for that). A think tank is neither a pressure group nor an association, but sometimes the dividing lines between the three types of organization are unclear. It is in this environment that we need to view the think tanks. That is, within the framework provided by a strong, centralized unitary state which needs to enter into a whole series of informal and semiformal relations with other sites of political activity, opinion, and expertise, because of its very centralization and the relative neatness of its political institutions. In short, a somewhat atomized nation-state with small political parties, very low union membership and little activity in local politics.

It is important to emphasize here that what determines the roles and aims of think tanks in this context is not vested interests, nor their source of funding, but their coherence of ideological belief and their expertise. It is, moreover, through these two fundamental characteristics that they acquire their third defining trait: political impact. Yet, as we shall see, this is not transmitted through the political system via formal channels and institutions alone.

For the purposes of analysis we shall therefore define a think tank in the French context as a group of experts who share an ideological orientation (and often similar educational and social background) and a wish for their research and reflection to influence the political process. This community's primary function is to engage in research projects, themselves informed by an ideological base, and to ensure that the results of the research or reflection have a political impact. Political impact can range from concrete policy proposals to electoral support for a particular candidate, to the fostering of public debate on particular topics. The defining features are therefore ideological coherence, expertise and impact. In our classification of think tanks in France some clearly share the characteristics of think tanks in other countries, while others are more exclusively French phenomena.

Definitional caveat

Before proceeding, however, we still need to bear in mind that identifying and classifying think tanks remains dauntingly difficult: associations, cercles, cercles d'étude, de réflexion, centres, clubs, alliances, conventions, forums, or simply groups with names or acronyms which resemble exhortations rather than an organization – Agir, Convergences solidarités, and so on – are everywhere; yet a phone number (so often unanswered) and a name (so often difficult to get hold of) do not in themselves constitute a think tank (or should not). The list, moreover, is endless and ever-changing. Such profusion and confusion is itself, however, significant and revealing of the overall situation: such activity and organization *assumes itself* to be politically consequential, and part of a vast and respected French tradition. It also bears witness to the French belief in ideas and their role in a politically healthy culture.

Ministerial *cabinets*

The ministerial *cabinets* place great strain on our definition of think tanks in France. Yet to miss them out would be to exclude from analysis a political institution, unique to France, which mimics, as it were, what think tanks yearn to be: groupings of experts, ideologically committed, practically oriented, who offer advice to government ministers, often short-circuiting that of the ministry's civil servants, and who have great influence upon agenda setting and policy elaboration (Gaffney, 1991). The *cabinets*, which are *ad hoc* groupings around newly appointed government ministers, have taken on a formal role within the governmental system (even though they have no basis within the Constitution).

They have existed in one form or another since before the Revolution, political entourages surrounding individuals. It was the Third Republic (1870–75 to 1940), suspicious of the Second Empire's civil servants, which saw the phenomenon embed itself in formal politics. The Third, Fourth and Fifth Republics have codified and regulated the *cabinets* (they now comprise a dozen or so advisors), and today they complement and rival the ministerial bureaucracy, providing all kinds of support, from legislative proposals to ordering taxis.

In many ways, the '*cabinet* ministériel' *is* the equivalent of the think tank in other countries. The member of the *cabinet* is, although normally civil service trained, invariably a member of a political party and has usually been associated with a particular principal personality, offering expertise, advice and support and therefore constituting part of his or her entourage. It is worth pointing out in the French context that the movement of individuals from the civil service, into politics, perhaps into business or the universities, and back again, has not been unusual, nor normatively questionable, as it is for example in the UK, on condition that certain procedural forms are observed.

Since the mid-1980s, there has developed a new phenomenon, what we might call the *cabinet*-in-waiting. With much greater alternation between the right and left in government, the ideological and personal groupings around a person or area of expertise need to be maintained while a government is out of office, hence the profusion since that time of small political clubs which mirror the *cabinets* themselves (Gaffney, 1988). It is clear that the *cabinets*' relationship not only to government but, even more importantly, to the political parties is of crucial importance. Let us turn then to the – again quintessentially French – phenomenon of the political clubs.

The political clubs

With respect to the role of political parties in France it is important to bear in mind the mistrust, if not disregard, in which parties have been held since their emergence. They were, in the first instance, held as a negative legacy of 1789, suspected of carrying forth into future eras the factionalism and back-stabbing politics of the darkest hours of the Revolution. In many ways, the parties were depicted as the enemies of the Republic: where the Republic was united, and embodied public concern and government for the people and by the people, the parties were disruptive, petty and the incarnation of individual or factional interests. The Third and Fourth Republics' weaknesses were seen as stemming directly from the power which the parties wielded within the National Assembly, to the detriment of strong efficient government.

Such hostility still exists, but from 1958 onwards, in a much reduced form. Ironically, de Gaulle, who so disdained the parties, was in large part responsible for their rehabilitation. His new Republic, although curtailing their influence – and effecting something of a showdown with them in 1962 when revising the Constitution to allow for the election of the president by universal adult suffrage – never posited an alternative to them. By heightening presidentialism within the Republic, however, he did institutionalize a kind of permanent antagonism between presidential and party principles. De Gaulle's mistrust of what he referred to as 'la politique politicienne' (party political machinations) and 'les féodalités' (parties as feudal lords) was accompanied by the curtailment of the National Assembly's powers and the relegation of the parties to their legislative and budgetary functions. Presidential politics, however, as designed by de Gaulle, went hand in hand with strong political parties in order to sustain potential candidates but also the democratic regime itself. In a regime built on the dual basis of Republicanism's historical legacy and strong presidential politics, political parties have had periodically to renegotiate their legitimacy.

Creating a club has been one of the ways in which parties have sought to be perceived as more than the apparatus of 'la politique politicienne'. This is even more true in the case of those clubs whose function is to promote the image and the opinions of a particular presidential candidate. In the 1980s and 1990s, for example, there were: 'Solidarité moderne' for Laurent Fabius; 'Convaincre' for Michel Rocard (later in 1996 Rocard founded 'ARES' – Action pour le Renouveau Socialiste); 'République moderne' for Jean-Pierre Chevènement; 'Club 89' for Jacques Chirac; 'Allons z'idées' for Jack Lang or 'Démocratie 2000' founded in 1985; and then 'Clysthène' for Jacques Delors.

Clubs in France reflect the need to elevate politics above partisan lines and the political club often depicts itself as being called into existence when the political party is seen to have failed in some of its essential functions: for example, offering the prospect of political power, providing policies, articulating an ideology, or, most importantly, defining or redefining political morality and 'vision'. The reasons for clubs serving a corrective function to political parties are complex, and raise questions about the premier importance of the role of the political party itself in the French polity. In the German case, the well-financed foundations are in a harmonious and permanent relationship to the political parties. In the UK, there are problems regarding their legitimacy vis-à-vis the party (the Fabians, for example, have always 'known their place' in terms of the British Labour movement and would face fierce criticism if they questioned it). In France, the legitimacy of the club is not contested. On the contrary, it is considered a vital part of the overall political process, but its *systematic* role vis-à-vis the political party is contested. It therefore resembles the UK think tank in one respect and the German in another, but its relation to the political party is, though organic, in many ways dynamically oppositional. The clubs therefore are always in an unstable, transitory, cyclical relationship to the political parties they 'serve'. As well as fulfilling their daily 'ordinary' tasks, the political parties, when 'healthy', are perceived as rallies of opinion – *rassemblements* – which rise and fall on the scale of political opportunity depending upon their 'fitness'. It is also worth noting that the nature of French political party rhetoric is very different from its Anglo-Saxon and Northern European counterparts. When this rhetoric seems no longer to correspond to political reality, that is, when the rhetoric remains 'moral' but action is perceived as not being so, there is a perceived fracture for which the club must offer a remedy. Good recent examples of this were the dislocations within the left as a result of repressive (often Socialist-led) government policy in Algeria during the 1950s, and the search for political purpose in the 1960s. The clubs in France thrive, therefore, in crises or perceived crises, and are always in a mutually legitimating relationship to political parties. This notion of crisis is underpinned by the fact that club activity invariably accompanies the loss of power by political parties, and the beginning of a period of regrouping and redefinition of aims, strategy and policy.

Two further points proceed from the preceding discussion. The first is that in the French case, for a whole variety of reasons related to history, political traditions, the electoral system, and political institutions, the parties are – when contrasted with comparable regimes – themselves relatively unstable, or rather vulnerable to shifts in opinion away from them to a rival party (for example in the 1980s and 1990s the Front National's gain in votes at the expense of the mainstream right and the Communists), or an alliance partner (for example the draining of support from the Communists to the Socialists as of the late 1970s and early 1980s; or the shift between the Rassemblement pour la Republique (RPR) and the Union pour la Démocratic Française (UDF) support from the mid-1970s onwards). The parties are also subject to surges of indifference or hostility, which are often followed by vulnerability to what the French call 'adventures' which may posit regime change and are normally accompanied by personal leadership appeals which contest party legitimacy.

The personal element we have just referred to within the overall political equation raises issues of fundamental importance, for just as personal leaders – especially during the Fourth Republic – could make anti-regime appeals for support and allegiance, in the Fifth Republic, because of the presidential system and its effects upon the polity, the personalization of power and of political allegiance have become the hallmarks of political activity. 'Persons' therefore work within the overall system as well as against it. This means two related things for clubs and political parties. The first is that the definition or redefinition of political activity and allegiance (and morality) traditionally undertaken by the club must address the question of the acute personalization of power in the Fifth Republic. The second related point is that individuals themselves will take on a more nodal function, making claims to be 'representative' of a tradition or part of it, and acting as brokers within parties, or between them, heightening their own position, and acting as rallying sites for opinion. 'Unstable' parties, or parties in complex alliance relations with others, witness this kind of activity constantly. So too do the clubs. Clubs set up by individual figures in the highly fractionated ecologist movement offer a good example – figures such as Brice Lalonde, Antoine Waechter and Noel Mamère moved throughout the 1980s and 1990s in perpetual relation to one another setting up *cercles de réflexion* ('Génération Ecologie', 'Le Mouvement des Ecologistes Indépendants', and 'Rassemblement pour une Ecologie Civique et Sociale' respectively) and claiming to represent various strands of ecologism in order to reinvigorate (and influence) the organized political movement. The same is true for individuals positioned *between* strong political parties. The site between the Socialist and Communist movements has long been one of proliferating *cercles or entourages* around figures such as ex-Socialist J.-Pierre Chevènement or ex-Communist Pierre Juquin. The irony in the case of ecologism, socialism, and communism lies in the claim of each to be fundamentally uninterested in following leaders for its own sake; once again we can see how the club imitates the structures it contests.

Like the ministerial *cabinets*, the political clubs are a hybrid phenomenon which, while not corresponding to a strict definition of think tanks, do however exhibit think tank characteristics (ideological coherence, political/policy impact and some research). They shed important light on the nature of relationships, formal and informal, political, ideological and social, and how these inform and structure politics in France. Often members of these political clubs are or have been members of ministerial *cabinets*, and are often involved in other groups and clubs.

Tracing the evolution of the political clubs in France from bona fide clubs to personalized political outfits sheds some light on the process through which many of these groupings designed to contest aspects of the political regime ultimately end up mirroring its defining features. The clubs of the 1960s, which sprang up right across the political spectrum in response to the Algerian war and the advent of the Fifth Republic, were themselves based upon a venerated French tradition of political clubs which thrived during the French revolutionary period of the late eighteenth century (themselves in part a version of the pre-revolutionary (and female influenced) *salons* of the

Enlightenment). This pedigree reflects a recurring (Parisian) insistence upon the role of the discussion of political ideas.

The most famous of the 1960s clubs was the Club Jean Moulin (founded in 1958 in reaction to the *coup d'état* in Algiers). It published a regular bulletin with a circulation of 2,000, produced in the course of the decade a dozen or so highly influential books (for example on constitutional reform and the rebuilding of the left), and saw transit through it most of the figures who were to play a role in left and centre-left politics in the subsequent decade (although in terms of what we said above about the subsequent personalization of club activity, few of the founding figures of the 1960s clubs went on to major political careers). We can make three points here: first, the Club Jean Moulin, like its contemporaries, was born in reaction to a perceived crisis (both of the regime and of the left more generally); second, it flourished in the absence of a strong left party, nurturing, redeveloping, 'keeping safe', as it were the torch of the non-Communist left; and, third, it was eclipsed at the moment the left united, and the clubs merged, in wave upon wave, into the new Socialist Party between 1969 and 1974.

Between 1958 and the late 1960s, scores of clubs were established. Many of them united with one another to form 'Unions', 'Conventions', or 'Federations' of clubs in order to give themselves more political influence at the national level (for example, François Mitterrand's 'Conventions des Institutions Républicaines'). In terms of their language and identity it should be mentioned that the 'voice' of the clubs was heavily influenced by, and in turn influenced, the emergence of neo-marxism as the main discourse of the left in the period 1960 to 1980. The rigour of marxism gave many of the clubs an intellectual integrity they might otherwise not have had, although such a discourse also added to the pretentiousness, inappropriateness, and ultimately the sterility of much club inquiry. Moreover, the teleology within marxian thought reinforced the idea that the clubs were so many tributaries flowing back to the main mighty river (a reunited left). It also eclipsed the other strong though younger tradition within the French left, that of Christian Democracy (Jacques Delors, a representative of this *tradition*, was himself a member of the second most important 1960s club, Citoyens 60, which claimed to provide a meeting-place for the centre-left).

The truly long-lasting effect of and upon the political clubs was their reconciliation of the left with the normative values of the Fifth Republic, the most dominant being that a person could represent a tradition or political family. It is not without interest to note that the clubs of the 1960s were superseded (1969–74) at the very point at which the left had reconciled itself to a *Gaullien* allegiance to an exemplary individual, in the case of the left the 'convert' to Socialism, François Mitterrand. The clubs, therefore, served a systemic function (which they would doubtless have denied), namely that rather than redefine the left in terms of rediscovering it beneath the rubble of the Algerian War and collapse of the Fourth Republic, their true 'function' was to align French socialism with the ideological parameters of the Fifth Republic, and take part in a mythical 'homecoming' of the left: the clubs, the trade unions, and the political parties, around the mythologized status of a heroic individual. This was to bring the left to power, but also present it and the club tradition with unexpected challenges.

Throughout the 1970s, with the reunification of the Socialist Party, the leadership of François Mitterrand, and the alliance between the Socialists and Communists, there was little club activity outside the rallying of opinion to the left. After the left gained power in 1981, winning both the presidency and a Socialist majority in the National Assembly, what had been apparent to some now became real for many and was to last throughout the 1980s and into the 1990s: socialism had lost its voice. There was an adage in British left politics after World War Two that socialism was whatever a Labour government happened to be doing at the time. In France, socialism in the 1980s, seemed to have become whatever François Mitterrand happened to be thinking.

Such as it was, the 'rethinking' that was being done was by groups of experts around the Socialist Party and members of the ministerial *cabinets*. Nevertheless, for most of them and for the left generally, there was little ideological terrain to occupy, simply a painful and dramatic conversion to the reality of government and the market economy. Modernization not socialism, rationalization not major social reform were the new watchwords.

The conditions, however, were being created for a renewal of the political clubs even though the left was to remain in government until 1993, with Mitterrand serving as president until 1995. By the mid-1980s, earlier wishful thinking about socialism had given way to several years of practical government and the experience of office. This was a curious phenomenon: the articulated voice of socialism had been handed over to the president because of the nature of the institutional system, the 'lyrical allusions' had been destroyed by the reality of office, and yet what we might call an unexplored discursive space had been created in which a new rhetoric, marrying republicanism and social democracy, for example, was now possible. The ministerial *cabinets* of the left had increased dialogue and exchange with other progressive thinkers such as trade unionists and members of associations. Furthermore, it was clear that the left would need to prepare for the post-Mitterrand period just as the Gaullists had to prepare for *l'après de Gaulle*. Social democracy, feminism, managerialism, localism, regionalism, republicanism; the revival of a leftist ideology or the creation of a new blend of political thought now had to address some of the successes of the left in the Fifth Republican government where once it had to address only its failures.

Nevertheless, these 'clubs' are now an active part of the political scene, and virtually every figure of any political significance is associated with a political club dedicated to the renewal of ideas within the Republic. All have shifted their focus from 'political' to 'social' questions reflecting the concerns of both the political class and the public, and the intractable and growing problems of unemployment, job insecurity, and the phenomenon of 'exclusion' – homelessness, poverty, ghettoization, and social marginalization. All have a secretariat, publicity material, sympathetic academics who write for or publicly support the club. Each have weekly or monthly evening debates, and day conferences, and some of them are very media conscious with prominent members taking every opportunity to appear on television, radio and in the columns of the national and regional press. In the post-1993 period, in opposition, many individuals and groups within the left began to contribute to a revival in club activity after a decade in power. In 1997, the left was unexpectedly returned to government, bringing the left's political clubs to the fore, many of them rather sooner than they had anticipated.

Think tanks and the longer-term perspective

The national research institutes

The national, state-funded research institutes such as the Centre National de la Recherche Scientifique (CNRS) – founded in 1939 – which is the mother organization to which many of these institutes are affiliated, or the Institut National de Statistiques et d'Études Économiques (INSEE) and a range of others, fulfil many of the functions carried out by independent research institutes in other countries. For example, the CNRS runs approximately 1,500 laboratories and research centres responsible for the majority of French scientific research. CNRS has extensive links to large nationalized French firms such as Electricité de France, Rhone-Poulenc and Matra, and this through 38,000 research and business contracts. The INSEE (founded in 1946) provides detailed social, economic and political statistics. The Conseil Scientifique de l'Audio-visuel (CSA) acts as both a media monitoring device and a research centre on the French media. The whole network of national institutes can be conceived as a research chain through which information is collected, analysed, diffused, and used for further research in other national research centres down the line. Regardless of the kind of activity carried out by the institutes, the nature of their staff provides continuity in that researchers and managers at every level are mostly recruited from the Grandes Ecoles (elite national colleges), thus ensuring that the system as a whole produces researchers with the skills and outlook concomitant with its aims.

The role of the national research institutes is of importance because it spans several sectors. The research chain has numerous links to other chains, that is, to other sectors in education, industry, politics, and culture. The scientific institutes provide expertise and research to the industries located both in the private and in the public domains. They also provide the staff for the Grandes Ecoles, some of which, such as the Ecole Normale Supérieure, tend to set – for better or for worse – France's cultural parameters. As such, their role is multiple and central. They resemble large North American think tanks such as the Hoover Institution or the Brookings. The links between these research institutes and the French state are so close as to make them an integral part of the state apparatus. Nevertheless, the personnel overlap between these institutes and the education sectors as well as with the ministerial *cabinets*, along with their claims to research and political/policy impact, warrants their inclusion in a survey of French think tank activity (for an overview of French think tanks see Table 2.1).

Table 2.1   *Select sample of French think tanks*[a]

Name	Staff	Budget (£)	Location
ADELS	14	unrevealed	Paris
AILES	11	£50,000	Paris
Convergence	6	£400,000	Paris
Club de l'Horloge	3	£200,000	Paris
CNRS	31,000	£13,452,000	Paris
GRECE	3	unrevealed	Paris

Note: [a] The data is indicative only but gives an illustration of the varying sizes and budgets (when revealed) of French think tanks.

The policy research groups

There are a number of think tanks in France whose roles and aims within the French political/policy process are as ill-defined as they are interesting. These groups have several characteristics in common. They are indeed epistemic communities and bring together a number of experts who carry out research in well-defined fields and who share values and principles. Often these experts are drawn from universities, but the groups in question seek to bring them together – and this very explicitly – with party-political actors, trade union representatives, social workers; in a word, with professionals who might be able to report on the state of a particular sector, based on their expertise, while also being well-placed to implement the results of any research emanating from the scholars active in the think tank. The desire to bring an element of pragmatism to politics is present in all of the groups we have included in this chapter. However, the policy research groups stand out in their belief that politics is overwhelmingly defined at the local or grass-roots level. Their practical stance is, therefore, necessarily highlighted by the nature of their ties to the local community, indeed by their very conception of the local community as the appropriate site of enabling political power. These groups are not neighbourhood-based or strictly local organizations: they share a national outlook and significant ties with universities and other groups across France. Nevertheless, part of their mission is to foster 'nationally applicable' research at the local level.

One such group is the 'Association AILES' (Autogestion Initiative Locale et Economie Sociale). Founded in 1986, AILES – an acronym meaning 'wings' – brings together former members of one of France's largest trade unions, the Confédération Française Démocratique du Travail (CFDT), and former members of the Communist Party and the PSU (Parti Socialiste Unitié). Most members are either linked to a national research institute, or to a university and combine various political activities and commitments with research activities. In the case of two of the association's three main co-ordinators, Michel Mousel, for example, was president of the Agence Française pour la maitrise de l'énergie while Dominique Taddei was both professor of economics and deputy mayor of the city of Avignon.

One of the characteristics of this group is its links with other similar groups. AILES has close ties to the Association pour la Démocratie et l'Education Locale et Sociale (ADELS) whose main activity is the dissemination of information about local democracy and political participation. Initiatives de Citoyenneté Active en Réseaux (ICARE) is another group involved on the one hand in formalizing ties between associations, research groups and local groups and on the other in promoting research on grassroots participation. Groups like ICARE, ADELS, and AILES (and there are many, many more) organize meetings and workshops, lobby national representatives for research and local initiative funds, and bring together experts in various fields who seek to apply their research to a common project.

Intellectual groups of the New Right: GRECE and the Club de l'Horloge

In France, the New Right was responsible for the creation of two contro-versial think tanks, both of which claimed to give new impetus to ideologies discredited by World War Two. The Groupement de Recherche et d'Etude pour la Civilisation Européene (GRECE), founded in 1968, and the Club de l'Horloge, founded in 1974, were the cornerstones of the French New Right. It is beyond the scope of this chapter to give an exhaustive descrip-tion of the ideological tenets of either of these (but see Duranton-Crabol, 1988; Taguieff, 1994). What is of relevance here is that the ideological incli-nations of these think tanks and how they encourage debate and disseminate their research offer striking examples of what we call the 'intellectual' think tanks. GRECE and the Club de l'Horloge sought to have an impact on politics not just through research and debate, but also through the adoption of an intellectual stance often seen as the preserve of left-wing intellectuals.

GRECE was a reaction to events even prior to 1968. In other words, the New Right precedes GRECE by several years. The New Right in France should be understood as originating around 1962–63 as a result of the Algerian crisis and, even more directly, as a result of the combined failures of the ultra anti-Gaullist movements for 'l'Algérie Française' (1956–62), and of the extreme right-wing parliamentary movements such as the Mouvement Nationaliste du Progrès and the Rassemblement Européen de la Liberté. GRECE was the intellectual expression of a frustration with the weakening of France's hegemonic strength, and the failure of the traditional nationalist right to deal with this decline. What was new in post-war France was the way in which this right wing expressed itself, both through GRECE and through the Club de l'Horloge.

The Club de l'Horloge is probably the most well-known and most respected think tank of the New Right. In a sense it is the bridge between the Old and the New Right bringing together political personalities and scholars in workshops and forums centred on political themes. Individual membership of the Club de l'Horloge often overlaps with membership of more centre-right parties (Yvan Blot, president of the Club de l'Horloge, was a leading personality of the RPR), and in many cases with membership of the GRECE. But where GRECE was highly active, technocratic, and robust if not abrasive in its intellectuality, the Club de l'Horloge presented a more classic scholarly face. Its members were older, more established political personalities, the scholars more quiet and less media-prone.

Despite their differences, both think tanks sought vigorous access to public debate. The manner in which this was done was, in part, through a kind of infiltration by the New Right of both the press and academic circles, in an effort to give currency to a specific vocabulary, thus familiarizing the public with the issues raised by the New Right. Central to their project was a 'cultural struggle' to unsettle or rather displace the ideology which constructed the post-war liberal and social-democratic consensus. In order to do so, GRECE and the Club de l'Horloge adopted a left-wing approach: a Gramscian strategy of molecular cultural change. It is probably true to say that, by bringing right-wing ideas centre stage, they succeeded.

Conclusion

We can draw six conclusions concerning the political think tanks in the Fifth Republic. The first is that they operate in a conflictual yet ultimately subordinate manner to the political party, itself perceived as prone to decline. The political institutions, even 'the state' in France, are also seen as vulnerable to the downward drive of Fortune's Wheel, and the think tanks are perceived as in a sense 'looking after' the Republic itself when it or its institutions or culture are sick or enfeebled. This is both a republican and deeply Gaullist view of politics, one which has spread across the political spectrum. 'Renewal' is the think tank's role, crisis the event which calls it forth. And never are they considered politically illegitimate. On the contrary, they are invariably treated as a bulwark against Bonapartist-style 'adventures'. The irony here is that they often exhibit the very personalization they were created to oppose, and in some cases offer one 'adventure' in order to avoid another.

Second, think tanks are best understood when seen within the overall political system; that is, one needs to see not simply their role vis-à-vis government agencies or political parties, but their place in the overall institutional and cultural configuration, both diachronically (in a rich tradition) and synchronically (within the Fifth Republic). Third, there is an element of wish-fulfilment on the part of contemporary think tanks, which raises the question of cause and effect in political relations. In a country with such a strong tradition of intellectually driven political renewal and the heroic role of the politically committed philosopher, it is difficult to disentangle teleological thought from enquiry, teleology from political action, and self-importance from significant political contribution. Even in the recent period, there is an assumption that just as the 1960s clubs led to the phenomenon of François Mitterrand's leadership and the renewal of the Socialist Party, so club activity in the 1990s will do the same. Irrespective of whether this is an accurate view of causality, such perceptions mean that the think tanks will have effects within the political system, whether or not they are the intended ones.

Fourth, and perhaps most significantly in terms of the essential character of contemporary think tanks and the Fifth Republic's influence upon them, is the tendency to personalization as an organizing principle within them. Today, many of them are just fan clubs with no proper reflection upon political questions. Sometimes they pretend to be less tied to their leader than they are, claiming that the personalization that exists is simply part of a deeper movement, or simply reflects the demands of the modern media. What is significant in terms of our analysis is to note that it is the Fifth Republic itself which has done this to the organization of political groups and political ideas.

Fifthly, in their often acute personalization but also in their specialization do they distinguish themselves from the think tanks of the 1960s. Sometimes mirroring the ministries of a government or the national secretariat of a political party, they often have 'groupes de travail' or sub-divisions concerned with, for example, housing, defence, and so on. As we have pointed out, many of the personnel are themselves highly trained specialists from ENA and similar institutions. Some of the think tanks therefore resemble the ministerial *cabinets*, producing reports on virtually everything, and sometimes, we might add, from every point of view, thus offering to leaders, ministries and government departments tailor-made positions, even policies, depending upon circumstances. There is, therefore, a tendency for the contemporary think-tanker to be a specialist rather than a generalist. The corollary to this is that along with the specialization has gone a shift from concern with the 'political' to the social, a shift which reflects both the acceptance of the Fifth Republic by most parts of the political spectrum and the growing specialization of the think tanks and perhaps of government itself – as well as the failure of government to solve the social problems it once claimed it could.

Finally, unlike so many evolving aspects of French society, politics and the economy, the phenomenon of French think tanks and their French character exhibit the continuing existence of the 'French exception'. The ministerial *cabinets* themselves are nodal in the maintenance of the exception. Around them, outside formal government, the polity bristles with a diverse range of think tanks that contribute to the political life of the Republic.

References

Duranton-Crabol, A. M. (1988) *Visages de la nouvelle droite: Le GRECE et son histoire*, Paris, Presses de la Fondation Nationale des Sciences Politiques.

Gaffney, John (1988) 'French Socialism and the Fifth Republic', *West European Politics*, 11(3): 42–56.

Gaffney, John (1991) 'Political Think Tanks in the UK and Ministerial "Cabinets" in France', *West European Politics*, 14(1): 1–17.

Haas, Peter (1992) 'Introduction: Epistemic Communities and International Policy Coordination', *International Organization*, 46(1): 1–35.

Polsby, Nelson (1983) 'Tanks But No Tanks', *Public Opinion*, April–May(14–16): 58–9.

Stone, Diane (1996) *Capturing the Political Imagination: Think Tanks and the Policy Process*, London, Frank Cass.

Taguieff, P. A. (1994) *Sur la Nouvelle Droite*, Paris, Descartes et Cie.

Think tanks, advocacy coalitions and policy change: the Italian case

Introduction

Although the recent transformations of the Italian political system have rekindled the interest of political scientists in the country's affairs, Italian think tanks have not as yet been the object of systematic academic analysis. Apart from the material produced by the think tanks themselves, a literature search on the topic yielded only two entries: a study on Censis, a Rome-based think tank, conducted in the early 1980s (Moscati, 1982), and an essay on agenda setting and policy change, which covers Italian think tanks somewhat tangentially (Regonini and Giuliani, 1994). This lack of attention could be symptomatic of the limited extent to which Italian think tanks have influenced public policy; alternatively, it could be merely a specific example of the more general neglect of policy formulation and evaluation in the literature on Italian politics.

Aside from the academic literature, the news media is an obvious place to look for signs of the activities of think tanks. Some presence of think tanks can indeed be found in the Italian press, but this is a far cry from the symbiotic relationship that the media has established with think tanks in other countries, particularly in the United States. In 1995, Censis, perhaps the most visible among Italian think tanks, was cited 101 times by the *Corriere della Sera*, the major Italian daily newspaper, and 85 times by *La Stampa*. The two newspapers cited the Centro Europa Ricerche (CER), another Rome-based think tank, 66 and 7 times respectively, and the Bologna-based Nomisma 43 and 12 times. In the same year, the Heritage Foundation was cited 2,268 times by the major US newspapers, and the Brookings Institutions 2,192 times (Dolny, 1996).

The analysis presented in this chapter attempts to fill the knowledge gap on Italian think tanks by drawing on two sources of information: a set of in-depth interviews with officials of five major think tanks, and a mail survey of Italian organizations, public and private, that are engaged in policy-oriented activities – a concept much broader than that of think tanks. Of the 104 organizations that responded to the survey, 69 can be classified as independent policy research institutes. Using this information, the chapter pursues three distinct lines of investigation. To begin with, we compare the qualitative features of the major Italian think tanks against the benchmarks provided by the comparative literature on independent policy research institutes. Later, we explore the quantitative dimensions of a larger number of Italian policy research institutes, using the results of the mail survey. More specifically, we investigate their size, main areas of policy interest, disciplinary approach, dissemination activities, media profile, type of personnel and funding. We also suggest a possible interpretation of how think tanks have affected public policy in Italy. In doing so, we build on the 'advocacy coalition' approach developed by Sabatier and Jenkins-Smith (1993). Finally, we make some concluding remarks.

The major think tanks in Italy: challenges and transformation

The most prestigious Italian think tanks are not a new phenomenon. Censis was set up in 1964, the Istituto per la Ricerca Sociale (IRS) in 1974, the CER and Nomisma in 1981. Among operating foundations, the Fondazione Carlo Cattaneo and Fondazione Giovanni Agnelli have been active in funding and producing research that is relevant for policy-making since 1958 and 1966 respectively.

The self-determination of research agendas – a typical feature of independent policy institutes – is comparatively limited in Italy. Stone (1996: 15) has observed that, in order to preserve autonomy in their research agendas, 'think tank managers often require that funding be untied so that they may be free in determining the questions they address and in arriving at their findings'. By contrast, most of the leading Italian policy institutes conduct research only when a client or group of clients asks for a particular product. In terms of Weaver's typology, Italian think tanks are more similar to 'contract research organizations' than to 'universities without students' (Weaver, 1989).

This statement must be qualified, however. Over the years, institutes such as Censis have developed their own interpretations of Italian society (Moscati, 1982). Moreover, the relationship between client and institute is dialectic. Typically, the client comes forward with a vague idea, and ample scope is given to the think tank manager for re-formulating the initial request. Indeed, one of the key slogans within policy institutes is that 'the supply educates the demand for research'. A further qualification is that evidence collected on a larger sample of independent policy research institutes indicates that untied funding could be more widespread than it may appear to be at first sight (see below). Finally, a small but significant percentage of the products of Italian think tanks is not tied to particular funding. Examples here include the activities of Fondazione Agnelli and the Censis annual report on socio-economic trends; the latter is produced by Censis itself with minimal levels of public funding.

Who are the intellectual leaders of think tanks? In a country where the number of university professors who serve in government is so high that the term 'government by professors' has been coined, it is hardly surprising that the presence of academics in think tanks is overwhelming. This has both positive and negative consequences. On the one hand, it reduces research costs, as academics only need to be paid 'at the margin' while all their fringe benefits are paid by the universities. On the other hand, academics frequently use these research centres as a base from which to obtain the administrative and logistic support they cannot obtain from their academic departments. Notwithstanding their undeniable expertise, these researchers also bring with them their heavy baggage of disciplinary affiliations and career incentives, which are not necessarily the ideal ingredients for research intended for use in the policy process.

Turning next to ideological orientation, the type of think tank characterized by a commitment to economic liberalism, aggressive language, and fierce competition for political impact has not yet materialized in Italy. Across the English-speaking world, these so-called 'new partisans' seized visibility and (some would argue) influence in the 1980s (Stone, 1991; 1996; Fischer, 1993). By contrast, the ideological propensity of Italian think tanks has remained low, when compared to the Adam Smith Institute in the UK, or the Heritage Foundation in the USA. To be sure, there have been examples of institutes promoting the diffusion of a free-market agenda in Italy, as illustrated by the Politeia Institute and the Centro Einaudi. However, in the case of Politeia, the adoption of the public choice paradigm was more a methodological option than an ideological commitment, and the Centro Einaudi has always argued for a moderate rather than a radical free-market approach. Moreover, these institutes have never acquired the same visibility in public debate as their British and American counterparts.

The absence or low visibility of this type of policy institute can be explained by the fact that a clear pro-market drive was almost completely absent from Italian politics in the 1980s (Regonini and Giuliani, 1994). Indeed, in our view, such strategies of overt ideological commitment would, in any case, have been far from optimal for think tanks operating in the Italian context. Italian ideological politics in the 1980s (and earlier) was dominated by stalemate and bitter confrontation between the left and the centre. Stressing ideology was useful for attracting votes in the electoral market of 'visible politics', but not for making public policy behind it. Public policy in

Italy was (and is) made in less confrontational arenas by policy networks (Dente and Regonini, 1987). Given that one of the aims of policy institutes is to achieve impact on the policy-making process rather than on the electoral market, Italian think tanks have always avoided the bitter confrontation of ideological politics. Almost invariably, their emphasis in policy discourse has been either on policy instruments or on the same mild conventional wisdom on economic policy advocated by international organizations (such as the International Monetary Fund and the Organization for Economic Cooperation and Development). In sum, we would argue not that Italian think tanks are completely isolated from the world of politics but that, in order to exercise more influence on policy-making, they have chosen to avoid the paralysing effects of overt ideological commitment.

The political transition

The avoidance of overt ideological commitment has aided policy institutes in the political transition. The latter is one of the challenges faced by think tanks in the 1990s. Not only has national politics changed dramatically, with once all-mighty political parties such as the Christian Democrats melting like snow in the sun, but occasionally the investigations of magistrates have made *tabula rasa* within public administration at the national and local levels. We refer here in particular to the massive legal operation against political corruption, dubbed Clean Hands.

For a typical institute, the external environment has changed dramatically in a very short period of time: senior civil servants with whom whole programmes of research had been conducted have been removed or sent to prison. Moreover, the huge turnover in parliament and among cabinet members that has taken place following the 1994 and 1996 national elections has severed many think tank leaders' long-standing connections with the corridors of power. In these conditions, the relative detachment from ideological politics has been an asset for policy institutes. Of course, this asset was not distributed evenly among think tanks. Institutes which have been traditionally perceived as more neutral than others have benefited most from the political transition. Censis, typically perceived as close to the 'old' political establishment, has lost ground, whereas IRS, with its specialization on policy instruments, has gained.

Arguably the most important result of the political transition concerns the proliferation of tenders in the market for research. Not only does a European Union directive require tenders for public procurement above ECU200,000 but, in the aftermath of the investigations on corruption, tenders have become more widespread, whereas they were virtually unknown even a few years ago. Simply put, tenders are a protection against allegations of using research contracts for political patronage.

Internationalization

This process has been 'pulled' by external factors rather than 'pushed' by think tanks. Undoubtedly, the main trigger has been the flow of research commissioned by the European Commission. Outside the European Union, tenders launched from the World Bank and other international organizations have rarely spawned a search for alliances between policy institutes.

Evaluation research is emblematic of the 'pulled' characteristics of internationalization. Before the European Commission started funding evaluation studies, the market for evaluation in Italy was practically non-existent. In this case, the demand has materialised before actors on the supply side developed a substantial methodological expertise. In many cases, internationalization has affected the sources of funding rather than the scope of research. Think tank managers have continued to study policy issues specific to the Italian context. However, in a limited number of cases the Europeanization of the market has prodded Italian institutes into looking for allies outside Italy and occasionally Italian think tanks have conducted research abroad. Bocconi University, Nomisma and Censis have recently won a tender from the World Bank for setting up a Polytechnic of Technology in Lebanon. The IRS has conducted research on foreign countries with the aim of drawing lessons for domestic consumption. Another interesting case is Progetto Europa, a small spin-off from Censis, which considers Europe its natural domain for research. Its researchers travel constantly in Europe for elite interviews, from the former Yugoslavia to Sweden, and its reports are dedicated to 'maps of European identities'.

In the process of internationalization, the predominance of academics has been an asset for Italian think tanks. Academics working in think tanks have employed their personal 'portfolio' of academic connections in Europe. However, the process of internationalization should not be overemphasized. Italian policy institutes remain essentially reactive rather than proactive as regards the international dimension of their activity. The level of funding from non-Italian sources in an institute such as the IRS has been stable at 10–15 per cent of total funding over the last few years. In sum, the drive towards the internationalization of research exists, but the capacity of Italian think tanks to stimulate collaboration with foreign institutes, to create European networks and consortia, and ultimately to 'push' the international market remains low.

A 'de-academization' of policy research institutes?

We have already argued that the presence of academics in Italian think tanks has been overwhelming. However, two observations lead us to conclude that in the future the role of academics within policy research institutes could be less crucial than it has been in the past. The first concerns a transformation in the market for social research. Most of the products which are now demanded in this market are not typical academic studies. To a large extent, evaluation research, cost-benefit analysis and feasibility studies are professional (not academic) activities. In turn, this may create the preconditions for an increased role of professionals (as opposed to academics) within think tanks. The case of IRS might be emblematic of this trend: in the 1980s, there were seven professors out of nine members on the executive board of the IRS, now there are two academics out of eight.

Our second observation is that in the 1980s and 1990s Italian public universities have created an extremely limited number of new academic positions: the government has imposed a zero rate of growth on most of the social science disciplines, which means that only rarely have new lectureships become available in political science and sociology. Thus a whole generation of young researchers has been excluded from the universities. Some of these researchers have ventured instead into the world of policy institutes. Members of this generation are professional researchers *tout court* and are not obsessed with disciplinary affiliations and loyalty to academic heavyweights. While it is impossible to detect a definitive trend towards the 'de-academization' of think tanks, certain pre-requisites for this appear to be already in place.

In sum, Italian think tanks have held on in a period of dramatic political transition and administrative change. The situation has been compounded by the necessity to internationalize, by new tendencies in the professionalisation of social research and by the post-Maastricht adoption in Italian economic policy of tight budgets, which has made the market for public funding more competitive. Perhaps, after years of relatively easy growth, the time for consolidation and adjustment has come.

A profile of Italian research institutes

The profile presented in this section draws on information collected through a mail survey of Italian organizations engaged in policy-oriented activities, conducted in 1996. The survey separately identified such policy-oriented activities as policy research, promotion of public debate, and education for public service. Of the 104 organizations that responded to the survey (approximately a third of eligible respondents) 69 can be classified as private stand-alone organizations, engaged in at least one of the three policy-relevant activities listed above (and in most cases in all three). The great majority of these organizations are also non-profit. We have also included the few that are nominally for profit, but which are not easily distinguishable in the way they operate in practice from their non-profit counterparts. The organizations excluded from this restricted group are research centres affiliated with the government, either central or local (25 of which responded to the survey), and those private organizations that are part of larger entities, like research centres that operate inside banks and trade organizations (10 in total).

In this section, we define as 'think tanks' all these 69 private independent organizations that carry out at least one kind of policy-oriented activity. Some might argue that this definition is too loose, because it includes organizations which do not have *all* the features normally associated with think tanks (at least those operating in English-speaking countries) such as control over their own research agendas, some degree of independence of government funding and an inclination to disseminate their research findings to a 'public' audience, particularly through the media, in order to affect the policy process. Our argument for applying such a broad definition is that, although in Italy there might be very few US or UK-type think tanks, most of the private independent organizations we have identified share some features of the traditional think tank model. Most of them have some control over their research agenda; many of them have access to non-government funding, or at least to untied public funding, which allows them to conduct independent analysis; and finally, most of them attempt to disseminate their research findings and devote resources to the promotion of public debate.

We argue with some confidence that the sample we analyse, while not representative from a strictly statistical point of view, provides a meaningful picture of the types of organization that use research and communication to inform and support policy-making in Italy. We examine the sample of 69 think tanks from several different points of view: their size, functions, main areas of policy interest, disciplinary approach, dissemination activities, media exposure, type of personnel and funding. Table 3.1 provides an overview of some of these organizations.

Size

The 69 think tanks vary very widely in size, as measured by their total annual budget for 1995. In 1995, the median size of their budget was about US$375,000 and the average about US$1.25 million. About 40 organizations (58 per cent of the total) had an annual budget below US$500,000, while only 12 surpassed US$2 million and only three the US$5 million mark. All the think tanks mentioned explicitly above (namely Censis, IRS, Nomisma, CER, Fondazione Agnelli, and Formez) had a budget above US$1.5 million, and were therefore in the top 20 per cent of the size distribution. Even the largest Italian think tanks would be considered of medium size in the US, where think tanks such as the Brookings Institution and the Heritage Foundation have annual budgets in excess of US$20 million, reach-

Table 3.1   *Italian think tanks*

Establish-ment	Name	Location	Expenditure 1995 (million lire)	Staff size (total)	Researchers	Other researchers employed as permanent consultants[a]
1965	Fondazione di Ricerca 'Istituto Carlo Cattaneo'	Bologna	535	5	1	5
1981	Nomisma S.p.A. - Società di Studi Economici	Bologna	6,000	30	12	50
1974	Prometeia: Associazione per le Previsioni Econometriche	Bologna	1,200	7	6	6
1973	Istituto per la Ricerca Sociale: IRS	Milan[b]	4,600	22	17	n.a.
1965	Centro di Formazione e Studi: Formez[c]	Rome and Naples	39,998	172	69	40
1981	Centro Europa Ricerche – CER	Rome	2,500	7	3	27
1964	Centro Studi Investimenti Sociali: Fondazione CENSIS	Rome	8,000	47	24	10[d]
n.a.	Politeia: Centro per la ricerca e Formazione in Politica ed Etica	Milan and Rome	250	n.a.	n.a.	5
1963	Centro di Ricerca e Documentazione Luigi Einaudi	Turin	800	5	1	5
1966	Fondazione Giovanni Agnelli	Turin	2,600	20	5	n.a.
1988	Fondazione Rosselli	Turin	1,200	6	1	4

Notes: [a] Active for at least 50 days per year. Due to Italian tax laws, full-time researchers are occasionally employed as permanent consultants. [b] A second IRS office is operative in Bologna. [c] Traditionally, Formez has been more a body set up by the government than a think tank, although it has recently moved in the direction of a think tank format. [d] 400 individuals participate yearly in the research activities of Censis on an ad hoc basis, but only 10 participate on a regular basis.

ing over US$100 million in the (admittedly extreme) case of the RAND Corporation (see Chapter 5).

Functions

The majority of the 69 organizations perform all three broad functions (policy research, promotion of debate, and education for public service.) More precisely, 93 per cent conduct policy research, 81 per cent promote debate on policy issues, and 54 per cent engage in some form of education for public service. The degree of overlap between these functions is obviously large: about 77 per cent engage in both policy research and promotion of debate, and almost 48 per cent perform all three functions. With respect to these broadly defined functions, therefore, it would appear that the degree of specialization among Italian think tanks is relatively low.

While most organizations engage in all three activities, they devote very different levels of resources to them, at least on average. If we look at the distribution of resources across the three functions, rather than the percentage of organizations reporting them, we get a better picture of their relative importance. Not surprisingly, policy research takes the lion's share, with 51 per cent of total resources. Activities labelled as promotion of debate account for an additional 17 per cent, while education for public service absorbs a substantial 32 per cent. However, the last figure is explained, to a significant extent, by the presence of a single organization, Formez – the largest think tank in our sample and one traditionally very active in providing education and training to public sector personnel. If Formez were eliminated from the sample, the distribution across the three functions would be very different, namely 67 per cent for policy research, 18 per cent for promotion of debate and a mere 15 per cent for educational activities.

Main areas of policy research

Respondents to the survey were asked to report the areas of policy research to which they devoted most attention in the 1993–95 period, choosing among a list of 28 pre-defined areas. They were also asked to rank the top five activities and to attribute to each their respective share of resources. Based on this information, we are able to calculate the total share of research resources going to each area of public policy among the 69 think tanks included in the survey. The top seven policy areas – that is, those absorbing the seven largest shares of resources across all 69 organizations – are health policy (14 per cent), transportation (13 per cent), urban development (8 per cent), local economic development (7 per cent), industrial policy, public administration reform and macroeconomic policy (6 per cent each). All other policy areas, including labour market, pensions and foreign policy, absorb fractions below 4 per cent. It should be noted that the top seven areas taken together absorb over 60 per cent of total resources, suggesting that the attention of most think tanks is rather concentrated in relatively few policy areas. Concentration does not necessarily imply specialization, however. Only six organizations reported devoting 75 per cent or more of their resources to one policy area, and only 16 as concentrating 75 per cent or more on only two.

We then sought to extend this analysis by grouping the 28 topics into four major broad policy areas, namely: (1) macroeconomic policy, including monetary and trade policy; (2) microeconomic policy, for example labour market, industrial and transportation policy; (3) social policy, including health, pension, and housing policy; (4) the traditional functions-of-government area, namely criminal justice, defence and foreign policy. Microeconomic policies came out ahead, with 48 per cent of resources, and macroeconomic policies add another 12 per cent. Social policy came next with 24 per cent of total resources (more than half going to health policy alone), while the remainder (16 per cent) was devoted to institutional policies.

The survey also asked whether or not the organization conducted, during the preceding three years, any research on six selected 'hot' policy issues, namely pension reform, privatisation of public enterprises, European economic integration, immigration, organized crime and electoral reform. Only nine organizations reported being active on three or more topics, while more than a third reported no activity on any of these topics, with an average of 1.3 topics per organization. Among the largest 12 think tanks, the attention to these issues increases only marginally, with an average of 1.7 topics per organization.

Disciplinary approach for policy research

Despite the prevailing focus on economic policies, about 75 per cent of these organizations indicate economics as a disciplinary approach used in their research, but a similar percentage also indicate statistics and sociology. Legal studies and political science still command a respectable 58 and 47 per cent, respectively. This would suggest a rather strong interdisciplinary inclination among think tanks. When asked to report their *main* disciplinary approach, 35 per cent indicate economics and 22 per cent sociology, with the others falling behind, 10 per cent for legal studies and 8 per cent apiece for statistics and political science.

In a subsequent question, organizations were asked to report on the use of statistical data in their research activities. A total of 88 per cent reported using statistics obtained from published material or on-line databases, and 65 per cent reported using microdata obtained from surveys, either existing or conducted by the organization itself. These figures might reveal a commitment to 'objective' (or at least fact-oriented) research. This finding is broadly consistent with the statement made above, that there is a low degree of ideological commitment on the part of Italian think tanks. Of course, the extent to which such 'objective' research actually influences the policy process depends on many other factors. These include the extent to which the media absorbs and publicizes the information produced by think tanks and the ability of the latter to market and disseminate effectively their research findings *via* their participation in 'advocacy coalitions' (see below).

Media exposure

The extent of media exposure is an important indication of how widely the research produced by think tanks is disseminated, and how visible think tanks are in public debate. Two-thirds of Italian organizations report that their research has been cited by the media more than five times a year, but only 20 per cent that it has been cited more than once a month. One would also expect the frequency of citation to vary with the size of the organization. As we noted in the introduction, the most prominent Italian think tank, Censis, was cited 101 times during 1995 by the *Corriere della Sera* alone. With one exception, all the large organizations reported being cited at least five times a year, whilst among the small and medium-sized think tanks the record is less impressive: a third of them are cited fewer than five times a year.

Promotion of debate

The same list of 28 policy areas used to identify the major topics of research was then used to identify the subjects on which these organizations mainly attempt to stimulate public debate. Although the data are not strictly comparable to those presented earlier, we can clearly see a different ranking. The seven areas most often cited as being among the top five for a given organization are, in decreasing order of frequency: local economic development (26 per cent), social services, industrial policy, European economic integration, education and labour policies, and public administration reform (18 per cent). Only three of these areas, local economic development, industrial policy and public administration reform, were at the top of the list as research topics. The top research topic, health policy, here drops to the middle of the list (12 per cent). This partial correspondence between research and public debate topics might be due to a different funding structure of the two activities: research might be mainly funded through contracts for a specific client, thus reflecting the preferences of the clients with more resources (for example, the Treasury, Transportation, and Health Ministries), whilst the promotion of debate might follow more closely the original mission of the organization or the cultural and professional preferences of its staff.

As far as the methods for promoting debate are concerned, our research has uncovered a clear orientation towards more traditional, academic-type means of communication. The methods most often cited among the top three for each think tank are the organization of conferences and the publication of specialized journals and books. All these forms are cited as among the top three by about 46 per cent of think tanks. Other forms of dissemination and promotion of debate, such as interviews given by staff members and testimonies in front of legislative bodies, appear well down the list (14 and 4 per cent respectively). Having an Internet home page is never cited among the top three means of communication. Only 25 per cent of the think tanks in our sample have a permanent public relations office.

The survey also attempted to ascertain whether or not these organizations consider it important to target their research findings to a wider audience. Respondents were asked to indicate their most significant research report of the last three years and whether or not it contained an executive summary. Only 34 out of the 55 organizations that cited a research report confirmed that it also contained an executive summary, a possible indication that effective utilization is not always a top priority in the minds of these researchers, perhaps owing to their academic orientation.

Personnel

These think tanks spend about 42 per cent of their resources on personnel directly employed by the organization and about 25 per cent on overhead expenses. The residual 33 per cent is spent on external consultants, a third of whom are 'permanent consultants' and two-thirds hired on a more occasional basis. The substantial presence of these permanent consultants might reflect a well-known characteristic of the Italian labour market, in which high labour costs and severe restrictions on dismissals discourage employers from hiring regular employees and encourage them instead to hire 'consultants', whose tax and legal treatment is identical to that of the self-employed.

About 30 per cent of the expenses for non-stable consultants go to persons that have a permanent academic position. As a percentage of overall labour costs, this amounts to about 9 per cent, which would suggest a limited presence of academics within these organizations. However, this figure represents only direct payments to individuals, and does not take into account the flow of services and other non-pecuniary benefits these academics might also obtain from working in the think tank sector, including office space and secretarial support.

Funding

The analysis of the funding sources of these organizations reveals that they are not as dependent on research contracts as one might anticipate. Contracts for specific projects on behalf of government clients were reported by 61 per cent of the organizations, the most widely quoted source of funding. However, 'untied contributions' are also reported from a variety of sources, central and regional governments, individual and corporate supporters, as well as proceeds from own endowment. The latter was reported in only 16 per cent of cases.

The survey asked each organization to report what proportion of their revenues comes from four different types of sources: research contracts for public and private clients, untied contributions from public and private sources, proceeds from sales of books and other commercial activities, and proceeds from own endowment. Across all organizations, 60 per cent of revenues come from untied contributions, 40 per cent from contracts, 6 per cent from commercial activities and only 4 per cent from own endowment. This pattern varies across think tanks of different size. Surprisingly, large organizations rely more on contributions and less on contracts than do smaller organizations. The share of untied contributions for small organizations is only 36 per cent, while that of contracts is 57 per cent: the corresponding figures for large think tanks are almost reversed (61 and 38 per cent respectively).

It is also interesting to note that relatively few of the research contracts received from governmental organizations are awarded through formal tenders. Almost 64 per cent of all organizations who reported government contracts also said that none of the contracts was awarded competitively, another 19 per cent said 'less than a quarter of the time' and only 10 per cent said 'more than half the time'. There is an apparent inconsistency between this evidence and what we argued previously about the increasing importance of tenders. The inconsistency can be explained by the fact that the mail survey was conducted in 1996 and the responses refer to the previous three years, whereas the interviews with senior officers from major think tanks were conducted in 1997, and thus reflect the more recent developments described earlier.

The overall impression that emerges from the mail survey is that Italian think tanks are only partially dependent on research contracts, the majority of which are assigned non-competitively. We do not know which mechanisms are used to select the contractors in these cases: we believe, but have no direct empirical evidence, that access to networks of expertise is crucial not only to gain influence on the policy process, but also to secure vital sources of funding which ensure the survival of these organizations.

Conceptualizing influence: think tanks and advocacy coalitions

Towards a framework for empirical analysis

Our aim in this section is to suggest an interpretation of the impact of think tanks. Do Italian think tanks make a difference? In attempting to answer the question, we confine our attention to the last decade and investigate if and how think tanks have affected policy. This means that we do not look at the other functions performed by think tanks. As shown by the comparative literature on this topic, not only do think tanks seek to influence policy, they also produce human capital, inform public debate, and give voice to minoritarian ideologies and paradigms which may, in a given period, be excluded from the political agenda (Stone, 1996; Cockett, 1995).

Here we examine theoretical issues first, and then turn our attention to the Italian case. The question of the influence or impact of think tanks on public policy has been debated at length in the comparative literature on this subject (Abelson and Carberry, 1996; Gaffney, 1991; Stone, 1991; 1996). Stone (1996: 219), for example, argues that: 'Rarely is there a one-to-one correspondence between a book or a study and a particular policy change. There are numerous intervening forces that mediate and alter the impact of research that shroud any cause and effect relationship that may exist between policy institutes and government decision-making.'

This view is consistent with that found in broader studies examining the impact of social science research on the policy process (Weiss, 1986; Wittrock, 1982; Radaelli and Dente, 1996). However, the implications of the 'elusiveness of influence' (Stone, 1996: 218) should be investigated thoroughly. Stone (1996: 219) asserts that 'influence cannot be measured': think tanks contribute to political life by shaping the climate of opinion and the terms of political discourse, but this form of broader influence (her argument goes on) cannot be measured, although it must be theorized. Measurement in a strict sense is probably impossible, but in our view this does not mean that empirical research cannot be done. Indeed, our contention is that the broader political influence of think tanks can be the object of systematic empirical research, provided that adequate models and conceptual frameworks are used. Stone herself points to the 'nascent discourse coalition literature' (Stone, 1996: 94; Hajer, 1993) which is precisely a conceptual tool for handling the tricky question of how ideas and research affect policy.

Another possible route to the analysis of knowledge utilization is the model of policy enlightenment put forward by Weiss (1979). According to this model, there is no policy impact of social science research in a narrow sense, yet challenging studies can offer new ideas, metaphors and evidence capable of altering the conceptual apparatus employed by policy-makers. Knowledge does not affect policy in the short term, but there is a long-term impact of policy analysis which is represented by the enlightenment of political actors and, more generally, by policy development (Weiss, 1979; Rich and Oh, 1994: 85).

These arguments are persuasive. However, concepts such as policy enlightenment remain vague when the analyst is mainly concerned, as in our case, with empirical analysis. Empirically, knowledge manifests itself in a symbiotic relation with power (Radaelli, 1995; Stone, 1996: 113) and consequently it is extremely difficult to detect whether policy institutes make a difference or not.

Nonetheless, there is a conceptual framework which seeks to acknowledge explicitly the symbiotic relation between knowledge and interests and aims to provide a model for empirical analysis. This framework is the 'advocacy coalition' approach (Sabatier and Jenkins-Smith, 1993; 1998). The model embraces the view that a narrow definition of political influence (above all, one that is limited to short-term impact) underestimates knowledge utilization. Therefore, the advocacy coalition approach emphasizes the long-term impact of policy analysis (thus drawing upon and extending the policy enlightenment model) and sets out to explain how knowledge is transmitted into the policy process. Transmission of knowledge occurs within, but also (as we shall see) across, advocacy coalitions.

Adversarial coalitions compete for the control of policy sub-systems. The result of the competition between coalitions, however, is not decided by power alone. Learning within (and, more rarely, across) coalitions, policy fora, and persuasion are at least as important as power. Sabatier and Jenkins-Smith formulate the hypothesis that policy-oriented learning across coalitions is facilitated by the existence of policy fora which are (1) dominated by professional norms and (2) prestigious enough to attract professionals from different coalitions. More generally, the cognitive element of politics is so crucial in this model that knowledge and beliefs represent a *constitutive* (that is, defining) aspect of advocacy coalitions (Sabatier, 1993: 25). One testable hypothesis offered by this approach is that non-incremental policy change requires (1) significant perturbations external to the subsystem (an exogenous shock) and (2) skilful exploitation of the opportunities generated by an exogenous shock by the (hitherto) minority coalition (Sabatier and Jenkins-Smith, 1993).

Turning to the Italian case, attention should be drawn to think tanks as policy fora. The first question to consider here is whether policy research institutes have spawned a debate on public finance and brought professionals from different coalitions closer, thus facilitating policy learning. The advocacy coalition approach, however, also alerts us to the fact that non-incremental change often requires an external shock and the capability of the previously minority coalition to capitalize on the shock itself. Hence a second question arises, namely whether think tanks have assisted minority coalitions (typically by providing ideas, language, data, information and other elements of the cognitive dimension of public policy) in their efforts to capitalize on external change. A third question is whether think tanks have been involved at all in the two more dramatic episodes of policy change, namely electoral-institutional reforms and fiscal adjustment. Did policy institutes play a role in these two episodes or not? It is to these questions that we now turn.

Advocacy coalitions in the Italian policy process

The details of the advocacy coalition approach are well-known. Moreover, review articles (Jenkins-Smith and Sabatier, 1994; 1998) and textbook treatments of the approach are available (Parsons, 1995). Hence it is our intention in what follows to *use* (rather than merely discuss) the approach. The Italian case appears fascinating in this respect. However, before we proceed further, some background information on policy change in Italy is in order.

Although the majority of recent studies have discussed the changes in the Italian political system from the narrow corner of party-systemic change (Bartolini and D'Alimonte, 1997), a couple of seminal papers have focused upon the changes in public policy (Dyson and Featherstone, 1996; Regonini and Giuliani, 1994). The main difference between the two studies is that the former examines the 1990s, and accordingly observes the radical change in macroeconomic policy, whereas the latter focuses upon the 1980s, and describes how electoral reforms and constitutional change became prominent issues on the Italian political agenda. Taken together, however, these two studies reveal much about the most important dynamics of policy change in Italy.

The main argument of Dyson and Featherstone is that, by accepting the European commitments enshrined in the Treaty on European Union signed at Maastricht, Italian policy-makers set the conditions for dramatic change in economic policy. The agenda of domestic economic policy was transformed by European Union commitments (especially the Treaty provisions on Economic and Monetary Union). More importantly still, this transformation of the agenda disempowered the old political parties. The power basis of the *partitocrazia* – Dyson and Featherstone argue – was curbed by the imperatives of Economic and Monetary Union, while at the same time a technocratic policy elite was empowered by the 'external constraint' on domestic policy accepted by Italian policy-makers at Maastricht.

Dyson and Featherstone propose an explanation of how an independent variable (the Economic and Monetary Union commitments) produced policy change (the dramatic change in economic policy) via political mechanisms of empowerment and disempowerment. However, their picture of the technocratic policy elite is rather limited, being confined to a group of technocrats working at the Italian Treasury and the Bank of Italy. As we elaborate further below, perhaps the advocacy coalition approach could have offered a more solid anchorage.

By contrast, Regonini and Giuliani (1994) do not stress independent variables but prefer to explain why the Italian debate has emphasized, since the early 1980s until now, the themes of constitutional engineering and electoral reform. These two authors argue that a community of academics actively involved in politics redefined the agenda during the 1980s in terms of institutional reform. Italy has changed its electoral laws in the first part of the 1990s and constitutional change has been dealt with by three high-level parliamentary commissions in the 1980s and the 1990s, the latest of which completed its work in June 1997.

Instead of looking at political parties and formal organizations, Regonini and Giuliani study influence by investigating a group of academics with different political affiliations, but with a similar socialization process and, most crucially, a common belief in the diagnoses and prognoses of the Italian crisis. Most of these academics have had a prominent role in parliament and in government in the last decade or so. Rather than using political parties as their main political vehicle, they have gained influence as a network of expertise. Although Regonini and Giuliani examine the 1980s, networks of expertise with political power have since become an entrenched feature of the Italian political system, as shown by the governments of the 1990s (for example, the Ciampi and Dini administrations) with a high presence of university professors relatively independent from political parties.

As already mentioned, in Regonini and Giuliani there is no external independent variable (such as, for instance, Economic and Monetary Union) determining change. Rather, Regonini and Giuliani's purpose is to show how the paradigm of institutional reform was transmitted into the policy process. Whilst Dyson and Featherstone's paper – notwithstanding its neglect of Jenkins-Smith and Sabatier's work – fits in neatly with the advocacy coalition approach (which emphasizes the role of external variables as the main cause of policy change over a decade), Regonini and Giuliani's study is more compatible with other models of policy change (Kingdon, 1984).

What is the role played by think tanks in the processes of change described by the above mentioned studies? To begin with, Regonini and Giuliani address an important element of agenda setting, namely the conceptualization of the Italian crisis as political crisis. The network of *professori* with political power described in their paper is epitomized by the current Prime Minister, Professor Romano Prodi, who shares with many of his academic colleagues in government and parliament the belief that Italy needs first and foremost electoral and constitutional reform.

It is important to ascertain whether or not this network of academics has been linked, in practice, to other actors: the advocacy coalition framework asserts that a coalition comes into existence only when a multitude of actors joins together, embraces a set of shared beliefs, and sets out to control a policy sub-system. This is precisely what happened in Italy. Between the second half of the 1980s and the beginning of the 1990s, this network of academics in politics expanded to a wider advocacy coalition which included the leaders of the mass movement supporting the electoral referendums of the 1990s, interest groups (such as the Confederation of Italian Industry, Confindustria), and magistrates fighting corruption. In other words, an advocacy coalition was formed. Yet think tanks as organizations did not get involved in electoral reform and debates on constitutional change because they have tended to specialize in social and economic policy and in intergovernmental delivery systems – not in macro questions of constitutional design. Italian policy institutes have always advocated bottom-up approaches to the Italian crisis (see the emphasis on societal mechanisms of change and development in the annual Censis reports), the reform of public administration (exemplified by the work of IRS on policy evaluation), and a micro debate on policy instruments rather than on macro-constitutional engineering. The Fondazione Agnelli has made the reform of the state one of its main areas of activity in the 1990s (Fondazione Agnelli, 1996). But this area of activity consists of research on the organization of the state, and the key issues are lesson-drawing in administrative reform (Dente *et al.*, 1995) and federalism – that is, two issues more compatible with a policy orientation than with constitutional engineering.

Our argument is that think tanks as organizations were at the periphery of (and in most cases excluded from) the *advocacy coalition for institutional reform*. However, by drawing attention to networks of expertise rather than to specific organizations, Regonini and Giuliani's study detects a crucial element of influence. Whereas think tanks as organizations were not participating in the coalition for institutional reform, some of their most charismatic leaders were *personally* involved in it. Individuals such as Romano Prodi, the founder of Nomisma, Luigi Spaventa of the CER, Arturo Parisi of Fondazione Segni and Fondazione Cattaneo, and even the apostle of bottom-up societal mechanisms (the leader of Censis, Giuseppe De Rita) were fascinated with the perspective of changing the Italian political system through electoral reform and institutional design in the 1980s and in the first half of the 1990s. To conclude, top members of think tanks have been instrumental in providing support for the institutional reform coalition. Their influence has been exerted through the channel of academics and experts in government described in detail by Regonini and Giuliani (1994).

Could it be argued that think tanks have been insiders in the other episode of policy change, namely fiscal adjustment? To begin with, we would argue that the technocratic policy elite promoting fiscal adjustment has included, in addition to the senior civil servants mentioned by Dyson and Featherstone, individuals from the CER, Nomisma, Prometeia, and the IRS. But what about think tanks as organizations? Throughout the last decade or so, think tanks have spawned a debate on the macroeconomic policy implications of Italian membership of the European Union, thus emphasizing the 'external constraint'. They have disseminated ideas, policy slogans, and data on European economic integration and the deterioration of Italian public finance. With the Treaty of Maastricht, the message of think tanks on the need 'to join Europe' became even more persistent. The CER reports and newsletters on public finance, the analysis of current economic trends provided by the IRS, and the project funded by the Fondazione Rosselli on 'the costs of non-Europe' (Amato and Salvadori 1990) have stressed the need for a radical change in the conduct of fiscal policy. Simply put, policy institutes have provided arguments and data, as well as a more conducive 'climate' of opinion, in support of the *coalition for fiscal adjustment*.

What members have comprised this coalition? As shown by Dyson and Featherstone (1996), the most powerful actors in the pro-fiscal adjustment coalition have been the Bank of Italy and the Treasury, with additional support – we argue – from employers' organizations. Knowledge and interests have been in a symbiotic relationship within this coalition, encompassing segments of the political system, such as the Republican Party, a small but very influential number of top socialists (for example, Giuliano Amato and Giorgio Ruffolo, who in turn participated in initiatives launched by Fondazione Rosselli and the CER in the 1980s and early 1990s) and even the technocratic rump of the Christian Democrats. Beniamino Andreatta, Minister, senior figure within the Christian Democrats and, at the same time, leader of the Agenzia di Ricerche e Legislazione (AREL), is a good example of a man bridging the worlds of knowledge and political action.

The battle over economic reform, however, was fought by two coalitions, one advocating radical reform of public finance and the other advocating the *status quo*, formed around what journalists labelled the *partito unico della spesa pubblica* (roughly, the grand party for public spending). The latter can be described as a cross-party coalition of politicians and constituencies with the aim of distorting public resources for micro-corporatist interests and electoral consensus.

Having broadly outlined the two coalitions, the question remains whether think tanks have played a role in economic policy change. We have already argued that they have contributed to the emergence of a climate of opinion in which a radical turn in economic policy has been perceived as indispensable for membership of the single currency club. In short, the 'external constraint' argument has been constantly fuelled by reports coming from think tanks. At the same time, the key actors within the fiscal reform coalition have been the Bank of Italy, the Treasury, and pressure groups, not think tanks. However, as mentioned earlier, economists from different parties have been 'socialized' into the discourse on fiscal reform through their participation in think tank initiatives.

This draws attention to our hypothesis that think tanks have operated as *policy fora*. Indeed, although think tanks have been closer to the fiscal reform coalition than to the public expenditure coalition, their role as independent and competent observers of economic policy has made them ideal policy fora. The latter – as explained by the advocacy coalition framework – are instrumental in generating cross-coalition learning. In the case of economic reform, think tanks have brought economists from different advocacy coalitions closer. A discourse on economic policy 'framed' in terms of 'objective' economic analysis has disenfranchised economists from political parties. Even economists relatively close to the parties then in government came to agree on the necessity of radical change in economic policy. It is no mystery that, in addition to the personalities mentioned above, senior economic advisors to the Socialist Party, the Christian Democrats and, as far as the opposition is concerned, the Communist Party, converged on their assessment of the Treaty of Maastricht. The first author of this paper conducted for a think tank a study based on a panel of experts in the aftermath of the Treaty of Maastricht (Prospecta, 1992) and found no evidence of disagreement on 'what should be done' among the experts interviewed, although they: (1) had very different party affiliations, (2) were active consultants of top politicians and (3) in some cases were directly involved in politics.

However, cross-coalition learning *per se* did not produce any policy change. Indeed, the turning point was represented by the robust ammunition provided by the Treaty of Maastricht. Clearly, the public expenditure coalition tried to ignore as much as possible the message coming from hundreds of alarming reports on public finance produced by policy institutes, but eventually had to surrender to the imperatives of Maastricht and their political implications. As argued by the advocacy coalition approach, an external shock (in this case, the Treaty on the European Union) altered the balance of resources available to the two coalitions. The fiscal adjustment coalition was empowered by the provisions on economic policy enshrined in the Treaty of Maastricht and was able to capitalize on this empowerment.

In sum, the advocacy coalition approach provides a conceptual framework for analysing knowledge utilization over the long term. The institutional reform coalition attracted individuals from think tanks. However, as Italian think tanks have specialized in social and economic policy rather than constitutional policy, their involvement as organizations was negligible. In the arena of economic policy, think tanks provided a policy forum and, in the long term, facilitated the emergence of an economic policy discourse based upon sound finance and convergence with the most powerful European economies. Their distinctive role has been that not of key actors within a coalition, but of policy fora.

Conclusion

What can be concluded at the end of this exploratory survey of Italian policy institutes? The first conclusion is that think tanks proliferated in the 1970s, and even more in the 1980s, but are currently undergoing a process of rationalization and consolidation. Their external environment has become more turbulent in the 1990s, due to the political crisis and the imperatives of internationalization.

The second conclusion is that think tanks have played a role in economic policy change, but not in electoral-institutional change. The analysis of two areas (fiscal reform and institutional engineering) has shed light on broader advocacy coalitions. Hence our third conclusion is that further research should not investigate policy institutes *per se*, but look instead at the wider political activity of advocacy coalitions in which think tanks operate as one set of actors. Specifically, we argue that think tanks should be characterized as policy fora rather than as members of one of the two coalitions in the debate on institutional change. Thus think tanks have been agents of learning in Italy: by acting as policy fora, they have generated across-coalition learning.

This leads to our fourth conclusion which emphasizes the need for an appropriate conceptual framework. In this chapter we have argued that an adequate framework should include the long-term impact of policy analysis, and the symbiotic relationship between interests and knowledge. We have made the choice of employing the advocacy coalition approach, but additional studies should test alternative approaches. In doing so, the study of think tanks could avoid the risk of becoming a 'cottage industry' and thus could contribute to crucial issues in theoretical policy analysis, such as policy change and knowledge utilization.

References

Funding for the survey utilized in this chapter was provided by the International Centre for Economic Research, the Associazione Iter Legis and the European Office of the World Bank. Special thanks to Pier Marco Ferraresi, Giovanna Garrone and Elisabetta Villa for their invaluable assistance with the implementation of the survey and analysis of the data. The financial support of the Nuffield Foundation (grant SOC/100/001577 on Think Tanks and the Politics of Expertise in Italy) to Claudio Radaelli is gratefully acknowleged. The authors are indebted to the editors and to Paul Sabatier and Marco Giuliani for extremely useful comments and suggestions; the usual disclaimer applies.

Abelson, D. E. and Carberry, C. M. (1996) 'In Search of Policy Advice. Why Presidential Nominees Turn to Think Tanks', paper prepared for the Annual Meeting of the PSA, Glasgow, 10–12 April.

Amato, G. and Salvadori, M. L. (eds) (1990) *Europa Conviene?*, Bari and Rome, Laterza.

Bartolini, S. and D'Alimonte, R. (1997) 'Electoral Transition and Party System Change in Italy', *West European Politics*, 20(1): 110–34.

Cockett, R. (1995) *Thinking the Unthinkable. Think Tanks and the Economic Counter Revolution 1931–1983*, London, Fontana–HarperCollins.

Dente, B., and Regonini G. (1987) 'Politics and Policies in Italy', in P. Lange and M. Regini (eds), *State, Market, and Social Regulation*, Cambridge, Cambridge University Press.

Dente, B. *et al.* (1995) *Riformare la pubblica amministrazione*, Turin, Fondazione Giovanni Agnelli.

Dolny, M. (1996) 'The Think Tank Spectrum: for the Media, Some Thinkers are More Equal than Others', *Extra!*, May–June.

Dolowitz, D. and Marsh, D. (1996) 'Who Learns from Whom: a Review of the Policy Transfer Literature', *Political Studies*, 44: 343–57.

Dyson, K. and Featherstone, K. (1996) 'Italy and EMU as Vincolo Esterno: Empowering the Technocrats, Transforming the State', *South European Society and Politics*, 1(2): 272–99.

Fischer, F. (1993) 'Policy Discourse and the Politics of Washington Think Tanks', in F. Fischer and J. Forester (eds), *The Argumentative Turn in Policy Analysis and Planning*, London, UCL Press, 21–42.

Fondazione Giovanni Agnelli (1996) *Programmi*, Turin, Fondazione Giovanni Agnelli.

Gaffney, J. (1991) 'Political Think-Tanks in the UK and Ministerial "Cabinets" in France', *West European Politics*, 14 (1): 1–17.

Hajer, M. A. (1993) 'Discourse Coalitions and the Institutionalization of Practice: the Case of Acid Rain in Great Britain', in F. Fischer and J. Forester (eds), *The Argumentative Turn in Policy Analysis and Planning*, London, UCL, 43–76.

Jenkins-Smith, H. C. and Sabatier, P. A. (1994) 'Evaluating the Advocacy Coalition Framework', *Journal of Public Policy*, 14(2): 175–203.

Kingdon, J. (1984) *Agendas, Alternatives and Public Policies*, Boston, Little, Brown and Co.

Moscati, R. (1982) 'Evoluzione e crisi della societa' italiana secondo i rapporti del Censis', *Stato e Mercato*, 4: 167–75.

Nomisma and IRS (1996) 'Governare la regolazione', report for the Civil Service Ministry, Bologna, typescript.

Parsons, W. (1995) *Public Policy*, London, Edward Elgar.

Prospecta (1992) 'Ideologie e prassi delle relazioni industriali prossime venture', Milan, 2 volumes, typescript.

Radaelli, C. M. (1995) 'The Role of Knowledge in the Policy Process', *Journal of European Public Policy*, 2(2): 159–83.

Radaelli, C. M. and Dente, B. (1996) 'Evaluation Strategies and the Analysis of the Policy Process', *Evaluation*, 2(1): 51–66.

Regonini, G. and Giuliani, M. (1994) 'Italie: Au-delà d'une démocratie consensuelle?', in B. Jobert (ed.), *Le Tournant Néo-Libéral en Europe*, Paris, L'Harmattan, 123–99.

Rich, R. F. and Oh, C. H. (1994) 'The Utilisation of Policy Research', in S. S. Nagel (ed.), *Encyclopaedia of Policy Studies*, 2nd edn, New York and Basel, Marcel Dekker, 69–92.

Sabatier, P. A. (1993) 'Policy Change over a Decade or More', in P. A. Sabatier and H. C. Jenkins-Smith (eds), *Policy Change and Learning. An Advocacy Coalition Approach*, Boulder, CO, Westview, 13–39.

Sabatier, P. A. and Jenkins-Smith, H. C. (eds) (1993) *Policy Change and Learning. An Advocacy Coalition Approach*, Boulder, CO, Westview.

Sabatier, P .A. and Jenkins-Smith, H. C. (1998) 'The Advocacy Coalition Framework: an Assessment', in P. A. Sabatier (ed.), *Theories of the Policy Process*, Boulder, CO, Westview.

Stone, D. (1991) 'Old Guards versus New Partisans: Think Tanks in Transition', *Australian Journal of Political Science*, 26 (2): 197–215.

Stone, D. (1996) *Capturing the Political Imagination. Think Tanks and the Policy Process*, London, Frank Cass.

Weaver, K. (1989) 'The Changing World of Think Tanks', *PS: Political Science and Politics,* 22(3): 563–78.

Weiss, C. H. (1979) 'The Many Meanings of Research Utilisation', *Public Administration Review*, 39(5): 426–31.

Weiss, C. H. (1986) 'Research and Policy-making: a Limited Partnership', in F. Heller (ed.), *The Use and Abuse of Social Science*, London, Sage, 214–35.

Wittrock, B. (1982) 'Social Knowledge, Public Policy and Social Betterment. A Review of Current Research on Knowledge Utilisation in Policy-making', *European Journal of Political Research*, 10: 83–9.

Think tanks in Germany

Introduction

Conventional wisdom about think tanks in Germany could be summarized as follows: there is no such thing as a German think tank. This view is based on a confusion of terms, and on the misleading assumption that only US-type think tanks fit the full definition of think tanks. Renate Mayntz, a prominent researcher on policy institutions, points out the alleged relative insignificance of German think tanks: 'the West German system has relatively little by way of a specialized infrastructure for policy analysis and advice' (Mayntz, 1987: 8–9). Mayntz and others, however, do not take into account the influence of the research divisions of political foundations, parties and interest groups. Instead, I shall argue in this chapter that the Federal Republic does, in fact, possess the *functional* equivalent of American-type think tanks.

The German political system has only a few institutions which correspond directly to the organizationally independent US-style think tanks. More typical are the research institutes and advisory bodies which are associated with a foundation or an interest group. Only a few think tanks are organizationally independent. Governmental and administrative advisory bodies dominate the policy arena. This is typical for a parliamentary system like the one in Germany, where legislatures do not 'legislate' – in the original sense – but serve mainly to scrutinize legislation emanating from the executive branch of government.

This discussion addresses the following questions. Which institutional constellations characterize the market for policy advice in the Federal Republic of Germany? Under what conditions do they operate? Which functions do they fulfil and which strategies do they adopt? After developing a practical typology, the main think tanks in Germany will be described and analysed according to their functions. The concluding section uses empirical material drawn from a survey of Bundestag MPs to assess the political use of think tanks.

A general framework

The influence of academics, journalists and federations on the agenda-setting process is usually underestimated. Kingdon (1984) argues that: (1) important information is used to support policy positions. Ideas or information are linked with a certain 'trend' in order to strengthen or weaken a particular argument; (2) the results of research rarely have a *direct* effect on the political process. They are integrated into existing practices rather gradually and with temporal delays (Sabatier, 1991: 148). More important than the results as such is their usage in the network of advocacy coalitions. Sabatier assumes that relatively stable advocacy coalitions constantly try to pursue their political goals. They consult think tanks in order to acquire academic and expert knowledge with a predictable value judgement. As Sabatier (1991: 151–3) argues:

> An advocacy coalition consists of actors from many public and private organizations at all levels of government who share a set of basic beliefs (policy goals plus causal and other perceptions) and who seek to manipulate the rules of various governmental institutions to achieve those goals over time. Conflict among coalitions is mediated by 'policy brokers', i.e. actors more concerned with stability than with achieving policy goals.

Think tanks are of particular significance in situations where political consensus is fragile. While existing internal advising committees are preferred for the 'political routine', periods of crisis provide think tanks with an *entrée* because their voice and competence is required to assist agenda-setting. Accordingly, Sabatier's approach serves as an analytical perspective to account for the aggregations of actors in specific institutional constellations in which persons from different organizations (including think tanks) have common normative ideas and co-ordinate their activities.

Think tanks contribute to the process of social agenda setting, through normative creation and discussion of political issues (Kepplinger, 1992). Those issues which arise on the agenda and the extent to which they dominate the political debate depend not on think tanks but on interest-driven preliminary decisions. In her systematic sociological analysis of academic institutes, Mayntz differentiates between: (1) non-university, non-profit, public policy research, (2) university research, (3) business research, (4) industrial joint-venture research, (5) commercial research, and (6) independent research by non-profit organizations (Mayntz, 1985: 9–10). Most of the institutes that will be dealt with here belong to the latter group, which, however, does not represent the field completely. Mayntz's study does not take into consideration academic research institutes of the political parties' in-house foundations, non-profit limited corporations and research undertaken by interest groups and organizations which conduct research, but not necessarily of a commercial nature.

In their study of the Federal Republic of Germany, Hohn and Schimank point out that, due to the lack of available data, the size and scale of activity in these institutes is extremely difficult to assess, especially where parties and interest groups are concerned. Moreover, the attempt to determine the members of advocacy coalitions poses difficulties that cannot sufficiently be solved with Mayntz's approach. Statements about the financial structure at best provide only a superficial insight into the actual role of think tanks and the way they see themselves. For this reason, think tanks seem most appropriately classified in accordance with three different functions which they accomplish in the political process, namely: to obtain and disseminate information and ideas (production and diffusion); to allocate and network (networking); and to recruit and transfer elites (transformation) (Gellner, 1995b: 499). The production of ideas and information is arguably the most important task of political think tanks. But even here, individual institutes differ with regard to the topics they select and the kind of personnel they employ to produce information.

At least as significant as the production of knowledge is its dissemination and marketing. This is especially so with regard to the agenda-setting process where the media are swamped with all kinds of publications (monographs, newspaper articles, TV commentaries, briefings, etc.). Apart from supplying and disseminating political ideas, think tanks also contribute to the recruitment and transfer of political and administrative leadership personnel in Germany. By organizing seminars, symposia, conferences and lectures, for example, they supply a forum for contact and mutual exchange between politicians, administrators and their staff. These different functions and institutional characteristics of think tanks can be expressed in the following typology: 'universities without students', 'interest-oriented' and 'interest-bound' institutes.

'Universities without students'

These organizations mainly employ scholars who could just as well be working for universities and state institutions; in fact, many of them alternate between think tanks and universities. Usually, they publish academic reference books or participate in current political debates by writing essays and articles. In the Federal Republic of Germany, this type of think tank is represented by the six big economic research institutes, the Stiftung Wissenschaft und Politik (SWP) in Ebenhausen, the Deutsche Gesellschaft für Auswärtige Politik (DGAP) in Bonn, and the Wissenschaftszentrum Berlin (WZB). All of these institutes focus primarily on academic research. Although political interests and preferences are discernible, they are rarely

explicit. However, in-depth interviews with representatives of these institutes have revealed that they are now competing with more interest-driven
institutes, particularly those focusing on socio-political issues. Hence, the
'universities without students' have tended recently to raise their profiles by
strengthening their public relations strategies. Holding press conferences
and publishing (mostly superficial) reports have become major instruments
in their quest for creating a stronger media presence, and thus influencing
the political agenda.

At the same time, the traditional channels of public policy research are still
operating, as the 'universities without students' continue to publish academic reference books through which they establish their scholarly reputation.
However, politicians and administrators complain about the length and academic flavour of these publications. By and large, these institutes have prepared themselves for changing working conditions without having altered
their overall aims and strategies.

'Interest-oriented' institutes

The second category of think tank comprises organizationally independent
institutes which are not directly dominated by political parties or interest
groups and which operate as public non-profit organizations: here they are
termed 'interest-oriented' institutes. Among these are the Oeko-Institut in
Freiburg, the Institut für Wirtschaft und Gesellschaft (IWG), and the Frankfurter and Walter-Eucken Institutes. All of these have in common a nominal
organizational autonomy, as well as a clear political and ideological alignment. While the Oeko-Institut is close to 'green' positions, the other institutes are aligned with generally market-oriented, liberal tendencies. In many
cases, these medium-sized institutions were originally 'one-man enterprises',
but have now secured for themselves a niche in the market of advisory
bodies.

Apart from seeking academic respectability, these think tanks increasingly
focus on normative aspects of public policy research. Their target group or
audience is clearly constituted by members of an advocacy coalition which
has to be equipped with arguments to maintain competitiveness in 'the
market of ideas'. A good example would be the close relationship between
the 'Frankfurter Institut' and the 'free-market' community. One of the main
outlets of this community is the prestigious daily newspaper *Frankfurter Allgemeine Zeitung*, where ideas from the institute are constantly spread by the
editors of the economics section. Even personal ties exist between institute
and newspaper. These 'interest-oriented' think tanks hardly ever produce
academic reference books, but have specialized in creating network infra-
structures. Besides their clientele they also address the general public, for the
most part by networking with sympathetic media representatives who may

even belong to the same advocacy coalition. Indeed, these institutions claim to deliver work of academic quality but are difficult to distinguish from the organizationally integrated institutes described in the next section.

'Interest-bound' institutes

'Interest-bound' think tanks offer research merely to supply partisan politicians and administrators with verbal ammunition. The production of academic work is pushed into the background of organizational activity. In the Federal Republic, these institutes are mostly aligned with the foundation of a political party or a certain interest group, such as the employer associations' Institut der Deutschen Wirtschaft (IW), or the trade unions' Wirtschafts- und Sozialwissenschaftliches Institut (WSI). While these institutes differ considerably in terms of composition, aims and strategies, they all have in common an explicit concentration on channelling and promoting their respective political objectives. They usually enjoy lavish funding.

Frequently, these so-called 'policy entrepreneurs' are difficult to distinguish from consultants or lobbyists. In most cases, they are small (in some cases, very small) enterprises led by a single person with an academic background. Their major objective is to uphold the interests of the funding bodies. They pursue interest politics with academic arguments. Here, good examples would be IW and WSI, owned by the German employer associations and the trade unions respectively. Their research is heavily controlled by the parent organizations. After pursuing divergent opinions about the trade union movement's future, the WSI, for instance, had to undergo serious reconstruction and was even threatened with dissolution (*Frankfurter Allgemeine Zeitung*, 12 December 1994).

In sum, German think tanks are characterized by their relatively close alignment to political parties and interest groups. The independent institutes which are best described as 'universities without students' are clearly dependent on the political executive. This holds true for the SWP, which is dependent on the Chancellor's office and the Foreign Ministry, as well as the six economic research institutes, which could hardly exist without the research contracts of the Ministry of Trade and Commerce. Unlike the presidential system of the United States, the Federal Republic's parliamentary system has relatively few think tanks. The most important German think tanks are discussed in the following section.

German think tanks

Founded mostly after World War Two, many of the 'universities without students' belong to the so-called 'blue list', a 'research-related political aggregate', or more exactly 'a summing of extremely heterogeneous and widely disjointed research institutes because of the "common ground of their financing"' (Hohn and Schimank, 1990: 142–3). The 'blue list' institutes are jointly financed by the Federal Government and the *Länder*. Their internal workings are heavily determined by the state. Table 4.1 shows in detail the actual size of the most important German think tanks in terms of personnel and revenues. It is evident that the 'universities without students', especially the big economic institutes, dominate the field, whereas the 'research-oriented' institutes are far smaller operations. Also, the comparatively strong position of the employer associations' institute IW becomes clear.

Table 4.1 *Personnel and revenues of German think tanks in 1992 (1991)*

Name	Personnel		Revenues (in million DM)
	research	total	
Universities without students			
IfW	89	333	28.5
IFO	110	220	25.2
WZB	140	250	24.7
DIW	100	202	23.8
HWWA	68	227	21.2
SWP	55	121	15.6
DJI (1991)	80	130	14.4
IWH	39	66	10.1
RWI	38	69	7.7
DGAP (1991)	11	30	4.6
Interest-oriented institutes			
Oeko-Institut (1991)	–	64	6
IWG	6	12	1.3
Walter-Eucken Institut	5	12	–
Frankfurter Institut	–	6	–
Interest-bound institutes			
IW	–	111	15.8
WSI	22	51	7.6

Sources: Annual reports, interviews, calculations.

Unlike the 'universities without students', the 'interest-oriented' institutes are relatively small concerns. However, they compensate for their shortage of staff and lack of financial clout through their excellent relations with the media. 'Interest-bound' institutes in the Federal Republic are the research centres of the big federations and trade unions as well as the research institutes of the political parties' in-house foundations. All of them are fairly well-equipped think tanks. Yet their dependence on the parent organization has a strong influence on their activities.

'Universities without students'

Most of the German 'universities without students' either belong to the 'blue list' or are supported by the Federal Government and the *Länder*. Other means of financing are not generally available to this sort of think tank. On the other hand, most of these institutes have started to explore additional sources of funding and new audiences for their advice. As mentioned above, at least some of them have to cope with increasing competition from consultants and 'interest-oriented' institutes which increasingly gain importance in conjunction with advocacy coalitions. That is why at least some of the 'universities without students' have started to adapt their strategies to the changed conditions in the market of ideas. All of the following are 'typical' German functional equivalents of American think tanks.

Stiftung Wissenschaft und Politik (SWP – Ebenhausen)

Shaped by the model of the American RAND Corporation, Ebenhausen is arguably the German political research institute and is reckoned to be 'Western Europe's largest international affairs think tank' (*Economist*, 21 December 1991). Although it does not belong to the 'blue list', the SWP finances itself mainly from the budget of the Chancellor's office. In 1990 it raised additional revenue of about 2 million DM. In view of its steadily increasing income and in comparison with other German research institutes, the SWP is financially strong. With around 55 research fellows (120 employees altogether), the SWP is not enormous as far as personnel is concerned.

Ebenhausen is led by a so-called 'foundation council', a committee of 19 members drawn from the *Bundestag*, the Chancellor's office, several ministries (Foreign Affairs, Defence, Economics, Research/Technology and Finance), representatives of science and economics and a representative from the *Land* of Bavaria. The representatives of the Federal Government have a two-thirds majority. They appoint the board whose chairman is the director of the institute. The SWP pursues four fields of research: West–East European and Atlantic politics, international security, international political economy and non-European affairs. Research findings are published in academic series and working papers as well as in secret dossiers. Particular importance is attached to the networking function of the SWP as an infrastructural planning panel (Ritter, 1978: 455–6).

Deutsche Gesellschaft für Auswärtige Politik (DGAP)

The SWP and the DGAP belong to the same advocacy coalition which supports the Federal Government on foreign affairs. This is illustrated not only
by the common personal networks linking the two institutes but also by the
very similar historical development of both institutes. The DGAP was
founded in 1955 as a non-partisan and independent association which was
supposed to serve as a public forum for discussions of foreign political relevance. The goal of the association is to integrate all circles with an interest
in foreign affairs in one single institution in order to discuss questions of
European security in a non-partisan atmosphere (DGAP, 1992: 5).

From 1960 onwards a separate research centre was founded. One of the
key figures in this process was Arnold Bergsträsser who later proved to be
one of the initiators for the foundation of the SWP. Furthermore, with the
Europa Archiv, founded in 1946 by Wilhelm Cornides the DGAP also had at
its disposal a renowned political journal. The DGAP is an elite network for
foreign affairs and consists of leading representatives from politics (including trade unions), economics and science. This is made clear by examining
the membership of the committee, the Academic Directory and the sponsoring firms, which reveals its character of a network similar to the Council
of Foreign Relations and the London-based Royal Institute of International
Affairs. Moreover the DGAP does not fulfil the function of producing and
disseminating ideas for the political process, focusing almost exclusively on
networking.

Only as far as financing is concerned can the DGAP be considered a 'university without students'. It charges membership fees and raises funds from
foundations and firms. The remaining 40 per cent – about 4.6 million DM
in 1991 – is raised by public institutions. The research institute of the DGAP
is the closest approximation to an ideas-producing think tank, and this is
where the most competitive points of contact with the SWP are located. The
fields of research are sub-divided into project teams and include problems of
foreign affairs, security and foreign trade – especially that of the United
States – international environmental issues, and problems of military proliferation and space research. The Academic Directory determines questions of
long-term research plans, individual research projects and publications. It
consists of first-rate academics from the relevant disciplines, among others
political scientists, economists and international lawyers.

Economic research institutes

The so-called big six economic research institutes (see Table 4.2) all belong
to the 'blue list'. They are well-known because of their regular reports concerning the economic development of the Federal Republic. These half-

yearly publications generally attract extensive media coverage and public debate about the reliability of the jointly presented predictions. Their 1992 assessment, for example, that the Federal Republic was not in a recession, caused a considerable stir in the press and consequently influenced the stock market. The economic research institutes were criticized for being influenced by the over-optimistic forecasts produced by the Federal Government. Other experts and federations reproached them for slipshod work (*Frankfurter Rundschau*, 14 November 1992) and 'mere wishful thinking' (*Frankfurter Allgemeine Zeitung*, 5 May 1993). The six economic research institutes are typical 'universities without students'. They are the closest equivalents to American think tanks such as Brookings or the American Enterprise Institute, except that the latter do not restrict themselves to economic questions.

Table 4.2   *Research institutes: year of foundation, location and legal status*

Name	Year	Location	Legal status
HWWA	1908	Hamburg	Public institution
IfW	1914	Kiel	Public institution
DIW	1925	Berlin	Non-profit organization
RWI[a]	1943	Essen	Non-profit organization
IFO	1949	Munich	Non-profit organization
IWH	1992	Halle	Non-profit organization

Sources: Annual reports
Note: [a] The RWI was founded in 1926 as the 'Western' department of the Berlin DIW; it has been legally independent since 1943.

The economic data concerning the size of the research centres already indicate a clear division: Kieler Institut für Weltwirtschaft (IfW), Information und Forschung Institut (IFO) and Deutsches Institut für Wirtschaftsforschung (DIW) may be classified as the dominant institutes, and this is matched by their respective journalistic significance. The Rheinisch-Westfälisches Institut für Wirtschaftsforschung (RWI) and the new Institut für empirische Wirtschaftsforschung Halle (IWH), for example, are hardly present in public discussions. Indeed, the Hamburgisches Weld-Wirtschafts-Archiv (HWWA) compares favourably with the leading institutes as far as size is concerned and also has close connections with Hamburg's opinion-forming newspapers and magazines. Its impact on the public agenda is limited, however, by internal problems. It has recently been criticized by an evaluation committee, consisting of leading economists, as being highly inefficient and having too little research output (*Frankfurter Allgemeine Zeitung*, 26 January1996).

Although differences exist, the working methods are strongly comparable. All of these bodies produce weekly or monthly reports on the economic situation. These are short statements designed for the broad mass of the population and enjoy extensive coverage in the German media. Hardly a day goes by without the leading newspapers mentioning at least one of the institutes' forecasts.

'Interest-oriented' think tanks

Oeko-Institut

The Oeko-Institut is a non-profit organization whose foundation goes back to the anti-nuclear movement of the late 1970s. Yet the most important incident for its growth was the Chernobyl disaster in 1986. The Oeko-Institut suddenly found itself the focus of public interest. The corresponding 'credibility bonus' catapulted the 'gym-shoe researchers' into the headlines: 'The people thought they [the institute] were right, so you have to listen to them' (*Frankfurter Rundschau*, 14 November 1992). The Oeko-Institut receives its research contracts from governments of the *Länder* (even conservative-governed administrative districts), the European Commission, environmental federations from Switzerland, communities from all over Germany, and Greenpeace. It appears that within the environmental advocacy coalition, the Oeko-Institut is regarded as one of its most important think tanks (*Forum*, 6/1992: 17).

The 'amazing growth of the critics of growth' is verified by the institute's economic prosperity. In 1991 it employed 64 research fellows. The annual budget amounted to 6 million DM (*Oeko-Mitteilungen*, 3/1992: 5). Before Chernobyl it had almost 1 million DM at its disposal. Between 1988 and 1991, when the Green Party and the ecological movement in general became increasingly powerful political actors and risk awareness in German society surged, the Oeko-Institut recorded a rise in orders for expert opinions of 150 per cent (*Oeko-Mitteilungen*, 1/1992). Unfortunately this 'alternative' institute does not give more explicit details. It does not reveal the origin of all these contributions, a familiar pattern with mainstream 'interest-oriented' and 'interest-bound' think tanks. As far as openness and accountability are concerned, the Oeko-Institut's 5,400 members tend not to exert much control or influence.

Institut für Wirtschaft und Gesellschaft (IWG Bonn)

The non-profit IWG Bonn was founded in 1977 by the then General Secretary of the Christlich Demokratische Union (CDU), Kurt Biedenkopf, and Meinhard Miegel. Leggewie is probably right to point out the rather selfish motives of Biedenkopf, who clearly hoped to build an image of a sober non-partisan expert: 'But in order to do so, even Biedenkopf has to do more than putting heavy theoretical tomes under his pillow. For ten years, since he lost political office in the power centre of the CDU, he has had his own Think Tank' (Leggewie, 1987: 80).

The institute does not seem too affected by direct political intervention. It is a typical 'interest-oriented' think tank which supplies its advocacy coalition with academic advice: 'With its pragmatic approach the IWG Bonn wants to shed light upon the economic and social backgrounds of political and entrepreneurial work in order to make strategic planning easier' (IWG brochure). The *Economist* points out an alleged tendency in the Federal Republic to conceal one's interests behind a sophisticated research image. In the case of the IWG, the orientation is clear. 'Inevitably, given [Biedenkopf's] background, its research has found its most appreciative audience among Christian Democrats' (*Economist*, 25 May 1991). The membership of the advisory council likewise clarifies the general orientation pursued by the institute. It consists of Friedrich Ebert Stiftung supporters and publicists of determined free-market provenance, such as C. C. von Weizsacker, E.-J. Mestmacker, J. Gross and H.-D. Barbier.

Despite the small number of employees (12, including six research fellows, in 1993 when its budget was a relatively modest 1.3 million DM), its significance within its own advocacy coalition seems considerable. When asked about the target group for the IWG's work, Miegel talked of a 'non-partisan modernising coalition' (Leggewie, 1987: 84). The institute tries to 'feed' these 'upholders of essential decisions in social and economic policy ... with data, models and concepts and, of course, to exert influence in a certain way' (Leggewie, 1990: 68). The IWG apparently attaches great importance to the national and international press. No other German institute is mentioned as often in *The Washington Post*, *Business Week* or *Time* and *Newsweek* as the IWG. In German newspapers full-page articles in *Die Zeit* or *Focus* are as regular as book reviews and reports of other activities.

'Interest-bound' think tanks

In this group the institutes of business and trade unions dominate. Perhaps the best examples of this type of institute are the peculiarly German quasi-party think tanks. All established German party foundations have created research institutes which perform (or try to perform) the functions of a think tank in many different ways. They fulfil the purposes of networking and elite transfer and 'are engaged in pure social science research as well as in applied research to support the political opinion-forming of the respective party, that is, they provide "ruling knowledge"' (Von Arnim, 1991: 100).

Konrad Adenauer Stiftung (KAS)

Until 1992 the KAS supported different institutes with different political orientations. The Institut für Kommunalwissenschaft, for example, has always been very strongly focused on pragmatic policy advice whereas the foundation's research centre considered itself to be an academic institute. The current director Hans-Joachim Veen has clearly maintained the social-science orientation of the institute. He also leads the newly created field of 'research and advice' which itself is sub-divided into four policy departments – one each for domestic and international policy, a third for local policy and lastly a political academy.

Two main concerns are discernible in the foundation's stronger policy orientation. The KAS has its largest impact on questions of strategic and security policy. Another central issue – championed by Werner Kaltefleiter in the 1970s – concerns public opinion polling and electoral research. These activities attract special public attention (Pinto-Duschinsky, 1991: 208), and influenced the CDU campaign during the 1990 elections in the still existing but already evaporating German Democratic Republic. Whereas almost all polling organizations predicted a landslide victory for the Social Democrats, the KAS consistently predicted that the Conservatives would benefit from the Chancellor's positive image as a key player in German reunification. The campaign concentrated on Helmut Kohl and resulted in a celebrated victory for the Conservatives in the East and thereby made it much easier to reunify Germany on West German terms.

Elite transfer is another important aspect of the KAS. After Bernhard Vogel lost power as Prime Minister in the Bundesland of Rheinland-Pfalz, he was made Chairman of the KAS – a position he still holds, despite his subsequent election as Prime Minister of the new eastern Bundesland of Thüringen.

Friedrich Ebert Stiftung (FES)

In comparison with the KAS the research institute of the FES (established in 1959) is a more traditional and non-partisan institute. According to its director, G. Stumpfig, the FES is not anxious to be seen as a Social Democrat think tank; it would rather see the universities as a yardstick for its activities. Neither is the FES very interested in networking. In spite of occasional co-operation with the Brookings Institution, for example, these contacts are not intended to establish anything like a strategic partnership. Unlike other foundations in this category, the FES also does not have a systematic election research department. It is forced to support itself through contract research and therefore tries to avoid political commitments (Vieregge, 1980: 29). The position of the FES in the Social Democrat advocacy coalition is further weakened by competition from the trade unions, especially the already mentioned WSI, which has a high reputation as the mainstream social democratic research institute (Pinto-Duschinsky, 1991: 207).

The research centre of the FES was founded in 1959. Its main fields of work have been social and contemporary history, foreign affairs, and questions concerning the German Democratic Republic, developing countries and economic policies. The FES is supported by the 'classic' sponsors of university research like the Deutsche Forschungsgemeinschaft (DFG) and the foundations of Thyssen and Volkswagen. Despite its non-partisan approach, in the late 1970s the FES played an important role in helping the Sozialdemokratische Partei Deutschland (SPD) to defeat the ideological challenge of the marxist left (Vieregge, 1980: 29). Apparently the institute is still characterized by this moderate orientation (Pinto-Duschinsky, 1991: 208). This was further accentuated when Holger Börner, a former Prime Minister of the Bundesland of Hessen, was made chairman of the institution, another example of the political elite transfers which are the hallmark of German think tanks.

Friedrich Naumann Stiftung (FNS)

The FNS is a foundation which deliberately tries to emulate the functions of a 'liberal' think tank. According to its executive committee member, Fliszar, the foundation will develop more as a source of forward-looking advice for the solution of political and social problems. The FNS, founded in 1958, is the only foundation in Germany which has a clear networking relationship with liberal think tanks all over the world, particularly those in the USA. Hence it organizes conferences and research projects together with the CATO Institute, for example. The FNS also strives for co-operation with the Frankfurter Institut, especially through the *Frankfurter Allgemeine Zeitung*'s influential editor H.-D. Barbier, who is a member of both executive boards. A first conference of politically like-minded think tanks took place in October 1992. Among the participating institutes were the Adam Smith Institute and the Institute of Economic Affairs from the UK, the CATO Institute from the USA, the Carl Menger Institut from Austria, Timbro from Sweden and the Liberalni Institute from Prague (Czech Republic). The Federal Republic of Germany was represented by the Frankfurter Institut, the Kieler Institut für Weltwirtschaft and the Walter-Eucken Institut. Undoubtedly these think tanks are members of a liberal advocacy coalition, and all are associated with the Mont Pelerin Society. The purpose of the conference was to set up a network around these like-minded institutions.

The research institute of the FNS seems to have a marked influence on liberal party politics, influence which is more direct within a parliamentary faction than the leadership (Pinto-Duschinsky, 1991: 209). The small staff is no obstacle to this. Many of the research contracts won by the FNS are deliberately assigned to external institutions and individuals in order to decrease personnel costs (FNS *Annual Report 1991*, 1992: 22).

Again, also, the FNS works as an elite transfer institution, having made the former Minister for the Economy, Graf Lambsdorff, its chairman, when he had to resign from his post on charges of fraud.

Summary

On the whole, one can confirm Pinto-Duschinsky's conclusions about the German parties' in-house foundations. These 'small universities' (Pinto-Duschinsky, 1991: 180) build a bridge between the areas of social science and politics. They vary greatly in size – from the 100 employees of the KAS and the 60 staff of the FES, to the 8 employed by the FNS (including only four academics) – yet they all carry out functions typical of think tanks. On the other hand their actual impact on the policies and strategies of their parties is quite marginal. As Pinto-Duschinsky (1991: 242) argues, 'Despite the undoubted quality of many of their researchers, the departments do not generally appear to enjoy the prestige of some of the think tanks in Washington. Policy-makers within the German parties frequently seem to rely on research emanating from the universities rather than from the Stiftungen.' As we shall now see, this finding is corroborated by empirical research on members of the German *Bundestag* (MPs).

Members of parliament and think tanks: a case study

In the summer of 1993 I investigated the extent to which members of the *Bundestag* were consulting political and economic research institutes. The main objective of this survey was to find out how 'research' is used and which forms of research are particularly helpful. The use of extra-university research and the academic work of interest groups were of particular interest here. The survey was also designed to discover which institutes were regarded as influential, whether there was a conscious demand for 'advocacy' research and how the *Bundestag* members considered that the studies should be presented.

General findings

The institutions which deal with research differ very much in their utility for members of parliament. The research institutes are by far the most significant sources of advice, whereas the Commissions (especially the Enquête-Commissions, the German equivalent to the British Royal Commissions) and, to an even greater extent, the universities and the parties' in-house foundations are of rather marginal importance. This holds true not only for special problems, but also for the daily work of MPs.

As shown in Figure 4.1, the replies illustrate a dominance of the research institutes of federations and trade unions. By contrast, the parties' in-house foundations and universities are less important. While this is not surprising in the case of the universities, the results for the political foundations clearly show that they have a very modest impact in comparison with the 'interest-bound' institutes of federations and trade unions. This evidence argues strongly for the transfer of knowledge between the parties' in-house foundations and the MPs.

Apart from the Max-Planck-Institutes and the Fraunhofer-Gesellschaft, both institutes for natural sciences and therefore not covered here, which were named most frequently, the big economic research institutes and the SWP dominate their respective fields. The data show that the 'interest-

Figure 4.1   *Preferred sources for research (%)*

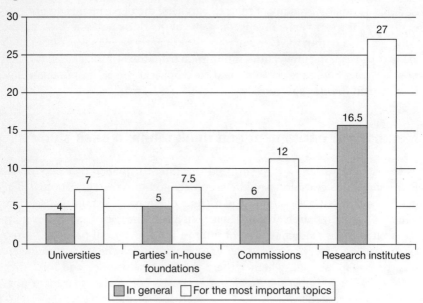

Note: n=241 (for general work); n=244 (for the most important topics).

bound' institutes are less important, but have clear advantages over the 'interest-oriented' ones (see Figure 4.2). As influential as they may be for policy advice in the USA, the 'interest-oriented' think tanks in the Federal Republic are still a relatively minor force, at least in the view of the surveyed MPs.

Figure 4.2 *Importance of German think tanks*

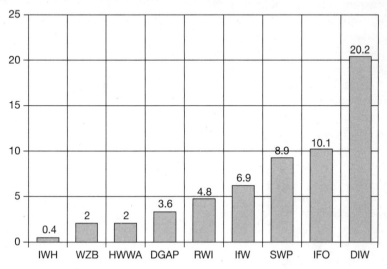

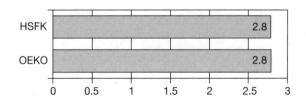

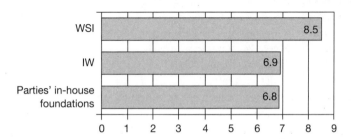

Note: n=248

However, most of the MPs are aware of the possible value of academic research, and increasingly try to make use of it. More than 54 per cent of the surveyed MPs were convinced that the results of academic research inevitably differ due to their origin and contain a certain bias, whereas only 40 per cent explicitly reject this assessment. A majority of the interviewees subsequently admitted that they consciously look for academic research which supports their political stance. Furthermore, 45 per cent of the MPs do this 'always' or 'frequently', whereas only 19.4 per cent stated that they 'never' or 'seldom' did so.

The relatively modest importance of both the 'interest-oriented' and the 'interest-bound' think tanks in Germany is due not to the cautious analysis of their fellows, but to other factors. The way the institutes present their research findings, for example, is often considered too academic. Only 19 per cent of the MPs find traditional presentations of science in reference books and journals helpful. They declared themselves clearly in favour of highly readable and journalistic information (47 per cent) and, even more decisively, that they prefer normative and pragmatic results of academic research (more than 51 per cent). At least as far as the research institutes are concerned, information obviously is transformed by different media. Press reports, in fact, are read most frequently, but the institutes' publications and academic journals also appear to attract an audience.

If we apply the metaphor of the 'market of ideas', then the field of institutionalized policy advice is certainly diverse, and only a few MPs believed that they came across the same sources time and again. There are apparently no advocacy coalitions which completely monopolize certain issues or parties. Instead, there appear to be competing advocacy coalitions.

These findings are confirmed by the responses of MPs to the question of the concrete influence of think tanks. The FES, for example, seems to be more important for the representatives of the SPD than the KAS or the FNS for members of the Federal Government. The impact of research institutes of federations and trade unions is also more significant in the case of the SPD. This is also true for the other external research institutes. The universities in contrast gain similar rates of interest in all of these groups.

The differences in importance become even more obvious if we consider the highest rates of the scale. The FES is quite important for more than 40 per cent of the SPD MPs, whereas only 30 per cent (of the conservative CDU and Christlich Soziale Union (CSU) members) and less than 20 per cent (of the liberal Freie Demokratische Partei (FOP) members) of the government faction assign comparable ratings to their respective foundations. Similarly, the research institutes of federations and trade unions are considered quite significant by more than 60 per cent of SPD MPs, in contrast to only 37 per cent of CDU/CSU representatives. The FDP MPs lie somewhere in the middle.

As expected, the trade unionist WSI is of major importance for SPD MPs. The employer association's IW, on the other hand, receives higher ratings from the representatives of the government parties, especially from the FDP, but – on the whole – is far less consulted. The evaluation of the big economic research institutes follows this pattern: the DIW is most frequently mentioned by SPD MPs, but the IfW in Kiel and the HWWA-Institut für Wirtschaftsforschung Hamburg very rarely. At least with regard to the IfW the findings are unambiguous and indicate its participation within an advocacy coalition, as this institute is clearly preferred by members of the government parties (see Figure 4.3).

By contrast, the RWI is mentioned more often – yet on a lower level – by SPD MPs. The IFO-Institut actually gains more of a hearing among government representatives, but it also scores respectably among the occupational parliamentarians. The SWP, on the other hand, enjoys a high level of acceptance among all factions. Conspicuous, though, is the large share of FDP MPs. This may indicate the existence of an advocacy coalition which is

Figure 4.3   *Question: On a scale between 1 (very much) and 5 (very little), to what extent do the publications of and contact with the following institutes influence your parliamentary work?*

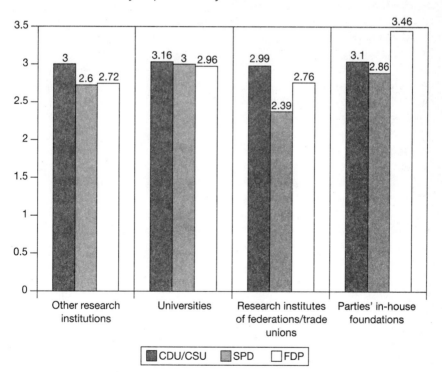

determined by a political preference for the 'official' foreign policy of the Federal Republic which has been deeply influenced by the former FDP Foreign Minister H. D. Genscher. Also the percentage of MPs who share a special interest in foreign affairs is particularly high among the FDP contingent. The Wissenschaftszentrum Berlin, an academic offspring of the WZB, by contrast, is mentioned very rarely. This institute is considered an academic research institution rather than a think tank. With the exception of the IfW the other institutes of this type only show a few characteristics of a think tank.

Among 'interest-bound' institutes, the WSI most clearly constitutes an important part of an advocacy coalition with the SPD parliamentarians. The IW, by contrast, cannot be rated in the same category, although certain tendencies are discernible. In comparison to the SPD MPs, more than twice as many CDU/CSU/FDP representatives consider this institute important. The modest significance for the SPD is probably due to the different clientele that the IW tries to address. MPs, at any rate, merely seem to constitute a minor addressee in comparison to the media. This confirms a finding from the institutional analysis, in which the IW was said to consider itself much more of a think tank than the WSI.

In comparison to the 'interest-bound' think tanks, the parties' in-house foundations were rarely mentioned. They are more concerned with networking than with research functions. As far as their general importance is concerned, they score considerably higher. This contradictory finding is informative insofar as it indicates significant differences between the two biggest foundations. The important networking function of the FES corresponds with its poor standing as a research institute. The KAS, on the other hand, serves as a centre of research; its networking capacities are of minor importance to MPs, but important in academic circles. This also confirms a finding from the institutional analysis, according to which the research institute of the FES in comparison to the KAS is regarded as quite insignificant.

The 'interest-oriented' institutes in general are mentioned very rarely. They might have a certain influence, but the parliamentarians do not seem to be aware of it. In no respect can these institutes compete with the significance of the 'universities without students'. This again bears out the institutional analysis which suggested that the German 'interest-oriented' think tanks were the least significant group.

MPs and advocacy coalitions

Advocacy coalitions consist of various participants whose common intention is to influence the political opinion-forming process. The membership of these coalitions is determined by the sources and channels of information, the orientation of the corresponding think tanks (and other actors) and the topic. With regard to sources and channels of information, German MPs reveal clear preferences which have been alluded to in the previous section. Unlike the opposition, which provides itself with policy advice mainly through academic literature, the parties' in-house foundations, research institutes, commissions and the media, the governmental majority tends to rely on ministries, the parliamentary factions and committees. If we now examine the extent to which this channelling of information correlates with the most important topics, some obvious patterns are discernible. Those parliamentarians who deal with research and technology make extensive use of academic literature. Politicians who specialize in the areas of defence, foreign affairs and foreign aid on the other hand hardly assign any significance to such sources. Table 4.3 gives detailed information about the preferred sources.

These politicians obviously prefer other sources of information, especially the parties' in-house foundations and research institutes. That these institutes in turn score considerably among the European politicians indicates a

Table 4.3 *Preferred sources of information according to the parliamentarians' main fields of activity (%)*

	Academic literature	Parties' in-house foundations	Ministry	Federations
Environment	56.3	12.5	40.6	28.1
Labour and social policy	44.1	11.8	35.3	38.2
Europe	63.0	18.5	48.1	33.3
Domestic affairs	63.0	7.4	22.2	29.6
Foreign aid	47.6	23.8	52.4	9.5
Defence	36.4	13.6	54.5	9.1
Research	74.1	7.4	44.4	22.2
Foreign	50.0	30.0	26.7	3.3
	Faction	Research institutes	Committees	Commissions
Environment	15.6	56.3	34.4	31.3
Labour and social policy	17.6	26.5	26.5	5.9
Europe	22.2	29.6	48.1	14.8
Domestic affairs	33.3	11.1	48.1	14.8
Foreign aid	28.6	28.6	33.3	9.5
Defence	31.8	27.3	50.0	9.1
Research	18.5	66.7	29.6	22.2
Foreign affairs	50.0	30.0	55.3	13.3

connection with the inter- and transnational questions. It appears that the political foundations and research institutes are well-equipped for these demands.

As the political parties do not simply neglect individual topics, other reasons must account for the different forms of information-channelling. Consequently, research institutes and political foundations are least frequently consulted by politicians who specialize in domestic affairs. Other important sources of information for the 'transnational community' are the media. This group of MPs on the other hand assigns almost no importance at all to universities and federations. By contrast, there is one group of parliamentarians who deal mainly with environmental matters and socio-political questions. These MPs prefer foundations, commissions and research institutes, and to some lesser extent the political foundations. For them, the media, academic literature, factions and commissions are of minor importance.

With regard to the channels of information and the main political focus, we can therefore distinguish between two groups: parliamentarians with 'international' orientation on the one hand and parliamentarians with domestic 'socio-political' orientation on the other – both of them with separate 'rules of the game' which may indicate the existence of different kinds of advocacy coalitions in these fields. This assumption is supported by the MPs' evaluations of the research institutes' significance.

It is very clear that the parties' in-house foundations are extremely important for both groups. Differences do exist, but are not significant statistically. Conspicuous, however, is the behaviour of the defence politicians, whose answers do not fit into this pattern. They possibly avoid explicit mentioning of partisan institutes for reasons of state. Experts on foreign affairs at any rate seem less restrained in this respect. But perhaps there are merely fewer offers for defence politicians. This assumption is supported by their careful evaluations concerning the role of 'other research institutes', which again is assessed much more highly by politicians whose main concern is foreign affairs. In comparison to other parliamentarians, however, both groups regard these institutes as relatively important. The 'other research institutes' are particularly important to MPs who focus on environmental affairs. This indicates that, despite the infrequent mentioning of institutes such as the Oeko-Institut, there is indeed something like a political market for this kind of advocacy coalition. Table 4.4 shows the significance of individual research institutes for the different advocacy coalitions. It is surprising, however, that those MPs who concentrate on social policy and labour have only average scores here, although they do have the considerable resources of the 'universities without students' at their disposal. This may indicate a certain degree of scepticism, to which we will return later. The 'other research institutes' of the 'international coalition' mainly consist of the SWP and the

DGAP. Concentrating primarily on social policy, labour and environmental affairs, the research institutes of trade unions and federations understandably are of only marginal importance. The IW and the WSI are the preferred think tanks of these groups and we can assume an increasing demand for 'interest-bound' policy advice.

Table 4.4 *Significance of individual research institutes for advocacy coalitions (means)*

	Parties' in-house foundations	Federational institutes	Universities	Research institutes
	'International' advocacy coalitions			
Foreign affairs	2.10	3.37	3.10	2.67
Defence	2.90	3.33	3.52	3.19
Foreign aid	2.45	2.95	5.52	3.15
Europe	2.67	2.77	3.00	2.65
	'Socio-political' advocacy coalitions			
Environment	3.03	2.48	2.76	2.21
Labour/social affairs	2.68	2.02	3.26	3.06
Education	2.55	2.38	2.27	2.44

It is apparent, notwithstanding the internal differences mentioned above, that we can speak of two groups – the 'international' and the 'socio-political' forms of advocacy coalition – with similar channelling and usage of information. As these coalitions cannot be identified with a certain partisan alignment, there must be another reason for those similarities. The market might in fact be organized by the political issues, or by the think tanks who have shaped this market themselves. As a foreign affairs politician, for example, one tends to consult the SWP, the DGAP or the political foundations, since these think tanks readily supply the desired answers, whereas someone with a more socio-political orientation will inevitably draw upon the advice of the WSI, the IW or (again) the political foundations. Apart from environmental affairs, hardly any other institute can create its own niche in the 'market of ideas'. Both groups therefore consist of persons who consult the same sources of advice and presumably know each other well. They would probably agree on issues such as the Federal Republic's commitment to the West, or the right to free collective bargaining. At the same time this might be proof of the strategic importance of these advocacy coalitions. Their common intention would be to maintain political community in these policy fields.

Conclusion

The central argument of this paper has been that, whereas think tanks have
emerged and developed in the USA on a scale unmatched by any other country, there are functional equivalents of these institutions in other countries
also. Moreover, institutions of this kind are gaining increasing importance
for agenda setting. This is evident in the Federal Republic of Germany.

The results of the descriptive analysis of the personal and institutional
constellation of think tanks in Germany are these: integrated in advocacy
coalitions, they act as mediators between social science, politics and the
media. Tendencies to politicization and professionalization are discernible
within German think tanks. As interviews with representatives of the 'universities without students' have indicated, the pressure from private competitors increases and enforces adjustments. In most cases research has
increasingly been replaced by normative statements as clients demand clear
and pragmatic advice. This, of course, is especially true for the 'interest-oriented' and 'interest-bound' institutes. At the same time these institutes are
intensifying their efforts to market their products.

One of the reasons for the increasing importance of political think tanks
is the latent crisis of the political parties of the Federal Republic. Where
interest articulation and aggregation of parties is in a state of crisis they can
no longer claim legitimacy, and a vacuum develops – a vacuum which could
be filled by specialized think tanks in Germany, among other bodies. The
necessary preconditions do exist, at least as far as the so-called 'international' and 'socio-political' advocacy coalitions are concerned.

Bureaucrats are not merely the recipients of expert knowledge. They are
rather deeply involved in the process of balancing and articulating interests.
Especially in the Federal Republic, they bring political interests into the
political process, and argue on the basis of consistent convictions (that is,
ideologies), whereas politicians have to try to keep up with the expert
knowledge of the top bureaucrats. We can observe not only a politicization
of bureaucracy but also a bureaucratization of politics. These developments
are linked by advocacy coalitions whose task is to carry out co-ordinating
and interest-aggregating functions. As the empirical results indicate, German
think tanks are a significant component, albeit not dominant in this respect.
Another reason for the 'Americanization' of German think tanks is recent
developments in the media. Both the press and television have taken over
patterns from the USA which are extremely receptive to think tanks and
their inexpensive 'soundbite' answers.

In sum, the Federal Republic still lacks polished strategies of marketing
and dynamic internal processes which characterize the diversified market in
the United States. It is a matter for speculation whether these will also
become apparent in the near future; this will depend on whether or not

German parties are capable of adapting themselves to specific patterns of demand from their clientele. But as there undoubtedly is a market for the think tanks' products, the development of corresponding institutional constellations may be only a matter of time.

Bibliography

Arnim, Hans Herbert von (1991) *Die Partei, der Abgeordnete und das Geld*, Mainz, von Hase & Koehler.

Friedrich, Hannes (1970) *Staatliche Verwaltung und Wissenschaft: Die wissenschaftliche Beratung der Politik aus der Sicht der Ministerialburoktarie*, Frankfurt/M., Suhrkamp.

Friedrich Naumann Stiftung (1992) *Annual Report 1991*, Koenigswinter.

Gaffney, John (1991) 'Political Think-Tanks in the UK and Ministerial "Cabinets" in France', *West European Politics*, 14(1): 1–17.

Gellner, Winand (1995a) *Ideenagenturen für Politik und Offentlichkeit: Think Tanks in den USA und in Deutschland*, Opladen, Westdeutscher Verlag.

Gellner, Winand (1995b) 'The Politics of Policy: Political "Think Tanks" and Their Markets in the U.S.–Institutional Environment', *Presidential Studies Quarterly*, 25(3): 497–510.

Gray, John (1993) *Beyond the New Right: Markets, Government and the Common Environment*, London, Routledge.

Heclo, Hugh (1987) 'The In-and-Outer-System: A Critical Assessment', in G. Calvin MacKenzie (ed.), *The In-and-Outers: Presidential Appointees and Transient Government in Washington*, Baltimore and London, Johns Hopkins University Press, 195–216.

Hohn, Hans-Willy and Schimank, Uwe (1990) *Konflikte und Gleichgewichte im Forschungsystem: Akteurskonstellationen und Entwicklungspfade in der staatlich finanzierten außeruniversitären Forschung*, Frankfurt/M., Campus.

Jann, Werner (1988) 'Politik als Aufgabe der Bürokratie: Die Ministerialbürokratie im politischen System der Bundesrepublik Deutschland im Vergleich zu anderen westlichen Demokratien', *Politische Bildung*, 21(2): 159–73.

Kavanagh, Dennis (1990) *Thatcherism and British Politics: The End of Consensus?* Oxford, Oxford University Press.

Kepplinger, Hans Mathias (1992) *Ereignismanagement: Wirklichkeit durch Massenmedien*, Zurich and Osnabruck, Edition Interform.

Kingdon, John (1984) *Agendas, Alternatives, and Public Policies*, Boston, Little, Brown, and Co.

Leggewie, Claus (1987) *Der Geist steht rechts: Ausflüge in die Denkfabriken der Wende*, Berlin, Rotbuch.

Leggewie, Claus (1990) 'Think Tanks – Wie und was produzieren (rechte) Denkfabriken?', *Forschungsjournal Neue Soziale Bewegungen*, 3(3): 66–75.

Mayntz, Renate (1985) *Forschungsmanagement – Steuerungsversuche zwischen Scylla und Charybdis: Probleme der Organization und Leitung von hochschulfreien, öffentlich finanzierten Forschungsinstituten*, Opladen, Westdeutscher Verlag.

Mayntz, Renate (1987) 'West Germany', in W. Plowden (ed.), *Advising the Rulers*, Oxford and New York, Blackwell.

Meusel, Ernst-Joachim (1992) *Ausseruniversitäre Forschung im Wissenschaftsrecht: Unter Mitarbeit von Thomas Koestlin*, Cologne, Carl Heymann.

Pinto-Duschinsky, Michael (1991) 'The Party Foundations and Political Finance in Germany', in F. Leslie Seidle (ed.), *Comparative Issues in Party and Election Finance, Volume. 4*, Royal Commission on Electoral Reform and Party Financing, Toronto and Oxford, Dundurn.

Ritter, Klaus (1978) 'Politikbezogene Forschung als Aufgabe: Anmerkungen zu Entstehung, Organization und Tätigkeit der Stiftung Wissenschaft und Politik', in Stiftung Wissenschaft und Politik (ed.), *Polarität und Interdependenz: Beiträge zu Fragen der Internationalen Politik*, Baden-Baden, Nomos, 447–58.

Sabatier, Paul A. (1991) 'Toward Better Theories of the Policy Process', *Political Science & Politics*, 10(2): 147–56.

Spieker, Wolfgang (1986) 'Gewerkschaften, Wissenschaft und Öffentlichkeit: Das WSI des DGB', *NZA*, 10(13): 417–19.

Veen, Hans-Joachim and Jürgen Hoffmann (1992) *Die Grunen zu Beginn der neunziger Jahre: Profil und Defizite einer fast etablierten Partei*, Bonn and Berlin, Bouvier.

Vieregge, Henning von (1980) *Gesellschaftspolitische Stiftungen in der Bundesrepublik*, Cologne, Deutscher Instituts-Verlag.

Vieregge, Henning von (1990) 'Die Partei-Stiftungen: Ihre Rolle im politischen System', in G. Wewer (ed.), *Parteienfinanzierung und politischer Wettbewerb: Rechtsnormen – Realanalysen – Reformvorschläge*, Opladen, Westdeutscher Verlag, 164–94.

Think tanks in the United States

Introduction

The rapid rise of think tanks in the United States and their growing presence in the political arena has attracted a flurry of scholarly attention in recent years (Smith, 1991; Ricci, 1993; Fischer, 1993; Gellner, 1995; Abelson, 1996; Newsom, 1996; Stone, 1996). Though once largely neglected in the literature on the internal determinants of American public policy, think tanks are enjoying unprecedented coverage. The much overdue acknowledgement by social scientists that public, private and university-based think tanks are worthy of scientific inquiry (Robinson, 1992; 1993) can in part be attributed to the close ties that have been established between several think tanks and recent presidential administrations (Wood, 1993; Abelson and Carberry, 1997). Indeed, as dozens of members from think tanks accepted high-level positions in the Carter and Reagan administrations, observers of American politics began to question the extent to which think tanks have defined, shaped and at times implemented policy ideas. Moreover, when Bill Clinton publicly endorsed the Progressive Policy Institute's (PPI) blueprint on how to govern the United States following the 1992 presidential election, scholars and journalists began to speculate even further about the growing influence of think tanks in American politics.

Evaluating the contribution think tanks make to policy development in the United States is a daunting task. As several observers of think tanks have discovered, even if it were possible to reach a consensus on what constituted a think tank – an unlikely outcome – it is difficult, if not impossible, to assess accurately the influence of particular institutes on specific policy decisions. Recognizing this, many scholars have consciously avoided or made only passing reference to the impact think tanks have in the policy-making process. Others have simply asserted that think tanks exercise influence without demonstrating how they actually achieve it.

The purpose of this chapter is not simply to describe what activities think tanks in the United States engage in, nor is it to speculate on how much or little influence directors of think tanks or disinterested observers believe these institutions have. Such an undertaking would do little to advance the literature in this field. Rather, my purpose here is two-fold: to examine and explore the evolution and proliferation of American think tanks and to highlight the extent to which they have become involved in the policy-making process. Establishing a *causal* relationship between the policy recommendations proposed by various think tanks (or think tank personnel) and decisions made by political leaders remains a formidable task, given the methodological difficulties involved. Nonetheless, as this study will demonstrate, it is possible to make informed judgements about the public and private influence of think tanks in the policy-making process. The distinction between private and public influence is useful in demonstrating how think tanks interact with policy-makers and the public at large. It also provides scholars with greater insights into the various environments that think tanks inhabit.

In the first section of this chapter, a brief history of the origin and evolution of think tanks will be provided. The purpose of documenting the history of think tanks is to trace the emergence of four generations of think tanks in the United States. By comparing think tanks created in the first decades of the 1900s such as the Brookings Institution, the Council on Foreign Relations (CFR) and the Hoover Institution to those established during and after World War Two, including the American Enterprise Institute (AEI) and the Heritage Foundation, one can observe the transformation of think tanks from non-partisan research institutions to avowedly ideological organizations committed to influencing Washington's political agenda. Once this has been done, the discussion will shift to the various factors that have contributed to the proliferation of both domestic and foreign affairs think tanks in the United States. In the second section, the many channels think tanks rely on to shape and mould public opinion and public policy will be discussed. The distinction between public and private influence will be made and applied in this section. Finally, the many methodological problems that must be overcome in order to assess and evaluate the impact of think tanks will be addressed.

A brief profile of four generations of US think tanks

Chronicling the origin and evolution of the estimated 1,200 think tanks competing for power and prestige at the local, state and national level in the United States is far beyond the scope of this chapter. However, it is not necessary to document the mandate, research agenda and outreach activities of hundreds of think tanks to identify their principal function in the policy-making process. A more manageable approach is to identify, as Kent Weaver

(1989: 563–78) has done, the key motivations and institutional characteristics or traits associated with each generation of think tanks.

Classifying generations of think tanks according to specific institutional criteria does pose certain problems, however. To begin with, some organizations possess characteristics common to more than one generation of think tank; whereas few scholars have encountered difficulty in distinguishing between the work of the Brookings Institution and the Heritage Foundation, both institutions engage in similar activities. They both conduct research and, to varying degrees, market their findings. The main difference is in the emphasis these institutions place on scholarly research and political advocacy. To argue, then, that the Brookings Institution is a policy research institution and the Heritage Foundation an advocacy think tank is, to some extent, superficial and even misleading.

It would be more appropriate to identify the central function of these think tanks, rather than to isolate their 'unique' institutional traits. Like chameleons constantly changing their complexion to suit new environments, think tanks have altered their behaviour to compete more effectively in the market-place of ideas. To enhance their visibility, some first and second generations of think tanks have adopted certain strategies employed by third and fourth generation think tanks. Conversely, some newly created institutes have looked to older generations of think tanks for ideas on how to manage their operations. In short, one generation of think tanks in the United States has not been replaced by newer generations. Rather, they co-exist in the policy-making community. Recognizing that think tanks can be classified according to their principal function in the policy-making community, it is possible to observe the emergence of four generations of think tanks.

The first generation: think tanks as policy research institutions

Since there is no consensus as to what think tanks are or how they differ from the hundreds of other organizations in the United States that share an interest in studying and making recommendations on public policy (Wallace, 1994), it is not surprising that scholars have been unable to agree on when the first think tank in the United States was created. While some maintain that organizations engaged in policy analysis initially emerged in the early 1900s, others contend that the seeds of contemporary think tanks were planted well before the end of the nineteenth century (Dickson, 1972; Smith, 1991).

Although scholars have been unable to agree on the origin of America's first think tank, a handful of institutes, professional associations and civic federations were founded in the mid to late 1800s which performed many of the characteristic functions of contemporary policy research institutions. By engaging in policy analysis and providing policy-makers and academics with a forum to discuss and debate a wide range of issues, the Franklin Institute (1832), the American Social Science Association (1857), the American Historical Association (1884), the American Economics Association (1885), the Chicago Civic Federation (CCF, 1894) and its successor, the National Civic Federation (NCF, 1900) represented the first wave of think tanks that graced America's political landscape. The institutional goals and objectives of these organizations differed considerably, but they nonetheless shared a common desire to provide a forum for policy-makers and social scientists to discuss and debate a wide range of public policy issues. They also recognized the importance of applying scientific principles to the study of public policy, a commitment which later became the hallmark of social scientists during the Progressive era.

While the activities of the NCF, the CCF and several other smaller organizations deserve to be recorded in the early history of American think tanks, it was during the first two decades of the twentieth century that the true impact of think tanks as policy research institutions began to be felt. Five think tanks in particular left a lasting impression on the formulation and implementation of public policy prior to and in the aftermath of World War One: the Russell Sage Foundation (1907), the Carnegie Endowment for International Peace (1910), the Institute for Government Research (1916, which merged with the Institute of Economics and the Robert Brookings Graduate School of Economics and Government to form the Brookings Institution in 1927), the Hoover Institution on War, Revolution and Peace (1919) and the CFR (1921).

These organizations, according to McGann (1992: 733), were 'rooted in the social sciences and supported by private individuals and foundations [and were seen] as part of a larger effort to bring the expertise of scholars and managers to bear on the economic and social problems of this period'. Developing their own areas of expertise in an environment insulated from the partisan interests of board members and from the vicissitudes of American politics, each of these organizations dedicated itself to the advancement of knowledge. This is not to suggest that think tanks created during the Progressive era should be regarded as the sole guardians of the public interest, devoid of any political motivations. Rather, it appears that several institutes created during this period assigned a higher priority to providing government officials with policy expertise than to lobbying members of Congress and the Executive or appeasing influential donors. The Hoover Institution's pioneering research on the causes and consequences of twentieth-century warfare, the Brookings Institution's contribution to the creation of a national budget system and the CFR's War and Peace Studies Project stand as testaments to the vital assistance early research institutions offered political leaders in charting, in each instance, a new course for America's future.

Moreover, while these institutions attracted policy experts committed to a wide range of political beliefs, the organizations themselves were rarely transformed into ideological battlefields. Individual scholars at times overtly supported or opposed governmental policies, but their primary goal and that of their institutions was not to impose their political agenda on policy-makers, but to improve and help rationalize the decision-making process. As John R. Commons, co-founder of the Bureau of Industrial Research, acknowledged in reflecting on the problems which can arise when academics masquerade as politicians, 'the place of economists [is] that of advisor to the leaders, if they [want] him, and not that of propagandist to the masses' (Smith, 1991: 36).

By engaging in policy research instead of political advocacy, early twenti-eth-century think tanks helped foster close and lasting ties to policy-makers. The willingness of philanthropic organizations such as the Carnegie Corpo-ration and the Ford and Rockefeller Foundations to support many of these research institutions also contributed to a more stable and permanent link between policy experts and government (Berman, 1983; Nielsen, 1989). Providing research institutions with the financial security of million-dollar endowments allowed think tanks such as the Brookings Institution, the Hoover Institution and the Carnegie Endowment for International Peace to devote more of their time and resources to studying the long-term implica-tions of particular governmental policies, a luxury few contemporary think tanks and government departments enjoy. Moreover, since these institutions did not solicit and rarely received government funding, they could comment on and criticize government policy without jeopardizing their financial future. Indeed, unlike the vast majority of think tanks which depend on cor-porate, government and individual donations to survive, policy research institutions supported by generous endowments are less vulnerable to the partisan pressures of donors. Some philanthropic foundations have refused to renew grants to research institutions, whereas endowments normally remain in place indefinitely.

The major distinguishing characteristic of most think tanks created during this period was, and for the most part is, their commitment to scholarly research. The Brookings Institution and the Hoover Institution, which next to the RAND Corporation are the largest think tanks in the United States, function, in Kent Weaver's words (1989: 566), much like 'universities with-out students'. They hold conferences, seminars and workshops, maintain close ties to the academic community and require their scholars to publish articles and books. Moreover, they identify and pursue long-term research programmes and allocate the majority of their funding to this purpose. Their preferred target audience is policy-makers, but their voluminous research findings tend to attract more attention in the scholarly community.

The Brookings Institution, like many other policy research institutions created in recent decades, may encounter difficulties convincing policy-makers to absorb information contained in their often weighty studies (Smith, 1991; Newsom, 1996: 153–6). However, when government departments and agencies provide millions of dollars to think tanks for their research and analysis, policy-makers and bureaucrats are more inclined to digest their findings. This may in part explain why studies released by government contract research institutions such as the RAND Corporation in Santa Monica, California, tend to generate considerable attention in Washington's policy-making circles. As the following section will illustrate, the major difference between first generation think tanks and those that emerged in the immediate post-World War Two era was the principal source of their funding.

The second generation: the emergence of government contract research institutions

Government contract research institutions emerged in the United States following World War Two, largely in response to growing international and domestic pressures confronting American policy-makers. Acknowledging the invaluable contribution defence scientists made during the war, the Truman administration recognized the benefits that could be derived from the funding of private and university-based research and development centres. By tapping into the expertise of engineers, physicists, biologists, statisticians and social scientists, policy-makers hoped to meet the many new challenges they inherited as the United States assumed the role of a hegemonic power after the war. It was in this environment that the idea for creating the RAND (for research and analysis) Corporation was born.

Chartered in 1948, the RAND Corporation's principal client in the immediate post-war years was the Department of Defence. Using systems analysis, game theory and various simulation exercises, RAND scientists began to 'think about the unthinkable'. Faced with the prospects of a nuclear exchange, RAND devoted much of its resources to advising the air force on how best to defend the United States against enemy attacks (Kaplan, 1985).

In addition to making several important contributions to strengthening America's nuclear deterrent, the corporation also served as a prototype for other research and development organizations including the Hudson Institute and the domestic policy-oriented Urban Institute. Hired by federal and state government departments and agencies and by private companies to conduct research on issues ranging from the safe removal of toxic waste to the technical feasibility of installing a space-based defence system, the RAND Corporation, the Hudson Institute and the Urban Institute have assumed a prominent role in the policy-making process.

The extent to which think tanks depend on federal funding varies considerably, yet the continued dependence of some think tanks on government contracts makes them highly vulnerable to political and budgetary pressures. As a result, although research and development organizations perform the same function as first generation think tanks, their reliance on government grants and contracts may create the perception, rightly or wrongly, that their policy advice is slanted.

Since many of America's leading economists and scientists were employed at prominent universities or independent research centres after the war, it is not surprising that Washington was willing to provide these institutions with generous funding in exchange for their expertise. Yet, while research and development organizations were able to rely on their contractual relations with government departments and high-level officials to establish strong ties with political leaders, the policy-making community did not become dominated by federally funded research institutions in the post-World War Two era. Although a handful of government contractors such as the RAND Corporation and the Urban Institute became key players in the political arena during the 1950s and 1960s, by the mid to late 1970s Capitol Hill had become inundated by a small but vocal group of highly aggressive and ideologically driven institutes, commonly referred to as advocacy think tanks.

The third generation of think tanks: from policy research to political advocacy

Breaking with the traditions established by Robert Brookings, Andrew Carnegie and founders of other early twentieth-century think tanks who were determined to insulate their scholars from partisan politics, several organizations, often described as 'advocacy think tanks' because of their ideologically derived policy agendas, have consciously avoided erecting a barrier between policy research and political advocacy. Rather than promoting scholarly enquiry as a means to better serve the public interest, advocacy think tanks such as the Heritage Foundation and the Institute for Policy Studies have come to resemble interest groups and political action committees by pressuring decision-makers to implement policies compatible with their ideological beliefs and those shared by their generous benefactors. No longer content with observing domestic and foreign affairs from the comfort of their book-lined offices, advocacy think tanks have made a concerted effort to become part of the political process.

Unlike traditional policy research institutions, advocacy think tanks are not driven by an intense desire to advance scholarly research. On the contrary, their primary motivation is to engage in political advocacy (Abelson, 1995). In short, they do not covet attention in the scholarly community, but are deeply committed to imposing their ideological agenda on the electorate. As Heritage President Edwin Feulner points out, 'our role is trying to influence the Washington public policy community ... most specifically the Hill, secondly the executive branch, thirdly the national news media' (McCombs, 1983).

Although think tanks, as non-profit, tax-exempt organizations, are prohibited by the Internal Revenue Service from influencing specific legislation, many advocacy think tanks have made a concerted effort to do so. As a director at a major policy institute stated, think tanks are 'tax-exempt cowboys defying the sheriff with their political manipulations. They don't want to stimulate public dialogue, they're out to impose their own monologue' (Linden, 1987).

Through various governmental and non-governmental channels, advocacy think tanks have attracted considerable attention in the political arena. Moreover, as a result of the meteoric success of the Heritage Foundation, the quintessential advocacy think tank, dozens of other institutes determined to leave their ideological imprint on Washington have entered the policy-making community.

The fourth generation: vanity and legacy-based think tanks

Vanity and legacy-based think tanks perform similar functions to first and third generation think tanks, but appear to have a more defined and limited mandate than traditional research institutions and advocacy centres. Created by aspiring office holders (or their supporters) and by former presidents intent on advancing their political and ideological beliefs well after leaving office, fourth generation think tanks are beginning to attract some attention in the policy-making community. While legacy-based think tanks such as the (Jimmy) Carter Center at Emory University, and the (Richard) Nixon Center for Peace and Freedom have developed a wide range of research programmes, vanity think tanks appear more concerned with engaging in political advocacy. Vanity think tanks are particularly interested in generating or at the very least repackaging ideas which will help lend intellectual credibility to the political platforms of politicians, a function no longer performed adequately by mainstream political parties (Gellner, 1995). They are also established to circumvent spending limits imposed on presidential candidates by federal campaign finance laws (Chisolm, 1990). Think tanks which fall into this category include Senator Dole's short-lived institute, Better America, and the Progress and Freedom Foundation, the ideological inspiration for Speaker of the House Newt Gingrich's 'Contract with America' (or 'Contract on America' as several Democrats claim). Ross Perot's United We Stand organization, the intellectual arm of his Reform Party, can also be added to this growing list.

Within a relatively short period of time, several of these institutes have established a strong institutional infrastructure with sizeable budgets. For instance the Carter Center, founded by President Carter in 1982 to study poverty, hunger, oppression and conflict, employs over 200 researchers and has an annual budget exceeding $10 million. With less than one-tenth of the staff at the Carter Center, the conservative Progress and Freedom Foundation, established in 1993, has a budget with a range of $2–5 million (see Table 5.1).

Vanity think tanks are the latest generation of public policy institutes in the United States, but it is unlikely they will be the last. Think tanks exhibiting a combination of characteristics common to the various types of institutions discussed in this section will, in all likelihood, join the hundreds of thinks tanks competing for recognition in the policy-making community. At the very least, existing think tanks will modify their institutional behaviour to meet new demands and challenges in the political arena.

Explaining the growth of US think tanks

In the first half of the twentieth century, policy-makers did not require a directory to contact experts at various policy research institutions. After all, between 1907 and 1950, less than two dozen think tanks existed in the United States. However, by the early 1980s, think tanks had become a virtual cottage industry. Over one hundred think tanks had been established in Washington DC, and several hundred more were created throughout the United States. But why did such a massive proliferation of think tanks take place following World War Two? A number of possible explanations are worth exploring.

First, as a result of casting aside its isolationist shell to assume the global responsibilities of a hegemonic power after World War Two, the United States had to rely increasingly on policy experts for advice on how to conduct its foreign relations. The demand for foreign policy expertise contributed to the creation of several institutes including the RAND Corporation (1948), the Foreign Policy Research Institute (1955), the Institute for Defense Analysis (1956) and the Center for Strategic and International Studies (CSIS) (1962).

Second, the impact of the anti-war and civil rights movements in awakening the public conscience to political and social turmoil at home and abroad also appeared to contribute to the proliferation of think tanks. Not unlike interest groups mobilizing popular support against the Vietnam war, many so-called 'liberal' think tanks, including (although by no means limited to) the Institute for Policy Studies, were created to provide scholars with an opportunity to challenge many of the underlying motivations of American domestic and foreign policy (Muravchik, 1987).

Similarly, during the late 1960s and early 1970s, as several conservative

Table 5.1   A selected profile of American think tanks

Institution	Location	Date founded	Staff[a]	Budget category (1995/96) $millions
First generation: policy research institutions[b]				
Russell Sage Foundation	New York	1907	3FTR; 22S	2–5
Carnegie Endowment for International Peace	Washington DC	1910	22FTR	Over 10
The Brookings Institution	Washington DC	1916	80FTR; 140S	Over 10
Hoover Institution on War, Revolution and Peace	Stanford, CA	1919	80FTR; 30PTR; 200S	Over 10
National Bureau of Economic Research	Cambridge, MA	1920	325PTR; 50S	5–10
Council on Foreign Relations	New York	1921	75FTR; 75S	Over 10
American Enterprise Institute for Public Policy Research	Washington DC	1943	75FTR; 50S	Over 10
Center for Strategic and International Studies	Washington DC	1962	80FTR; 60PTR; 75S	Over 10
Second generation: government contractors				
RAND Corporation	Santa Monica, CA	1946	525FTR; 425S	50–100
Hudson Institute	Indianapolis, IN	1961	66FTR; 10PTR	Over 10
Urban Institute	Washington DC	1968	125FTR; 95S	Over 10
United States Institute of Peace	Washington DC	1984	5FTR; 45S	Over 10
Third generation: advocacy think tanks				
Institute for Policy Studies	Washington DC	1963	15R; 4S	1–2
Institute for Contemporary Studies	San Francisco, CA	1972	18R and S	5–10
Heritage Foundation	Washington DC	1973	80R; 20S	Over 10
Rockford Institute	Rockford, IL	1976	10R; 8S	1–2
CATO Institute	Washington DC	1977	17R; 20S	5–10
Progressive Policy Institute	Washington DC	1989	17R; 3S	1–2
Empower America	Washington DC	1993	10R; 25S	5–10
Fourth generation: vanity and legacy think tanks				
The Carter Center	Atlanta, GA	1982	200R and S	Over 10
The Progress and Freedom Foundation	Washington DC	1993	13R; 5S	2–5
Nixon Center for Peace and Freedom	Washington DC	1994	4R; 2S	N/A

Source: Lynn Hellebust, *Think Tank Directory: A Guide to Nonprofit Public Policy Research Organizations*, Topeka, Kansas, Government Research Service, 1996.
Notes: [a] FTR=Full-time researchers; PTR=Part-time researchers (these figures are only included when the number of part-time researchers is over 10; S=Support staff. [b] According to several scholars, a number of think tanks could be considered as first and/or second generation think tanks.

academics were becoming increasingly disillusioned with what they considered to be a growing liberal bias among the faculty at American universities, an increasing demand for autonomous research institutions emerged. Accordingly, the Institute for Contemporary Studies (1972), the Heritage Foundation (1973) and the CATO Institute (1977) were founded to allow conservative academics to pursue their research interests in a more congenial environment. The growth of conservative, neo-conservative and liberal think tanks during this period clearly reflected a breakdown in consensus in the foreign policy-making establishment over America's role in world affairs (Ehrman, 1995).

Fourth, generous corporate financing and tax exemptions for non-profit organizations provided an impetus for policy entrepreneurs, political leaders and aspiring office holders to create think tanks. By establishing private think tanks as non-profit organizations and employing sophisticated direct mailing techniques, founders of third and fourth generation think tanks could encourage corporations, philanthropic foundations and private citizens to contribute thousands of dollars to support and advance their institution's particular ideological and political perspectives on domestic and foreign policy issues.

The tremendous growth in the number of think tanks in the United States can also be attributed to the declining role and importance of political parties in providing members of Congress and the Executive with sound policy advice. As Weaver (1989: 570) points out: 'Weak and relatively non-ideological parties have enhanced think tanks' role in several ways. The most important effect of the U.S. party system is that parties have not themselves taken a major role in policy development by establishing sizeable policy research arms of their own. Think tanks have helped fill this void.'

Unlike in Germany where political parties have created their own political foundations to conduct policy research, or in Canada and in the United Kingdom where members of parliament are bound by strong party unity, decision-makers in the White House and on Capitol Hill are not required to follow a defined set of party principles. As a result, they can and often do actively solicit policy expertise from think tanks and other institutions capable of providing policy-relevant, though not necessarily empirically sound, advice. Many presidents have turned to think tanks for policy expertise and for ideological validation (Abelson and Carberry, 1997). In fact, as noted, dozens of members from think tanks have served in high-level positions in recent administrations. In their attempts to fill the ideological void left by political parties, third and fourth generation think tanks have also inundated members of Congress and the bureaucracy with their policy recommendations. Indeed, the willingness of the policy-makers to rely on contract research institutions and consultants for advice on issues ranging from the economic implications of de-regulating the airline industry to the utility or futility of developing and deploying a space-based defence system has stimulated the creation of dozens of think tanks.

The highly decentralized and fragmented nature of the American political system should also be taken into consideration in explaining the proliferation of think tanks. In a system based on separate branches sharing powers, and one in which politicians are not constrained by the philosophical goals of political parties, think tanks are provided with multiple channels to convey their ideas to several hundred policy-makers. The opposite situation exists, for instance, in Canada, where political power is not widely dispersed, but formally concentrated in the cabinet. This may help to explain in part why think tanks in Canada have a limited presence in the policy-making process.

The booming think tank industry in the United States following World War Two not only altered the complexion of the policy-making community, but more importantly, it fundamentally changed the relationship between policy experts and policy-makers. In an environment where think tanks had to compete aggressively to promote their ideas, their priorities began to change. As new generations of think tanks emerged, they realized that developing effective marketing techniques to enhance their status in the policy-making community, rather than providing decision-makers with sound and impartial advice, had to become their main priority. In the following section, the various strategies all generations of think tanks employ to influence the direction of American politics will be discussed.

Competing in the market-place of ideas: the public and private influence of think tanks

In observing the increasingly crowded think tank industry in the United States, several scholars and journalists have stated, often with little or no supporting evidence, that think tanks exercise considerable influence in the political arena. Particularly in the months and weeks leading up to presidential campaigns, think tanks, especially those that have established close ties to candidates, are frequently portrayed as the architects of new and sometimes innovative ideas. Indeed, we are left with the impression that think tanks are largely responsible for shaping the political and economic agenda of incoming administrations. Unfortunately, in their efforts to monitor the behaviour of these organizations, few scholars have attempted to explain how they operationalize influence, or at the very least how think tanks seek to achieve it (an exception is Higgott and Stone, 1994).

Although it is difficult to assess accurately how much or little influence think tanks wield in the policy-making process, it is nonetheless possible to make informed judgements about the nature of think tank influence. A useful point of departure is to examine how think tanks attempt to exercise both public and private influence in the United States. By making this distinction, scholars can at least begin to think more critically about the methodological problems that must be addressed in studying the influence of think tanks in American politics.

Public influence

Though once portrayed as elite organizations composed of scholars pursuing research in relative isolation, think tanks have become increasingly visible in the political arena. Indeed, many contemporary think tanks have descended the ivory tower to assume an active role in American politics. To this end, several contemporary think tanks have employed a wide range of strategies to shape and mould public opinion and public policy. While some of these strategies are concealed from the public, many can be identified. To varying degrees, think tanks employ some or all of the following strategies to influence public attitudes and beliefs.

- Holding open public forums and conferences to discuss various domestic and foreign policy issues. Many of these forums are televised and available to viewers through satellite television. This strategy is part of the educational function some think tanks perform.
- Encouraging scholars to give public lectures and addresses at universities, rotary clubs and other organizations.
- Testifying before committees and sub-committees of Congress. Several experts from think tanks are frequently called upon to give testimony. Their remarks and written reports become part of the official public record.
- Enhancing their media exposure by submitting op-ed (opposite the editorial page) articles to major American newspapers. Some think tanks have even hired ghost writers to submit articles for particular scholars. Members of think tanks also appear frequently on network newscasts, political talk shows and radio programmes to discuss the implications of various domestic and foreign policy issues.
- Publishing opinion magazines, newsletters, policy briefs and journals that have wide distribution. For instance, the CFR and the Carnegie Endowment for International Peace publish *Foreign Affairs* and *Foreign Policy* respectively. Moreover, several think tanks including the Brookings Institution, the AEI, the CATO Institute and the Heritage Foundation publish a variety of opinion magazines.
- Selling audio tapes to the public which summarize key policy issues. The Heritage Foundation for instance sells *Monthly Briefing Tapes* to inter-

ested listeners. In his endorsement of this product, Speaker of the House Newt Gingrich stated, 'A monthly dose of conservative common sense. You'll wonder how you ever got along without it.'

- Creating home pages on the Internet. This is a new medium which think tanks representing various ideological views are relying on to reach thousands of Internet users. Several think tanks including the Brookings Institution, the CATO Institute, the Heritage Foundation, the CFR, the Hoover Institution and the PPI have created home pages. By 'going on-line', think tanks have provided the public with an opportunity to find out information on their ongoing research programmes, staff and institutional resources. Some think tanks also include recent speeches and reports. Others have even gone so far as to advise people on how to find jobs in Washington.
- Targeting the public during annual fundraising campaigns. In exchange for sizeable donations, some think tanks will allow members to join exclusive clubs which will provide them with access to key policy-makers.

Private influence

The many channels think tanks rely on to exercise public influence are relatively easy to observe and document. However, it is often difficult to monitor closely how think tanks seek to influence policy-makers in the corridors of power. The following list provides some examples of how think tanks and scholars affiliated with them have attempted to exercise private influence. These include:

- Accepting cabinet, sub-cabinet or bureaucratic positions in administrations. Some think tanks, including the Heritage Foundation, monitor job vacancies in the bureaucracy and try to fill them with individuals who share their political and ideological views. Writing letters of reference on behalf of colleagues being considered for high-level positions is also frequently done.
- Serving on policy taskforces and transition teams during presidential elections. Many scholars from think tanks who participated on taskforces during the 1980 campaign were later invited to serve in the administration.
- Maintaining liaison offices with the House of Representatives and the Senate. This allows think tanks to establish close ties to policy-makers and to provide them with current analyses of major domestic and foreign policy issues. It also allows think tanks to discuss various legislative bills with congressional aides.
- Inviting selected policy-makers to participate in conferences, seminars, workshops and to head up fundraising campaigns.

- Offering former policy-makers positions at think tanks. Several think tanks have become retirement homes for important policy-makers. Their presence at think tanks helps to enhance the prestige of institutes. It may also help to generate funding from philanthropic and private donors.
- Inviting bureaucrats to work at think tanks on a limited-term basis. For instance, the Diplomat in Residence Program overseen by the State Department has resulted in several ambassadors accepting research positions at think tanks.
- Preparing studies and policy briefs for policy-makers. This is the main function of research programmes at several advocacy think tanks.
- Developing specialized programmes for key policy-makers. The CSIS's Transition project in 1988 to advise the president-elect on how to govern a new administration is an example of such a project.
- Maintaining direct correspondence with policy-makers.

Although this list is by no means exhaustive, it does provide some insight into how think tanks attempt to assert private influence. Having said this, two central questions remain. What are some of the major problems in assessing influence? How can scholars properly assess the impact of think tanks in the policy-making process?

Assessing the impact of think tanks

In developing an informal method to measure how much influence think tanks have in the foreign policy-making process, Howard Wiarda notes (1990: 171):

> Government runs, in part, on the basis of memos. If a State Department or Defense Department official, or an analyst at the CIA or the National Security Council, has your study in front of him and open at the time he is writing his own memo to the secretary or the director or perhaps the president himself – if, in short, he is using your ideas and analysis at the time he writes his own memo – then you have influence. If your study is not open in front of him or, worse, you do not even know who the responsible official is, you do not have influence. It is as simple as that.

But *is* measuring the influence of think tanks in the policy-making process really as simple as Wiarda suggests? Wiarda is correct in stating that the circulation of memos plays an important role in facilitating communication between government officials. In fact, some presidential records from the Reagan years indicate that correspondence between members of think tanks and policy-makers may have had a direct impact on presidential behaviour. For instance, in a memo, Robert MacFarlane, Reagan's third national security advisor, instructed his staff and colleagues to incorporate poll findings sent to him by the Committee on the Present Danger (CPD) on the Strategic Defense Initiative (SDI) (Star Wars Project) into all 'future presidential speeches' (Abelson, 1996: 63–4). Yet, Wiarda's contention that think tank scholars can only exercise influence if their study is quoted in an internal memo is a gross generalization. A number of factors, including how responsive government officials are to the views of certain policy experts and the perceived benefits and costs of adopting their recommended course of action, are among the innumerable factors which could determine the extent to which think tanks influence policy development. The frequency with which members from think tanks distribute reports on particular issues to policy-makers, appear on network newscasts and testify before congressional committees, may, along with several other indicators, be useful in assessing the importance think tanks, media executives and policy-makers assign to specific policy matters. Moreover, for scholars studying policy communities and issue networks (Heclo, 1978; Lindquist, 1992), assembling data on these and other forms of private and public influence provides a crude measurement of how actively think tanks are engaged in particular policy debates. These statistics may also be helpful to think tanks as they court potential donors for funding. Nonetheless, such an approach by itself sheds little light on how influential think tanks are.

One of the major problems of assessing influence in this manner is that think tanks and policy-makers have different perceptions of what constitutes influence, not to mention how it can best be measured. For some think tanks, particularly those that are much smaller in scope than the Brookings Institution and the RAND Corporation, having one of their reports cited in a major newspaper, or a staff member appointed to a bureaucratic post, may be used as criteria to justify their institution's influence relative to other think tanks in the policy-making community. Other think tanks such as the Hoover Institution and the AEI keep statistics on how many of their staff members are recruited to serve in administrations, as an informal, though frequently cited, measurement of their political influence. The Heritage Foundation, on the other hand, relies on other indicators to convince the public and policy-makers of their influence. For instance, during the first term of the Reagan administration, Heritage President Edwin Feulner proudly proclaimed that over 60 per cent of the policy recommendations proposed in the institute's encyclopaedic study *Mandate for Leadership* had been or were in the process of being implemented by the government. Few scholars bothered to reveal that a majority of the recommendations outlined in the study had been developed and refined several years before by other individuals and organizations.

A related problem is that policy-makers frequently refer to the influence of think tanks without indicating how, what or whom they actually influenced. For instance in the *Congressional Record*, Senator Ted Kennedy stated that the Council on Hemispheric Affairs (COHA), a Washington-based think tank specializing in Latin American Affairs, is 'one of our nation's most respected bod[ies] of scholars and policy-makers' (Abelson, 1996: 96). Despite Kennedy's gracious endorsement, COHA is rarely mentioned in the literature on America's most prominent think tanks. This is not to suggest that COHA and other smaller think tanks have not made their presence felt in key policy-making circles. Indeed, as the controversial debate surrounding US foreign policy toward Latin America during the Reagan years demonstrated, several think tanks working in concert with other non-governmental organizations actively lobbied members of Congress to oppose White House policy. Rather, it suggests that COHA does not possess the institutional resources to allow it to compete with the Brookings Institution, the Hoover Institution and several other policy research institutions. COHA's activities must thus be evaluated by other criteria.

Some policy-makers prefer not to focus on the contributions of one think tank, but to pay homage to many. For instance, on 6 January 1981, in the same week he took the oath of office, President Reagan acknowledged that he called on more people from the Hoover Institution to help in his campaign and in the transition than from any other institute. Seven years later, shortly before leaving the Oval Office, Reagan stated that no think tank had been more influential in the policy-making community than the American Enterprise Institute (Abelson, 1992: 867).

Reagan's confusion as to which think tank exercised the most influence in his administration could be attributed to several factors. However, what it does reveal is the lack of consensus on the part of policy-makers as to which think tanks exercise influence, under what circumstances, and to what degree. These are questions that scholars must begin to address and to which this chapter will now turn.

Given the number of methodological problems scholars encounter in assessing the impact of think tanks in the policy-making process, it is not surprising that this avenue of enquiry has been largely neglected. It is far simpler and less problematic to infer from the growth of think tanks in the United States that these institutions wield considerable influence. Yet little can be gained by making general observations about the nature of their influence.

Although it may not be possible to demonstrate that a specific think tank was directly responsible for influencing a particular policy decision, given the number of domestic and external factors that may affect policy outcomes, scholars can provide far more insight into the impact of think tanks in a number of ways. For instance, by examining specific domestic and foreign policy areas, such as education, health and nuclear strategy, scholars can isolate the various organizations that have made a concerted effort to shape the content and outcome of government policy. This can be done by observing the many channels think tanks rely on to exercise public and private influence. Since the majority of think tanks in the United States offer specialized expertise, it is not difficult to compile a preliminary list of those institutions most actively engaged in a particular policy area. In other words, it is highly unlikely that 1,200 think tanks will have a vested interest in influencing every conceivable government policy. Once a list has been compiled, scholars can pursue one of many options. They can interview (or send questionnaires to) both members of think tanks and policy-makers involved in a particular policy debate to determine how extensive a role think tanks played. Or, alternatively, they can compare the policy recommendations proposed by think tanks to the actual decisions made by government. This may provide additional insight into the impact certain think tanks may have had in a given policy area.

A similar approach can be employed in assessing the influence of think tanks during presidential campaigns. Moreover, by accessing materials stored at presidential archives, it is possible to acquire a far more comprehensive understanding of the key individuals and institutions that helped shape and mould campaign platforms and administration agendas. In fact, these issues are frequently raised in newspaper and magazine articles months and weeks before elections. These avenues may not allow us to reveal completely how significant or negligible a role think tanks play in American politics, but they will take us far beyond the limited treatment of think tank influence in the current body of literature.

Conclusion

The growth of think tanks in the United States and their active involvement in American politics has compelled social scientists to think more critically about their role and function in the policy-making process. It has also forced scholars to reflect on the implications associated with the politicization of policy expertise. Yet, to date, few scholars have paid close attention to how think tanks seek to influence the political agenda. Even less attention has focused on the extent to which think tanks have made a significant impression on public policy. To address these and other deficiencies in the available literature, this study has explored, among other things, how think tanks attempt to wield public and private influence. In the process, some preliminary suggestions on how to study the influence of American think tanks have been made. Think tanks have become permanent fixtures in the policy-making process. Future researchers must now determine the most effective methods to evaluate their behaviour.

References

Abelson, Donald E. (1992) 'A New Channel of Influence: American Think Tanks and the News Media', *Queen's Quarterly*, 99(4): 849–72.

Abelson, Donald E. (1995) 'From Policy Research to Political Advocacy: The Changing Role of Think Tanks in American Politics', *Canadian Review of American Studies*, 25(1): 93–126.

Abelson, Donald E. (1996) *American Think Tanks and their Role in U.S. Foreign Policy*, London and New York, Macmillan and St Martin's Press.

Abelson, Donald E. and Carberry, Christine M. (1997) 'Policy Experts in Presidential Campaigns: A Model of Think Tank Recruitment', *Presidential Studies Quarterly*, 27(4): 679–97.

Berman, Edward H. (1983) *The Influence of the Carnegie, Ford and Rockefeller Foundations on American Foreign Policy: The Ideology of Philanthropy*, New York, State University of New York Press.

Chisolm, Laura Brown (1990) 'Sinking the Think Tanks Upstream: The Use and Misuse of Tax Exemption Law to Address the Use and Misuse of Tax-Exempt Organizations by Politicians', *University of Pittsburgh Law Review*, 51(3): 577–640.

Dickson, Paul (1972) *Think Tanks*, New York, Atheneum.

Ehrman, John (1995) *The Rise of Neo-conservatism: Intellectuals and Foreign Affairs 1945–1994*, New Haven, CT, Yale University Press.

Fischer, Frank (1993) 'Policy Discourse and the Politics of Washington Think Tanks', in Frank Fischer and J. Forester (eds), *The Argumentative Turn in Policy Analysis and Planning*, Durham, NC, Duke University Press Press.

Gellner, Winand (1995) '"Political Think-Tanks" and Their Markets in the U.S.–Institutional Setting', *Presidential Studies Quarterly*, Summer: 497–510.

Heclo, Hugh (1978) 'Issue Networks and the Executive Establishment', in A. King (ed.), *The New American Political System*, Washington DC, The American Enterprise Institute for Public Policy Research.

Higgott, Richard and Stone, Diane (1994) 'The Limits of Influence: Foreign Policy Think Tanks in Britain and the USA', *Review of International Studies*, 20: 15–34.

Kaplan, Fred (1985) *The Wizards of Armageddon*, New York, Simon & Schuster.

Linden, Patricia (1987) 'Powerhouses of Policy', *Town and Country*, January: 99–179.

Lindquist, Evert A. (1992) 'Public Managers and Policy Communities: Learning to Meet New Challenges', *Canadian Public Administration*, 35(2): 127–59.

McCombs, Phil (1983) 'Building a Heritage in the War of Ideas', *The Washington Post*, 3 October.

McGann, James G. (1992) 'Academics to Ideologues: A Brief History of the Public Policy Research Industry', *PS: Political Science and Politics*, December: 733–40.

Muravchik, Joshua (1987) 'The Think Tank of the Left', *The New York Times Magazine*, 27 April.

Newsom, David D. (1996) *The Public Dimension of Foreign Policy*, Bloomington, IN, Indiana University Press.

Nielsen, Waldemar A. (1989) *The Golden Donors: A New Anatomy of the Great Foundations*, New York, E. P. Dutton.

Ricci, David M. (1993) *The Transformation of American Politics: The New Washington and the Rise of Think Tanks*, New Haven, CT, Yale University Press.

Robinson, William H. (1992) 'The Congressional Research Service: Policy Consultant, Think Tank and Information Factory', in Carol H. Weiss (ed.), *Organizations for Policy Analysis: Helping Government Think*, Newbury Park, CA, Sage.

Robinson, William H. (1993) 'Public Think Tanks in the United States: The Special Case of Legislative Support Agencies', paper presented for the Conference on Think Tanks in the USA and Germany: Democracy at Work: Where and How Do Public Decision-makers Obtain Their Knowledge? Philadelphia, University of Pennsylvania.

Smith, James A. (1991) *The Idea Brokers: Think Tanks and the Rise of the New Policy Elite*, New York, The Free Press.

Stone, Diane (1996) *Capturing the Political Imagination: Think Tanks and the Policy Process*, London, Frank Cass.

Wallace, William (1994) 'Between Two Worlds: Think-tanks and Foreign Policy', in Christopher Hill and Pamela Beshoff (eds), *Two Worlds of International Relations: Academics, Practitioners and the Trade in Ideas*, London, Routledge and the London School of Economics.

Weaver, R. Kent (1989) 'The Changing World of Think Tanks', *PS: Political Science and Politics*, September: 563–78.

Wiarda, Howard J. (1990) *Foreign Policy Without Illusion: How Foreign Policy-Making Works and Fails to Work in the United States*, Glenview, IL, Scott Foresman/Little, Brown.

Wood, Robert C. (1993) *Whatever Possessed the President?: Academic Experts and Presidential Policy, 1960–1988*, Amherst, MA, University of Massachusetts Press.

A quarter century of Canadian think tanks: evolving institutions, conditions and strategies

Introduction

Canadian think tanks are a relatively young group of organizations, having only started to emerge in the early 1970s. In some cases, Canadian think tanks and their leaders have aquired something close to celebrity status; their leaders and senior staff appear frequently on television and comment regularly in the print media. Think tank leaders and senior analysts are important elements of elite networks, sometimes injecting expertise into the policy-making process and public debate, and sometimes interpreting policy research and developments to the public. However, despite the prominence of think tanks, most policy elites and citizens know relatively little about how they attempt to exercise influence, and how they manage to survive.

This chapter attempts to convey the character and distinctive features of Canadian think tanks both as a collectivity and as individual organizations. It also provides readers with a sense of how the environment of think tanks has changed during the past quarter century (1972–97) and influenced their activities. It does not attempt to assess the effectiveness of Canadian think tanks, provide detailed historical accounts of think tanks, or set out a conceptual framework to compare and assess the outputs of think tanks, which would require considerably more space (but see Lindquist, 1989; 1991; 1993a; 1994a). However, I pose questions about Canadian think tanks which I hope are interesting, and perhaps useful for reflecting on the experience of think tanks in other jurisdictions. Accordingly, this chapter has four themes: first, it provides an overview of the size and structure of social and economic policy institutes; second, it outlines think tank diversity in size and structure; third, it discusses how the Canadian political, economic and institutional environment constrains and promotes their development; and, finally, it addresses some contemporary issues facing think tanks such as the emergence of a new generation of 'virtual' institutes.

A quarter century of think tanks in Canada: a synopsis

Most Canadian accounts of the emergence of modern Candian think tanks begin with the Ritchie report. In late 1968, Ronald Ritchie was directed by the Canadian government to consider the feasibility of creating an independent policy institute. He surveyed the status of policy research in Canada and compared this with institutional arrangements elsewhere. Ritchie acknowledged that royal commissions, taskforces, government councils, universities, and several non-profit organizations undertook activities relevant to public policy analysis, but he concluded there was insufficient multidisciplinary and policy-oriented research in Canada. His report, submitted in 1969, led to the creation of the Institute for Research on Public Policy (IRPP) (Ritchie, 1971). But, even as the IRPP was established during the early 1970s, the institutional landscape was already beginning to change.

Four established organizations underwent significant transitions that produced part of the first wave of Canadian policy institutes. Until 1971, the Canadian Welfare Council functioned as a peak interest association, housing three national associations in the social services field, two divisions on ageing and family and child welfare, and a small research branch. In response to mounting internal tensions, it became the Canadian Council on Social Development (CCSD) and was transformed into a social policy institute by granting independence to the associations. In 1954, the New York-based Conference Board established a small Montreal office to serve member companies having interests in Canada with studies on economics, personnel administration, and business practices, with its membership and staff growing steadily. In 1971, under a new president, its offices were moved to Ottawa, and the Canadian branch grew rapidly, transforming into a more autonomous research operation anchored around a short-term economic forecasting model, and improved meeting and information services for members. The C. D. Howe Research Institute was formed following a merger of the Private Planning Association of Canada and a small foundation, becoming a centre for short-term economic policy analysis, and continuing to serve three private sector councils. Finally, the profile of the Canadian Tax Foundation (CTF), founded in 1946 to conduct and sponsor research on taxation, increased significantly during the early 1970s due to the national debate stimulated by the Royal Commission on Taxation on the economic and social policy objectives of the tax code.

In the early 1970s, three new policy institutes were established. In 1972, the Institute for Research on Public Policy was created by the federal government to become Canada's equivalent to the Brookings Institution. The plan was to secure a hefty endowment with contributions from the federal government, provincial governments, and private sector donors. In 1973, the Canada West Foundation (CWF) was established in Calgary to focus more attention on the role of the West in the Confederation. A year later, the Fraser Institute was established in Vancouver to conduct research, to educate Canadians about the viability of market solutions to policy problems and to draw attention to the growing and allegedly counterproductive presence of government in the economy.

A second wave of institutes arrived in the late 1970s and early 1980s. The Canadian Institute for Economic Policy (CIEP) was formed in 1979 by Walter Gordon, a former finance minister, to sponsor a five-year research programme revolving around the themes of economic nationalism. In 1980, the Canadian Centre for Policy Alternatives was established by supporters of the union movement and social democratic principles to counter the influence of the free-market Fraser Institute. Finally, following the defeat of the Progressive Conservative government in early 1980, several party loyalists sought to create an institute dedicated to conservative principles in the analysis of economic, social, and international issues. However, the National Foundation for Public Policy Development soon foundered because of shifting party priorities.

Since the late 1980s, several more institutes have emerged. In 1987, the Public Policy Forum was established to improve the performance of the Canadian government and its public service, to expand the constituency for public service reform in the private sector, and to foster greater understanding across the business, labour, academic and public service sectors. In 1990, the Institute on Governance developed a niche in drawing on Canadian expertise to advise governments in developing nations to better manage public services and train executives, served as broker for Canadian agencies seeking to assist such governments, sponsored seminars and provided advisory services for Canadian policy-makers. In 1992, the Caledon Institute for Social Policy was created in Ottawa, with the financial support of the Maytree Foundation, to enable Ken Battle, a former executive director of the federal government's National Council of Welfare to develop a research agenda without the distractions and constraints of serving a government council. In 1994, the Canadian Policy Research Networks (CPRN) Inc. was formed by Judith Maxwell, the former head of the Economic Council of Canada (ECC, an advisory and research institution which fell victim to federal cutbacks during the early 1990s), to sponsor longer-term, interdisciplinary policy research programmes on social and economic policy issues, and to lever research capabilities across Canada.

During the early 1990s, several think tanks underwent significant transformations of one kind or another. IRPP's new president consolidated its operations into an office in Montreal, reshaping its structure more like the Howe Institute, but focused on issues such as education policy, urban policy and governance. The CCSD floundered as the federal government cut grants and contributions during the early 1990s, sold its building in Ottawa, and restructured so that it could survive on the basis of research contracts. In 1993, the Conference Board of Canada absorbed the Niagara Institute, which had been dedicated to organizing conferences for many different clients and developing new techniques for improving the dynamics of such events. Finally, the Public Policy Forum established a separately funded, autonomous Public Management Research Centre in 1995 to commission research on private sector approaches to management and on comparative practice in public management.

In the late 1990s, there certainly is no shortage of Canadian think tanks. Like most observers, I have focused on think tanks with relatively broad policy interests. I have not reviewed think tanks with interests in foreign policy, nor have I accounted for the many, many more think tanks working in particular sectors on specific subject matters. To date, no census on think tanks has been attempted, but it is conceivable that a hundred non-profit policy think tanks exist in Canada.

Think tanks are prominent in policy and political debates. The media regularly report on the release of their studies and the proceedings of their public conferences and seminars. Their presidents, executive directors and senior staff analysts are regularly interviewed for television, radio and print coverage of major issues. Finally, several think tanks hosted public conferences for the federal government as part of national consultation exercises during the early 1990s (see Russell, 1993; Lindquist, 1994b). These, and other think tank events, are often televised on the Canadian Parliamentary Channel, thus providing additional public exposure.

The diversity of Canadian think tanks

It should be evident that Canadian think tanks vary considerably in terms of mandate and ideological orientation. But equally important sources of variation involve financial resources, as shown in Table 6.1, and their respective portfolios of activities.

The best place to begin is by reviewing some figures that indicate revenue flows and staff complements. Some think tanks – such as the old CIEP, the Canadian Centre for Policy Alternatives, and the Caledon Institute for Social Policy – are quite small, with limited budgets (in the order of $500,000 each year) and rely on anywhere from four to five staff. The CWF and the Public Policy Forum have budgets that are roughly twice as large. The next cluster of think tank budgets – that of the CCSD, CPRN, Fraser Institute, C. D. Howe Institute, IRPP, and Institute on Governance – range anywhere from $1.4 million to just under $2 million, employing from 10 to just over 20 staff. The CTF falls into the same range, in terms of staff, but its revenues are double the latter group of think tanks. Finally, as has been the case for

Table 6.1 *Selected Canadian policy think tanks*

Think tank	Established	Location	1995 revenues	1995 staff (FTE)
Caledon Institute for Social Policy	1992	Ottawa	550,000	3
Canadian Centre for Policy Alternatives	1980	Ottawa	650,000	5
Canada West Foundation	1973	Calgary	718,408	9
Public Policy Forum	1987	Ottawa	1,000,416	10
Canadian Centre for Philanthropy	1981	Toronto	1,573,000	16
Institute on Governance	1990	Ottawa	1,444,595	11.5
Canadian Council on Social Development	1971	Ottawa	1,816,626	24
Institute for Research on Public Policy	1972	Montreal	1,822,000	12
C. D. Howe Institute	1973	Toronto	1,875,471	16
Canadian Policy Research Networks Inc.	1994	Ottawa	2,024,613	4.5
Fraser Institute	1974	Vancouver	2,534,787	20
Canadian Tax Foundation	1946	Toronto	3,745,000	23
Conference Board of Canada	1954	Ottawa	22,995,000	190

Sources: Annual reports, telephone interviews.
Note: These figures were obtained from the annual reports of think tanks and from telephone interviews. In some cases, the financial year of think tanks did not correspond to the calendar year, and in those cases I relied on figures from the financial year that overlapped most with the calendar year.

some time, the Conference Board of Canada dwarfs the others: its 1995 revenues exceeded $22 million and it employed 190 people, thus rivalling major US research institutions.

Canadian think tanks vary with respect to the enquiry they undertake. When observers conjure up images of 'typical' think tanks, they probably envision a critical mass of in-house staff who, in collaboration with a larger network of researchers and supporters, produce a variety of research studies, short-term policy analyses, newsletters, seminars and conferences. This image applies to several think tanks – the CCSD, Canadian Centre for Policy Alternatives, Fraser Institute, Howe Institute and the consolidated and relocated IRPP all come to mind – but it does not account for their full diversity. Consider these examples:

- The CIEP adopted an information-centred strategy focused almost exclusively on producing research. Over five years, CIEP published more than thirty monographs by contracting to outsiders, usually academics. Even responsibility for managing the institute was contracted out.
- The Public Policy Forum, which organizes round tables, search conferences and other events to explore medium-term issues, generally seeks to be a catalyst for learning and for reforming the public sector, often by means of private–public partnerships. The Public Policy Forum has relied mainly on networking strategies rather than research.
- The Conference Board sponsors an impressive number of conferences and other meetings on an ongoing basis. Approximately 164 events were held in 1994. Almost three-quarters of these events involved regular meetings of 35 councils for senior executives to discuss issues in a certain domain, and occasionally sponsor studies. Other events include conferences and seminars, and the above figures do not include the 90-odd courses hosted by the Niagara Institute.
- The CTF sponsors several annual conferences across the country where research papers and analyses of recent tax developments are presented and published as proceedings. It also provides support for academics and others to conduct extensive research, often published in either the *Canadian Tax Paper* series or its scholarly journal, and it has a superb research library. Staff produce important reference volumes on national, provincial, and municipal finances. CTF has many features similar to organized research units at a major research university.

The key point is that there are many different 'social technologies' employed by Canadian think tanks to achieve the objectives of their supporters and leaders. Some think tanks are managed more like conglomerates. This may be achieved either by locating programmes in different cities, or by giving programmes considerable autonomy. Consider these examples:

- The IRPP provided a spatial model of a research holding company until the late 1980s. IRPP had a rolling set of five or six broad programmes, such as social policy or governance. Each had a director, obtained funding from separate sources, was located in different cities across Canada, and functioned like autonomous 'mini-institutes'.
- The Conference Board had nine separate research centres in 1995 (now expanded to sixteen, after several councils were given status as centres). Each is supported by a separate membership fee structure and has an advisory council (Conference Board of Canada, 1995).
- The CPRN has established several autonomous networks of researchers across Canada who work in different institutional environments. Each network has a director and perhaps one or more research fellows

(depending on the funding streams) who typically do not reside at the head office but are connected electronically.

Despite this diversity, it is possible to discern some patterns. First, very few institutes generate their own data. Only the Conference Board is heavily involved in producing data not available from other sources. It produces national and provincial economic forecasts, surveys of business investment and consumer spending, regular reports on a variety of corporate practices and various 'outlook' documents. Some institutes, such as the CCSD and the Fraser Institute, 'mine' and repackage existing data available from Statistics Canada, putting it in a more accessible format for members of the public, or in the case of the CTF, making it available as a valuable library resource.

Second, policy research tends not to be conducted by institute staff; such work is usually undertaken by outsiders (again, the Conference Board is a notable exception). There are good reasons for this practice. Institute staff are often hired as generalists who can dabble in many policy areas, and attend to the day-to-day demands of managing contracted research projects and the publication programme, organizing conferences and forums, meeting the demands of members, seeking funding opportunities, and responding to requests from the media. Moreover, some experts may be too expensive or unavailable to work on a full-time basis, so it makes sense to contract out the responsibility for undertaking major research projects.

Finally, policy analysis tends to be more implicit than explicit since it may be provocative and have implications for an institute's image. Some think tanks – such as the Conference Board – avoid producing policy prescriptions (though they seek to influence policy debates by supplying new information), while others indicate that recommendations in studies do not represent the 'official' position of the think tank and its directors. Conversely, think tanks that regularly produce prescriptive policy analyses typically ensure that such work is undertaken by staff or trusted outsiders.

Evolving environments for Canadian think tanks

In the period since the first Canadian think tanks emerged, significant changes have occurred in their broader policy and institutional environments. The trajectory of the welfare state, as well as public confidence in government leadership, has changed markedly, which, in turn, has affected the 'market' for think tank outputs.

During the 1960s and early 1970s, the federal government and its programmes grew rapidly. These developments were inspired by the optimism and activist governments in the United States, complemented by a relatively

general interest in building capacity to comprehend and solve social and economic problems, and reinforced by a belief that solutions could be found.
The result was the proliferation of policy planning, analysis and evaluation
units in federal departments and central agencies, as well as the creation of
arm's-length advisory organizations – the Economic Council of Canada
(1963), the Science Council of Canada (1966), and the National Council of
Welfare (1969) – intended to marry policy research capabilities with the
promise of consensus. Not unrelated was the drive to create the Institute for
Research for Public Policy and the emergence of the CCSD, the latter relying heavily on federal funding during the late 1960s and early 1970s. It was
in this context that think tanks critical of government policies – the Fraser
Institute, the C. D. Howe Institute and the CWF – emerged, relying primarily on private sector support. In short, economic and government growth
created a relative abundance of funds which, together with a general confidence in the social sciences and policy analysis, supported the emergence of
this early group of think tanks. Yet these early think tanks did not challenge
government bureaucracies or influence policy debates, largely because they
were young, fledgeling organizations.

The national mood of optimism was shaken by events during the rest of
the 1970s and the 1980s. Like many other Western industrialized nations,
Canada grappled with two energy shocks and the severe recession of the
early 1980s, thus leading to declining confidence in economic policy. Federal
policy-makers added to the mix the regionally divisive National Energy Program of the 1980s, a failed attempt to reform the tax code, and a bruising,
but ultimately successful, initiative to patriate the equivalent to the Canadian
constitution from the United Kingdom in 1982. Government political leaders and their public service advisors steadily lost credibility with the public
and interest groups; the capability and wisdom of governments to remedy
social and economic problems was increasingly questioned. The growing
sense of malaise provided fertile ground for several new institutes – the
Canadian Centre for Policy Alternatives, the CIEP, and the National Foundation for Public Policy Development – and provided increasingly receptive
audiences for the Fraser Institute and the C. D. Howe Institute.

As the 1980s unfolded, the sense of malaise deepened. Despite worsening
national finances, even a Conservative government could not take tough
measures to reduce deficits and to restructure important programmes
because it did not have sufficiently strong public support. One strategic
response was 'managerialism': during the late 1980s, the government
announced a succession of expenditure restraint measures, launched internal searches for efficiencies in government operations, and undertook piecemeal efforts to modify existing programmes. The government did negotiate
a Canada–US free trade agreement and announced significant tax policy
reforms following considerable public debate, but since these measures had

medium to long-term implications for the structure of Canadian governments and the affordability of programmes, the debate about the specific choices seemed rather academic. Finally, there were sustained attempts to mollify Quebec following its objections to the adoption of the 1982 Canadian Constitution. Canadian think tanks were prominent players in the free trade, tax reform and constitutional debates, receiving grants and contributions to undertake studies and host conferences and seminars, probing the economic and social implications of various options, and providing media commentary.

These constitutional deliberations diverted the governments from grappling with the poor state of the finances of federal and provincial governments, and the need to rethink many programmes and policy regimes, even though the C. D. Howe Institute and the Fraser Institute continually sought to draw attention to these problems. Constitutional matters were set aside after 1992, when Canadian governments started taking concerted steps to balance budgets and initiate debt repayment programmes in the context of public worry about the deficit and growing resistance to increased levels of taxation. Policy-makers were faced with very difficult and long overdue decisions about how programmes should be reshaped or whether they should continue, and about the role of government. At the federal level, ministers and senior officials concluded that policy capacity of the public service had withered due to the effects of managerialism (deputy ministers re-allocated scarce resources from policy units to programmes areas) and the fact that Conservative governments distrusted bureaucratic policy advice (the policy capabilities of ministerial offices) and sought external advice from consultants and lobbyists. In late 1993, a newly elected Liberal government sought to rely more heavily on the public service for policy advice, but it soon became clear that many departments could not fully meet the challenge (Government of Canada, 1995; Cappe, 1995).

These developments created interesting cross-pressures for Canadian think tanks during the early 1990s. On the one hand, the drive to review and restructure federal programmes, the federal public service and federal-provincial arrangements in all sectors led to the elimination of several prominent government research bodies (the Economic Council of Canada, the Science Council of Canada and the Law Reform Commission of Canada) and a significant reduction in unencumbered funding for outside bodies. On the other hand, policy-makers have had to rely more heavily on outside organizations to assist with policy research and analysis, and the organization of conferences and seminars. In short, a healthy 'public market' has developed for the provision of 'policy inquiry' services at the expense of sustaining grants (Pierre, 1995; Halligan, 1995).

The concept of market implies competition, and Canadian think tanks have been exposed to increased competition over the last 25 years. One source has come from the emergence of more generalist and specialist think tanks. There has also been a dramatic increase in the number of universities, but more importantly, in the number of specialized research units, many of which have a decided policy orientation. Indeed, several governments have funded 'centres of excellence', often linking researchers located at different universities. The number of business, labour and other associations – not to mention special interest groups – involved in policy debates has greatly expanded, and they often support or sponsor policy research and analysis. Finally, there has been an explosion in the number of integrated and 'boutique' policy consulting firms in recent years, on which governments have increasingly relied for advice on policy and restructuring, and sometimes to manage projects (Bakvis, 1997).

Funding remains a critical issue for all Canadian think tanks, particularly for sustained projects that explore medium to longer-term issues. For think tanks that rely on government support, the shift to service contracts means they can divert fewer resources towards building new intellectual capital since many contracts are awarded on a competitive basis, and they can be undercut by other organizations not interested in deepening their research competence. There are government funds available for deeper research, but they are largely channelled through the Social Sciences and Humanities Research Council of Canada and it is difficult for think tanks to tap into this stream of funds since they mainly go to university professors, and peer review defers more to disciplinary and professional standards than to policy relevance. In contrast to the United States, there is relatively limited support in Canada from private foundations for policy research (there are fewer foundations, they tend to be quite small, and they have tended not to support policy research), and in the context of government cutbacks in so many domains, the competition to secure foundation funding is particularly intense. In short, the funding base for most Canadian think tanks remains tenuous and even the most successful ones struggle to retain members and secure support for important research topics.

Evolving images of Canadian think tanks: thematic reflections

This section examines some recent developments and issues for Canadian think tanks. These reflections, though stimulated by recent events, are also meant to be a prism through which one can reflect on the past activities of think tanks. They have been selected because they are probably the most intriguing, but should not be interpreted as a complete list of the most compelling management challenges for think tank leaders. Several enduring issues – particularly the critical role of leaders in ensuring organizational success, the uneasy relationship between values and enquiry, and measuring the relevance and impact of think tank activities – could be added to the list.

Think tanks as virtual networks: new or old idea?

The first annual report of the recently established CPRN, Inc. bills the organization as a 'virtual' institute, a think tank 'without walls' in the information age. CPRN is a transformed remnant of the Economic Council of Canada, a larger organization that had well over a hundred full-time employees and served a council with representation from many sectors of the economy. The ECC produced annual reviews of the economy and undertook a rolling portfolio of about five or six fundamental research projects that often lasted three years, producing consensus reports and many background studies. CPRN emerged, in part, as a reaction to the cumbersome nature of these arrangements, and, in part, to continue with the objective of undertaking definitive research projects. Its founding president, the former chair of the Economic Council of Canada, established a small head office with several networks looping across Canada and connected by electronic mail, fax machines and telephones. The questions I want to pose are, is CPRN really a 'virtual' think tank, and does this constitute an innovation in the Canadian context?

If 'virtual' means a think tank 'without walls', or not having many primary contributors working inside the organization, then there have been several such Canadian think tanks. The first was the CIEP, which functioned by contracting out the research and management responsibilities to outsiders, and maintained an even smaller head office than CPRN. For many years, the IRPP ran a de facto network of institutes guided by an elaborate governance framework; more recently it has relied on outside directors to commission and edit series of studies. Others, like the C. D. Howe Institute, rely on academics to contribute research monographs and analyses on a regular basis (although the Howe Institute has several core staff who also produce studies). Finally, the Fraser Institute and the Institute on Governance nurture international networks of practitioners and scholars. One strategy for developing Canadian think tanks is to eschew building a significant 'in-house' research capacity.

The other interpretation of 'virtual' is to rely on the Internet and web sites as research and communication tools, reducing the need for non-professional support staff. However, the Canada West Foundation, the CCSD, the Conference Board of Canada, the Fraser Institute, and the Public Policy Forum have established home pages or web sites. The CWF is perhaps most innovative in this regard. In late 1994, not only did CWF make its publications, notices and various lines of data available on-line, but it helped to establish 'free net' services in the Calgary area, advised other communities

on how to create such capabilities, and established a network among experts
across Canada to exchange information and discuss social policy alternatives
(Canada West Foundation, 1995). If CPRN is not unique as a surfing think
tank, in what ways is it a relatively unique experiment in Canada?

I would like to suggest two important qualities, and they are useful to discuss because they are *not* – in combination – a defining feature of Canadian
policy think tanks. The first is CPRN's objective of securing funding for
research projects with two- or three-year time horizons. To raise the necessary funding, its president must build a consortium of funders, including
government departments at the federal level, provincial counterparts, private foundations, and other sources. But other think tanks – such as the
Howe Institute and the Institute for Research on Public Policy – have supported research programmes resulting in a steady stream of studies over two
years or more. The key feature is that CPRN seeks to develop an *interdisciplinary* network of researchers, ones that will produce genuinely interdisciplinary research insights, something which (as I have noted elsewhere) few
think tanks ever accomplish (Lindquist, 1989). CPRN's main innovation and
insight has been to realize that unless a think tank can mobilize significant
resources – say, $500,000 over two years for a group of scholars with diverse
backgrounds working on a modest project – it is impossible to create a suf-
ficient 'in-house' critical mass for undertaking interdisciplinary policy
research. The alternative is to tap into an equally diverse group of scholars
who reside in their home institutions, to articulate clear research objectives,
and to facilitate the often difficult process of encouraging scholars to work
across disciplinary boundaries. It will be interesting to see how each of the
networks actually performs.

Technologies for 'thinking the unthinkable': think tanks and deliberation

On 30 October 1995, the citizens in the province of Quebec voted in a ref-
erendum on whether to give a mandate to the Parti Quebecois government
to negotiate sovereignty or independence from Canada. The vote was very
close, a slim 'No' against granting the government such a mandate, but the
country is still grappling with the implications. Several think tanks played
important roles in alerting the public and experts alike in the 'rest of
Canada' to consider seriously the plausibility of different scenarios and their
implications for Canada and Quebec, regardless of the outcome of the vote
(see Gibson, 1994; Robson, 1995; Vander Ploeg and Elton, 1994 and 1995).
The federal government, either due to miscalculation or because its leaders
believed the government should not be seen to be seriously considering and
therefore endorsing various options, did not see fit to stimulate a debate outside Quebec. Think tank contributions were thus useful and timely, though

several research centres at universities and independent researchers also made similar contributions.

These contributions were interesting because Canadian think tanks were involved, in varying degrees, in thinking more systematically about different futures, the quintessential think tank function. But I would like to argue that most think tanks have not acquired a reputation or solid track record for doing so. Although they have worried about the future and advocated proposals for new policy or institutional frameworks, they have tended not to develop scenarios and examine how they might unfold along dimensions of concern to citizens and policy-makers. Too often Canadian think tanks have simply decried one unacceptable future and advocated a single solution as a response. Indeed, as I have argued elsewhere, Canadian think tanks have been slow to develop new social technologies to help policy-makers and citizens grapple with complex problems and to propose possible solutions (Lindquist, 1989; 1993a).

However, the IRPP began making progress on this front as early as 1990. The Governance Program supported a two-year 'participatory action research' project that brought together several senior federal officials (with funding from their departments) to listen to a series of experts, probe the trends and implications of the emerging 'information society', and write a final report (Rosell et al., 1993). The second phase relied on participatory action research, but focused on scenario-building methods to assist senior officials, political leaders and citizens to chart courses in a rapidly changing social and economic environment. IRPP dropped the project not long after its move to Montreal, but it continued under the auspices of the new Meridian International Institute based in the San Francisco Bay Area.

More recently, and in different ways, Canadian think tanks are attempting to assist governments to better listen to, and facilitate, deliberations of citizens. The CPRN Family Network reviewed studies and opinion polling on Canadian values and commissioned 25 discussion groups to determine which values are changing and which are not. The next phase consisted of launching a 'public dialogue project' in partnership with several organizations across the country to engage more citizens in deliberative processes; a 'dialogue kit' was created to assist small groups in diverse settings to discuss the future of the social union (Peters, 1995). The Canadian Centre for Policy Alternatives has worked with a network of organizations to commission studies and then, through a deliberative process, develop an 'alternative budget' to challenge the position of the Minister of Finance. The Institute on Governance has sought support to undertake further work on deliberative polling and other processes. The Niagara Institute (now an arm of the Conference Board of Canada) experimented with technology that permits workshop or search conference participants to indicate the ranking of options as well as the strength of preferences. As noted, the CWF assisted local communities to establish electronic networking capabilities in order to facilitate increased dialogue among citizens and experts, and over the years it has often held town hall – and citizen – meetings related to its long-standing interest in reform of the Canadian parliament, particularly the senate, and other constitutional matters. Finally, IRPP has long published a magazine called *Policy Options* which has evolved in order to provide a forum for experts to comment on special thematic issues.

I have come a long way from discussing how some think tanks engaged on the future of Quebec in Canada. But encouraging more disciplined thinking by elites and citizens should be a primary concern of think tanks. Focusing on deliberative techniques and processes should not be their only 'line of business', although some institutes and foundations may well begin to specialize in this area, as has been the case in the United States. Policy analysis and research, as well as promoting networking among experts and policy-makers, will probably continue to be the most significant contributions of Canadian think tanks, but the recent interest in citizen deliberations constitutes exciting terrain.

Should think tanks 'dance with the devil'?

Some years ago I suggested that more Canadian think tanks, if not contrary to their mandates, should provide services to governments. By doing so, I thought leaders and staff would expand networks, obtain glimpses into the policy-making process, acquire information and intelligence to position themselves better to secure grants and increase the relevance of the work they published. Although many think tanks have long been reluctant to do so, others have assisted governments with major research studies, hosting public consultations, publishing the proceedings of meetings, co-ordinating the coming and going of foreign delegations investigating certain issues, delivering programmes and providing assistance to help prospective or newly elected governments deal with transition planning (Lindquist, 1993b). Such activities may range from constituting a very small to a significant proportion of a particular think tank's rolling portfolio of activities.

The key issue is whether or not the benefits of taking up such activities, even if consistent with the mandates of think tanks, outweigh the costs. Leaders must predict whether working for governments serves to increase or diminish the credibility or reputation of the think tank, and whether taking on contracts will create a dependency relationship that may ultimately compromise its independence. For smaller think tanks, the administrative challenges associated with meeting contract obligations can be all-consuming, and the net proceeds may not be sufficiently large to support the deepening of work-in-progress or moving into new lines of enquiry. For larger think tanks this presents less of a problem. However, there may not be many alternatives for think tank leaders, who cannot rely on securing grants available to university researchers from government funding councils or from foundations, unless they receive support from an enlightened individual or organization with deep pockets and similar interests.

If think tanks choose to 'dance with the devil', they must identify projects that build up organizational capital and credibility. This suggests that think tanks must search for projects which are almost proprietary, and negotiate contracts that deepen or broaden their expertise. The Conference Board has done this in great measure, although it avoids making policy prescriptions. A more modest example is the 'Governing in an Information Society' project which, by engaging policy-makers in deliberative processes, led to successive phases and work in other jurisdictions. Even if think tanks retain non-profit or charitable status, they must act like for-profit entities – if only because the latter now constitute an important source of competition.

'Getting caught by the wave': think tanks as emergent policy organizations

Implicit in my discussion is the model of think tanks led by entrepreneurs identifying new policy, process or service niches. But this belies the experience of some of Canada's earliest think tanks. During the late 1960s and early 1970s, the Canadian Welfare Council was transformed into the CCSD because of the dramatic increase in government social spending, and the profile of the CTF was enhanced due to increased interest in tax policy. The underlying dynamic at work in both cases was the ascendancy of a policy problem or domain, and the existence of institutions that could be transformed into policy think tanks. Rather than actively 'waiting for the wave' (Flanagan, 1995), some organizational leaders suddenly find themselves 'in the midst of a big wave'. To be sure, if such organizations are to take full advantage of the opportunity, they must be led by shrewd leaders who will identify niches compatible with the existing fabric of the organization while, at the same time, developing new capabilities to take up other niches.

The question I want to raise is, what organizations – not currently viewed as think tanks – are about to be engulfed by a wave, and may potentially be transformed? Such a development may not necessarily mean that an organization starts proscribing policy but, like the Conference Board, it can be relevant as a knowledge producer. The most dramatic changes in motion – and ones that will likely endure in Canada – are the restructuring and downsizing of governments, and the increasing pressure to have 'public services' delivered, if not financed and delivered, by the non-profit and voluntary sectors.

If I am correct, organizations like the Canadian Centre for Philanthropy, the Coalition of National Voluntary Organizations, and the Institute of

Public Administration of Canada – to name only a few possibilities – may assume more important roles and develop higher profiles outside their normal networks. Such transformations may happen not because leaders are the first to divine the possibilities, but rather because members insist that the organization deal more effectively with their needs. Such a path is more likely to occur in 'membership' organizations, but as the experience of the CCSD suggests, it may be a difficult transition to manage. However, if existing organizations cannot fill the needs of members, then pressure to establish new entities to provide think tank functions will mount.

Conclusion

This chapter has shown the ideological and structural diversity of Canadian think tanks by reviewing the activities and evolution of several economic and social policy institutes. Canadian think tanks resist easy categorization; it is difficult to generalize about practices, structure, and change. They are small when compared to the most prominent US think tanks (with the exception of the Conference Board), but they resemble the vast majority of smaller think tanks in the United States and in other countries. A think tank census has yet to be completed in Canada, but even if it were possible to include the full population of international and specialist think tanks in the discussion, similar issues and trends would be likely to emerge.

The broader policy and institutional environment in which think tanks work has changed dramatically: we have witnessed a dramatic shift from a growing, if troubled, welfare state and national economy to cash-strapped governments trying to placate an increasingly disgruntled and fractious public in the context of fundamental economic restructuring. This, in turn, has led to pressure to restructure governance in Canada at the constitutional, policy, and administrative levels. These changes and pressures have led to an expanding number of think tanks, and more opportunities and exposure for their outputs and staff in the media. However, this should not be construed as arguing that Canadian think tanks regularly influence policy debates and policy-making – that kind of assessment requires detailed case study. Even more importantly, the opportunities afforded by widespread change has not necessarily led to a better endowed or more financially secure group of organizations; financing remains a critical contingency for think tank leaders. Membership fees remain important for think tanks, but governments now tend to provide project-specific funding (for those think tanks that received such support) rather than sustaining grants, and foundations have started to fund policy research and think tanks.

At stake for the future of Canadian think tanks is whether governments, corporations, non-profit sector organizations, and individual citizens will support organizations dedicated to exploring issues and educating the public on policy matters. Think tanks are not simply competing with each other for funding support from the private sector and the public sector – they are now competing with university, nonprofit and consulting entities in almost every niche of policy enquiry and deliberative practice. Think tanks cannot wait for public sector and private sector leaders to become more enlightened in this regard; they must persuade their leaders to appreciate the value of policy enquiry, and they must support talented leaders, analysts, researchers, and facilitators by means of partnerships that spread costs and risk.

There can be no one model to guide such strategic and institutional development, since think tanks vary enormously with respect to normative and substantive aspirations and how they engage members. Despite the bewildering possibilities, a time of fundamental social, economic, and political change could mean greater support of think tanks in general in order to help comprehend rapidly changing environments, to assist in the search for new ways for policy-makers, experts, interest groups and citizens to comprehend shifting environments, to deliberate, to identify plausible scenarios and alternative courses of action, and to involve and groom a new generation of policy analysts and leaders. Sponsoring new think tanks may not fully meet the challenge: a critical issue remains what sort of critical mass and level of funding is required for truly innovative insights and perspectives to emerge from think tanks.

References

I would like to thank the editors of this volume and the leaders of several think tanks – Monique Jerome-Forget, Patrick Johnston, Thomas Kierans, Judith Maxwell, David Ross, Michael Walker, and David Zussman – for reviewing earlier drafts of this chapter and providing useful comments amidst busy schedules. I particularly want to thank Diane Stone for arranging funding to attend the (UK) Political Studies Association Conference at the University of Glasgow to present an earlier version of this paper in April 1996. I am solely responsible for any errors in fact or interpretation.

Bakvis, Herman (1997) 'Political–Bureaucratic Relations and the Role of Management Consulting Firms', paper presented to a conference on 'Political Control of the Bureaucracy in Democratic Systems', Beersheva, Israel, 16–18 February.

Canada West Foundation (1994) *Annual Report 1994*, Calgary, Canada West Foundation.

Cappe, Mel (1995) 'Managing Horizontal Policy Issues', mimeo, 16 October.

Conference Board of Canada (1995) *Annual Report 1995*, Ottawa, Conference Board of Canada.

Flanagan, Tom (1995) *Waiting for the Wave: The Reform Party and Preston Manning*, Toronto, Stoddart.

Gibson, Gordon (1994) *Plan B: The Future of the Rest of Canada*, Vancouver, Fraser Institute.

Government of Canada (1995) 'Strengthening Our Policy Capacity – Report', Task Force on Strengthening the Policy Capacity of the Federal Government, mimeo, 3 April.

Halligan, John (1995) 'Policy Advice and the Public Service', in B. Guy Peters and Donald J. Savoie (eds), *Governance in a Changing Environment*, Montreal and Kingston, McGill-Queen's University Press and the Canadian Centre for Management Development, 138–72.

Lindquist, Evert. A (1989) 'Behind the Myth of Think Tanks: The Organization and Relevance of Canadian Policy Institutes', doctoral dissertation, Graduate School of Public Policy, University of California, Berkeley.

Lindquist, Evert A. (1991) 'Confronting Globalization and Governance Challenges: Canadian Think Tanks and the Asia-Pacific Region', in John W. Langford and K. Lorne Brownsey (eds), *Think Tanks and Governance in the Asia-Pacific Region*, Halifax, Institute for Research on Public Policy, 189–213.

Lindquist, Evert A. (1993a) 'Think Tanks or Clubs? Assessing the Influence and Roles of Canadian Policy Institutes', *Canadian Public Administration*, 36(4): 547–79.

Lindquist, Evert A. (1993b) 'Transition Teams and Government Succession: Focusing on the Essentials', in Donald J. Savoie (ed.), *Taking Power: Managing Government Transitions*, Toronto, Institute of Public Administration of Canada, 29–51.

Lindquist, Evert A. (1994a) 'Balancing Relevance and Integrity: Think Tanks and Canada's Asia-Pacific Policy Community', in Stephen Brooks and Alain-G. Gagnon (eds), *The Political Influence of Ideas: Policy Communities and the Social Sciences*, New York, Praeger, 135–62.

Lindquist, Evert A. (1994b) 'Citizens, Experts and Budgets: Evaluating Ottawa's Emerging Budget Process', in Susan D. Phillips (ed.), *How Ottawa Spends 1994–5: Making Change*, Ottawa, Carleton University Press, 91–128.

Peters, Suzanne (1995) *Exploring Canadian Values: Foundations for Well-Being*, Ottawa, Canadian Policy Research Networks Inc.

Pierre, Jon (1995) 'The Marketization of the State: Citizens, Consumers, and the Emergence of the Public Market' in B. Guy Peters and Donald J. Savoie (eds), *Governance in A Changing Environement*, Montreal and Kingston, McGill-Queen's University Press and the Canadian Centre for Management Development, 55–81.

Ritchie, R. S. (1971) *An Institute for Research on Public Policy: A Study and Recommendations*, Ottawa, Information Canada.

Robson, William B. P. (1995) 'Change for a Buck? The Canadian Dollar after Secession', *Commentary*, 68 (March).

Rosell, Stephen A. *et al.* (1993) *Governing in an Information Society*, Montreal, Institute for Research on Public Policy.

Russell, Peter H. (1993) *Constitutional Odyssey: Can Canadians Become a Sovereign People?*, 2nd edn, Toronto, University of Toronto Press.

Vander Ploeg, Casey and Elton, David (1994) *The Quebec Question: A Roadmap of the PQ Agenda and the Questions for Canada*, Calgary, Canada West Foundation.

Vander Ploeg, Casey and Elton, David (1995) 'Suppose the "Yes" Side Wins: Are We Ready?', Calgary, Canada West Foundation, January.

The development and discourse of Australian think tanks

Introduction

Since the 1970s, there has been gradual growth in the number of Australian think tanks. This development has been complemented by greater public and political awareness of their activities. However, the development of think tanks in Australia is less extensive than the other countries discussed in this volume. There are a number of contributing factors rather than one single explanation. These factors include the federal structure of government, taxation laws, an under-developed philanthropic culture, and the strength of the policy-analytic capacity of the Australian state. Notwithstanding the adverse environment for private policy analysis in Australia, a handful of policy institutes have gained public prominence and some influence in advancing their ideological perspectives. In particular, the rise of the so-called New Right think tanks with their discourse of economic rationalism (that is, a market liberal policy agenda), has paralleled that of the British New Right think tanks.

The development of independent institutes in Australia has not been on the scale witnessed in North America, Asia or Europe. There are only a handful of older established institutes – the Institute of Public Affairs (IPA), the Australian Institute of International Affairs (AIIA) and the Committee for the Economic Development of Australia (CEDA). The latter two are modelled after the Royal Institute of International Affairs in London and the Committee for Economic Development in the USA respectively. While there are Fabian associations in Australia, the Australian Fabians did not develop a strong organizational presence unlike their British equivalent (Mathews, 1993). Furthermore, these older organizations did not evolve into large prestigious institutions like some overseas contemporaries such as the Brookings Institution or the British National Institute for Economic and Social Research (NIESR). The reduced size and standing of Australian think tanks could be attributed to the supposed 'anti-intellectualism' of Australian society (see Stokes, 1994: 10; Walter, 1988). However, institutional factors are more important. Indeed, that think tanks have been established, survived and proliferated testifies to the tenacity of Australian intellectual life.

The Australian think tank scene

Think tanks and think tank-like organizations have been present in Australia since the turn of the century. The Round Table and the Institute of Pacific Relations were engaged in the research and discussion of regional and international affairs. They are now defunct but may be described as proto-think tanks. One of the first think tanks (and the oldest still in existence) is the AIIA which emerged in 1933. Although it is not usually called a think tank, it has think tank attributes. It was designed to stimulate interest in and promote understanding of international affairs, including politics, economics and international law. While the AIIA has played a prominent role in Australian intellectual life concerning foreign affairs, the organization has experienced difficulties and some internal feuding over its mission since the late 1970s. Criticism and concern regarding its relevance in contemporary times has not always been met constructively within the Institute (Stone, 1996b). It has not adapted well to a changing environment and other think tanks have emerged as competitors. Unlike the AIIA, the IPA was established with overt political motivations and a clear link to a political party – the nascent Liberal Party of Australia. Despite its political connections, during the 1970s the Institute began to drift. The organization was revitalized in the 1980s through the proactive leadership of Rod Kemp (later a Liberal member of parliament), but recessionary conditions have made it difficult for the organization to grow. For example, attempts to spin off a new organization devoted to foreign and defence policy issues – the Pacific Security Research Institute in Sydney with Owen Harries (co-editor of the *National Interest* in the USA) as the president – failed. Similarly, the conservative Council on the National Interest, set up in the mid-1980s, closed after two years. It was unable to retain staff or attract funding. Its demise was 'confirmation that issues of foreign affairs and defence tend not to rate very high on the list of priorities in the Australian community' (*Weekend Australian*, 28 February, 1987). The CEDA is most closely associated with business interests but, like the AIIA, presents itself as an apolitical and independent forum for research and debate. It acts as a 'communications bridge' among private and public decision-making elites to facilitate an improved and co-ordinated approach to economic development (Mead, 1985).

From the mid-1970s, the New Right think tanks emerged. This development paralleled the emergence of free market institutes in Great Britain. The Centre for Independent Studies (CIS) was created in 1976 and most closely resembles the Institute of Economic Affairs in London with a scholarly rather than activist focus. The Australian Institute of Public Policy (AIPP) was founded in 1982 by a former Liberal Party federal politician, John Hyde, who wished to promote the principles of the free market and individual liberty. Both AIPP and IEA have been participants in the international network of free market institutes co-ordinated by the Atlas Foundation. The H. R. Nicholls Society (1986) is more of a proto-think tank that has not developed beyond its dining club character to have a stronger organizational presence. Addressing industrial relations issues, it gained notoriety and ongoing media attention when former Prime Minister Bob Hawke referred to the organization as a group of 'political troglodytes and economic lunatics'. The Tasman Institute in Melbourne has consolidated since 1990 with a relatively high national profile. With an evident free-market ethos, the Tasman Institute has a well established network of scholars extending beyond Australia. The Institute concentrates primarily on economic issues and is more research-oriented than organizations such as the IPA. Founded in 1989, the Sydney Institute was previously known as the New South Wales branch of the IPA. Claiming to be a mainstream public affairs forum devoted to opposing extremism, the Sydney Institute is less ideologically identifiable. While conducting some policy analysis and publication, it operates more as a policy discussion salon. Indeed, it has been described as a 'talk tank' rather than a 'think tank'. By comparison, CIS is more of a publications-oriented 'ink tank'.

The perceived impact of the New Right think tanks provoked the organizational restructuring and redirection of the Evatt Foundation. Created in 1979 as a training organization, the Foundation was transformed in the late 1980s into 'a public interest group to promote the ideals of the labour movement – equity, participation, social justice and human rights' (Evatt Foundation, n.d.). Evatt also maintains formal links with the Institute of Public Policy Research (IPPR) and Demos in the UK and stocks a range of their publications. The Sydney based WETtank (Women's Economic Think Tank) was established in 1992. Like the H. R. Nicholls Society, WETtank is a specialized proto-think tank. It is a very small organization, reliant upon the infrastructural and personnel support provided by the parent consultancy company and the unpaid research of women employed in universities and the public service. Another specialized think tank based in Sydney is the St James Ethics Centre established in 1989 to promote business and professional ethics. Launched in 1994, the Australia Institute is another with a 'progressive' orientation, and was established 'in part, because of concerns about the influence of well-funded right-wing think tanks on Australian policy formation' (Hamilton, 1996). Finally, in May 1997, a new business-funded organization was launched by the Australian Prime Minister to promote research on and links with Asia. Known as the AustralAsia Centre, this body is linked with the prestigious US-based Asia Society but is yet to develop think tank-like features.

Think tanks are not the only manifestation of the increasing salience of private policy advice. The Australian government has promoted academic input into policy (Marsh, 1995). University centres have proliferated, often with a strong policy focus. Individual academics have been incorporated into the policy process, invited to write reports, appointed to government agencies or to sit on committees of enquiry. Furthermore, during the 1980s a number of new consultancy companies emerged, most especially Access Economics, staffed by six former Treasury personnel. Finally, a number of pressure groups have boosted their policy analytic capacity, notably the Business Council of Australia and the Australian Council on Social Services. Non-state actors, like business associations, are 'moving beyond old-style lobbying functions and adopting more sophisticated roles in the public policy process' (Bell, 1995: 26).

In general, and as Table 7.1. reveals, Australian think tanks are not large organizations, and cannot be equated with establishments like the Heritage Foundation in the USA, C. D. Howe in Canada or the NIESR in the UK. Nor are they as well-funded. A 1994 review of think tanks found that 20 independent Australian institutes collectively spent $20 million (Marsh, 1995: 11). This compares poorly with the resources of university-based centres and, especially, 19 government policy research institutes with expenditures totalling $89 million (Marsh, 1995: 9). Australian think tanks may be small but they are often cross-subsidized by universities, private companies or bureaucracies and rely on the efforts of part-time and voluntary staff. The St James Ethics Centre was provided temporary office space by the State Bank of New South Wales as start-up assistance. Some of the new Australian institutes have attracted funds through contract research. An economic consultancy is attached to the Tasman Institute while Evatt attracts some contract work from trade unions.

Recent recessions have made the funding environment more unpredictable. Cost cutting at the IPA involved relocation from a central high rise office building in Melbourne to the fringes of the business district. Another response to the straitened financial environment has been amalgamation. Located in Perth, the AIPP had a local rather than national character and was very much reliant on the energy of its founding director, John Hyde. It never acquired an image of stability despite efforts to expand through a branch office in Canberra. AIPP was having difficulty retaining people of talent on low salaries and invigorating the support of members. In 1991, the AIPP amalgamated with the Institute of Public Affairs after the sudden death of the IPA Director. The process was cemented by Hyde filling the directorship of the new IPA.

One of the major problems that the smaller policy institutes confront is

Table 7.1 *Australian think tanks*

	Founded	Location	Expenditure ($)	Personnel
AIIA (1993)	1933	State capitals	130,000	3–4 admin. and voluntary
AIPP (1990)	1982–90	Perth	400,000	7
Australia Institute	1994	Canberra	n.a.	2 + research network
CEDA	1960	5 state offices	3,768,000	29 across all states
CIS	1976	Sydney	915,000	9 plus research fellows
Evatt (1991)	1979	Sydney	400,000	7 ft and pt; adjunct voluntary
H. R. Nicholls	1986	Melbourne	n.a.	
IPA (1991)	1943	Melbourne	1,470,000	17 ft equivalent
St James Ethics Centre	1989	Sydney	483,000	10 + volunteers.
Sydney Institute	1989	Sydney	650,000	4 ft
Tasman Institute	1990	Melbourne/Canberra	n.a.	8 research + admin.
WETtank	1991	Sydney	n.a.	No paid staff

Note: Data is for 1996 unless indicated otherwise.

the lack of a career structure for their research scholars, particularly as think tanks operate with a small core of executive staff. In most Australian think tanks, salaries do not exceed those found in the private sector or universities. It is unlikely that think tanks can guarantee an employment base allowing for predictable careers. It is easy to attract visitors (who have a secure base of employment elsewhere) and ex-politicians or bureaucrats seeking a pre-retirement post. For example, John Stone and Des Moore, both senior Treasury officials, found some solace after life in the bureaucracy through their association with the IPA. For Stone, the IPA was a 'half-way house' before becoming a Senator for the National Party. However, it is difficult to attract middle level people to make a long-term commitment. Instead, Australian think tanks have always relied upon the support of academics.

Institutes reliant on adjunct or associate scholars such as those connected with CIS, Evatt and AIIA are a contemporary think tank feature (Stone, 1996a). In other words, they are 'think tanks without walls' (see also Lindquist in this volume: Chapter 6). The typical Australian institute has a small staff and commissions academics or experts to write on topics. The advantage of the network organization is that management can draw upon a wider pool of expertise. At the same time, a wide range of viewpoints can be encompassed in the organizational product. Networking potentially curtails the problem of an institute developing an 'institutional line' and allows it to remain fresh by drawing upon new writers. While the network mode is efficient for small institutes with limited resources, a think tank has less control over scholars and few sanctions to ensure that a book or report is delivered on time. Furthermore, an organization will lack a strong physical presence where people can gather to hear speakers and interact. Notwithstanding these difficulties, the New Right think tanks have been important as organizational foci for networks linking previously isolated individuals in a broad, if not united, liberal movement or 'discourse coalition' (Hajer, 1993) from 1975 onwards (Kemp, 1988).

The tax and philanthropic environment

As in Canada, not all of Australian institutes have charitable status. Indeed, the Australian tax system undermines more extensive development of think tanks. The Income Tax Assessment Act allows 'the income of a religious, scientific, charitable or public educational institution' to be tax-exempt. Some think tanks such as the AIIA, the Australia Institute, the Tasman Institute and the CIS are categorized as charitable or public educational institutions (CCH Australia Ltd., 1992) on some or all of their activities. 'Approved research institutes' – including the AIIA, CIS, the Australia Institute and Evatt Foundation – are also exempt from tax whilst the gifts or subscriptions of donors are also tax-deductible for the individual. Neither the Tasman Institute nor WETtank have 'approved' status. Tax exemption is very difficult to acquire. Furthermore, Australian tax laws are not simple. Reduced personal and company tax rates have further reduced incentive for both individuals and corporations to give to institutes as there is less of a tax saving (Marks, 1988: 49–52).

In Australia, there is a poorly developed culture of philanthropy. The number of charitable foundations is believed to exceed one thousand, but these bodies are small by international standards. The Australian government has not encouraged private philanthropy through the tax system. Instead, the government's position has been to assist worthy causes through state expenditure rather than tax concessions. Consequently, 'it is almost impossible to establish a tax deductible foundation' (Dumais, 1995: 494, 504). Additionally, much private philanthropy has concentrated on social and welfare provision. As one Director of the AIIA lamented, 'it is much harder to get Australians and Australian institutions to give to a cause that has an intellectual appeal than to one that has an emotional appeal' (Millar, 1976: 15). The state is the dominant source of funding for research through universities, departmental research bureaux and scientific laboratories. Additionally, the corporate sector is not accustomed to funding research, and support for organizations such as the AIIA or WETtank is marginal. CEDA and the market liberal institutes such as CIS and Tasman have greater success in attracting business funding but not on the scale witnessed by their American or European counterparts.

While the philanthropic culture in Australia is markedly different from that in North America and Europe, since the 1980s Australian business has been more willing to fund independent research. Sections of the Australian business community consistently pay high membership fees to CEDA to ensure that a business perspective is represented in policy discussion. A further sign of changing attitudes towards philanthropy was the establishment in 1988 of a permanent secretariat for the Australian Association of Philanthropy indicating the increasing vitality of this sector. Government funding cutbacks in numerous areas since the 1970s has given private philanthropy a higher profile as it confronts greater demand to fill funding shortfalls (Dumais, 1995: 497–8).

Party competition and think tanks

An argument often heard concerning think tanks is that countries with strong political parties restrict the points of access at which policy institutes can participate in politics and policy development. In other words, think tanks potentially have greater impact on large parties with weak discipline that act more like electoral coalitions. By contrast, stronger parties are said to develop in-house policy machines and exert greater control over membership regarding policy platforms. This argument has some merit in the Australian context. The main political parties – the Australian Labor Party (ALP), the Liberal Party of Australia (LPA) and its coalition partner the National Party – are structured around detailed policy manifestos and tight party discipline. They are all relatively closed to outside inputs of policy advice. Yet, on the other hand, parties amplify the influence of an institute if that party is enlivened by the thought and writings of a particular think tank. This was certainly the case during the 1980s regarding the Thatcher government's patronage of the British New Right institutes. Potentially, think tanks introduce ideas into debate to see if they are unpopular or unworkable. It allows political parties and/or governments to 'test the water' with a policy idea before becoming closely associated with it. In Australia, however, the political parties have not developed an affinity with independent research organizations. There are no parallels to the kind of relationships that the Progressive Policy Institute or Economic Policy Institute enjoy with the Democratic Party in the USA. The links of the Liberals to the IPA and Labor to Evatt are weaker than the relationship of the Conservative Party to the Centre for Policy Studies, or the Labour Party to the IPPR, in Britain.

Nevertheless, there are historically specific circumstances of think tank influence. For example, during the 1940s the business-funded IPA was the catalyst for the reunification of anti-Labor political forces and was central in thwarting the perceived socialist advance of the ALP which was advocating extensive nationalization and economic regulation (Kemp, 1988). For Robert Menzies, subsequently to become Prime Minister, the IPA provided the policy rhetoric and ideologically informed platform with which to attract the electorate and rebuild conservative forces (Hay, 1982). Eventually, policy was formulated within the Liberal Party as it grew in size and electoral strength. The IPA temporarily filled a vacuum left by the disintegrating United Australia Party while conservative forces were re-established in a formal political sense. The IPA did not have direct influence over the new Liberal Party, business leaders or other elites but it was in a position to mobilize opinion (Walter, 1988). The IPA mustered a new economic philosophy and new symbols and beliefs into a cohesive plan for economic reconstruction. Neither business nor government fully subscribed to it, but it shaped policy debate and set the broad contours of post-war reconstruction.

During the 1970s, the emergence of a libertarian backbench group within the federal Liberal Party found ideological succour among groups such as the IPA and CIS. The 1970s and 1980s were a watershed in Australian policy developments. Both the coalition parties and the ALP increasingly turned towards economic rationalism (Pusey, 1991). Politics has always used 'legitimating patterns of ideas' (Walter, 1988: 267), and the free-market think tanks represented a contemporary form for the articulation of ideas that subsequently informed the policy paradigms of the 1980s and 1990s. They were a key component of an economic rationalist discourse coalition.

Despite its broad affinity with the ALP, the Evatt Foundation has not cultivated much favour at either the state or federal levels in Australia. Evatt had very limited access to the federal Labor government. The general ethos of Evatt research does not always reflect the economic beliefs and political values of the party's power brokers. Prime Ministers Hawke and Keating were more likely to consult their own advisors within the party than those outside it. Additionally, the factional system of the ALP fragments the party into contending sets of policy preferences. It is difficult for a think tank such as Evatt to address the party as a whole whereas identification with a faction can lead to marginalization. Instead of seeking a close relationship, the Foundation has maintained some distance from the ALP in order to preserve its independence. With the defeat of the ALP in the 1996 federal election, it is debatable whether any reassessment of party policies will be conducted in conjunction with either of the two 'progressive' think tanks. Much depends on the proclivities of party leaders. With Kim Beasley as the new Labor leader and Gareth Evans as deputy leader, this is unlikely as neither has personal links to Evatt or the new Australia Institute, and Beasley's political philosophy is probably more centre-right than could be said of these two organizations. Nevertheless, think tanks will continue to serve as a platform for politicians, and politicians will request these organizations to arrange meetings and briefings. For example, the Australia Institute has been called upon by politicians across the spectrum from Labor, the Greens and the Australian Democrats and has conducted discussions with senior Liberals on issues of mutual concern.

Architecture of the state

An important structural constraint on think tank development is the Australian federal system. In the USA, the federal structure has aided the proliferation of think tanks, particularly as growth has been fertilized by extensive foundation support. State or provincial level governments provide yet another arena in which think tanks can operate. This is not the case in Australia. For the older institutes, such as the AIIA and the IPA, a federal branch structure was an important feature at the time of establishment in building a strong membership and support base. However, there are significant disadvantages of de-centralization. Resources are spread thinly over several distant offices. It is instructive that the new Australian think tanks have concentrated their activity in one city, usually Sydney or Melbourne, with second offices located in the national capital, Canberra.

It is a commonly stated argument that parliamentary systems are closed to think tanks (Kay, 1989; Oliver, 1993). The decline of parliament and concentration of power within Prime Minister, cabinet and bureaucracy supposedly insulates policy-making from outside influences. An entrenched career public service with considerable control over information also acts as a gate-keeper to policy-making. Furthermore, the privacy in the advisory relationship between ministers and senior public servants enshrined in the principle of collective ministerial responsibility is symptomatic of a more cohesive and co-ordinated decision-making structure than in the USA system where there is a separation of powers. In Australia, the Department of Prime Minister and Cabinet has 'become something of a prime-ministerial think tank' while the rising influence and rapidly increasing numbers of ministerial 'minders' or advisors in the upper echelons of political policy-making have precluded the search for advice of senior political leaders outside government (Jarman and Kouzmin, 1993: 507–9). Think tanks are further constrained by the absence of conduits into government for the exchange of information and personnel.

Another important factor retarding the development of Australian think tanks is the analytic strength of research bureaux within government and parliament. For example, the Parliamentary Research Service (comparable to the US Congressional Research Service) provides Senators and Members of Parliament with 'analysis and advice on current and prospectives issues, policies, legislation and programs' and other services. With a budget of $2.28 million in 1990–91, and a staff of 55, the Service has resources at its disposal that far exceed those of the independent think tanks (Argall, 1990). Royal Commissions of Inquiry are well-known devices of policy advice while the development of policy research bureaux inside the Australian public service during the 1970s and 1980s has helped to meet greater government demand for policy analysis. Bodies such as the now defunct Priorities Review Staff or the Industries Assistance Commission (IAC), the Australian Bureau of Agricultural and Resource Economics and Economic Planning Advisory Council (EPAC) were created. The growth of internal government research bureaux is a more notable trend in Australia than the growth of think tanks (Jarman and Kouzmin, 1993; Marsh 1995). Policy positions in the Departments of Prime Minister and Cabinet, Finance, and Employment, Education and Training were also expanded, further enhancing the analytic capacity of government (Kemp, 1988).

The Australian parliamentary system is not impervious to think tanks. Parliamentarians, party officials and bureaucrats participate in think tank functions. Some are think tank members and others independently seek advice and information. Additionally, Commissions of Inquiry and the circulation of 'discussion papers' provide opportunities for policy research institutes to make submissions and contribute to public debate. The revivification of the

committee system in the Australian and British parliaments potentially represents a limited source of demand for think tank research and analysis
(Marsh, 1980). The Australian Senate, which acts as a house of review, has
shown a greater proclivity to draw on external sources of advice. Furthermore, as the number of research institutes grows, decision-makers in bureaucracies and political parties as well as leaders in interest groups may become
more conscious of and more open towards them. Changing mechanisms of
policy formation over time may present new opportunities for think tanks
but in the interim, institutional factors continue to limit political opportunities for think tanks.

Nevertheless, the New Right think tanks appeared in the 1970s and 1980s
in common with trends in the USA, Canada and Britain. Some of these organizations have played a part in the paradigm shift from Keynesianism to economic rationalism in Australian public policy. Progressive institutes emerged
in response to this development in the late 1980s and 1990s. As discussed
through the remainder of this chapter, think tanks are symptomatic of the
importance of ideas in fashioning policy. Furthermore, rather than having
decisive impact on policy development or political influence on politicians
or legislation, think tanks have played a greater role in shaping the climate
of opinion or establishing the terms of debate.

The impact of Australian think tanks

Given the cultural, legal and political impediments to think tank development in Australia, questions about the influence or impact of think tanks
have not taxed Australian social scientists. Of those accounts that do exist,
quite different interpretations are prevalent. These range from neo-marxist
perspectives that the New Right think tanks exert hegemonic control, to
more sceptical views that think tank influence is marginal. As discussed in
the introduction, power based on knowledge is notoriously difficult to
examine and measure. Accordingly, the following analysis commences with
three standard hypotheses concerning think tanks and the policy process.
Think tanks supposedly introduce 'greater rationality' (Dror, 1984), perform an 'enlightenment' function (Weiss, 1990), and offer 'alternative views'
to enhance the democratic functioning of policy debate (Parsons, 1995:
167). For reasons outlined below, Australian think tanks rarely achieve these
ambitions. Instead, it is more appropriate to consider think tanks as strategic organizations for policy entrepreneurship and networking.

Theoretically, think tanks can make the policy process more rational or
comprehensive in the sense that their analysis provides additional insights
for decision-makers, allowing them to address a wider range of possible
policy alternatives. Such a perspective assumes, firstly, that think tanks are

designed to produce unbiased recommendations on the basis of full investigation of an issue or problem. Secondly, there is the assumption that think
tanks can directly communicate research results to government; and, thirdly,
that government incorporates such analysis into its deliberations. However,
as noted by the Tasman Institute (1995: i) 'government often has an interest
in restricting debate and information in the interests of "a quiet life" and in
hiding limitations and failures'.

Nevertheless, a central theme in Australian policy discourse since the
1970s has been the need to improve the policy process given the pressures
on cabinet, ministerial overload and other institutional constraints that limit
the comprehensive discussion of long-term issues and priorities. A concern
has been to broaden perspectives within government and the nature of
inputs to decision-making. Although think tanks represent an additional
advisory system to counter bureaucratic bias within the system, in-house
advisors in government ministries continue to provide the bulk of policy
advice. Politicians and bureaucrats do not call upon private policy institutes
in a systematic fashion. Even if think tank ideas are adopted, these ideas are
shaped by the bargaining and conflict that occurs in politics as well as
bureaucratic inertia and incrementalism to such an extent that policy outcomes may differ considerably from the original think tank proposal.

The less ambitious claims of 'enlightenment' and proffering 'alternative
views' are more realistic assessments of think tank contributions to policy.
Enlightenment involves illuminating decision-makers with the best available
knowledge and social scientific research. This approach assumes that social
science has impact at the broader level of opinion and world-view through
a longer-term percolation of ideas into public policy (Weiss, 1990: 101). The
market–liberal institutes in Australia, for example, have collectively championed the economic rationalist agenda and tried to set the frame of discourse
for key public servants and media commentators. The CIS was created to
challenge Keynesian policy perspectives and government intervention
(Kemp, 1988: 344–8). In conjunction with the IPA, the H. R. Nicholls Society and Tasman Institute, these institutes were policy entrepreneurs in the
'liberal policy network', informing some of the ideas of the 'dries' (that is,
free market advocates and libertarians) in the Liberal Party (Kemp, 1988). In
particular, these institutes pioneered policies such as deregulation and pri-
vatization, labour market reform and trade liberalization, and were able to
provide decision-makers in federal and state governments with blueprints,
economic arguments and political justifications to legitimate the adoption of
such ideas (see Self, 1993).

Those arguing from a neo-marxist stance suggest that these institutes were
part of a hegemonic project to replace the discredited social democratic consensus with a new policy paradigm that would help build conservative political dominance and restore conditions for profitable capital accumulation.

The IPA, in particular, has been portrayed as a mainspring of ruling class mobilization (Connell and Irving, 1980). Another variation is that the ideological hegemony of capitalism is consciously sustained by the 'ideological management industry' which primarily works through think tanks and business organizations to promote free market enterprise and instil fear of socialism and trade union power (Carey, 1987). The impact of these think tanks was to 'shift the centre of political debate' and 'dislodge the ideological hegemony of the Keynesian regulators' (Sawer, 1990: 1). Whilst those associated with institutes such as IPA and CIS might agree that they played a role marketing and popularizing new terms of debate in the hope of generating 'attitudinal change' (Lindsay, 1996: 20), they have significant misgivings about their ability to shape the views of diverse business interests, let alone mobilize and unify this sector.

The effect of introducing the economic rationalist language of policy was to give currency to preferred policy perspectives and constrain the range of policy alternatives. That is, in 'reorganizing the public policy agenda along Anglo-American "free" market lines, continental European social democratic experience is excluded almost to the point of invisibility' (Pusey, 1991: 227). Additionally, think tanks have had a broader impact on the culture of debate among the wider public. The economic rationalist institutes have been important in articulating the premises of free market and limited government intervention. This role has been undertaken with two related aims. Firstly, these think tanks have facilitated a more regularized interaction between conservative and market liberal economic and political leaders, and leading scholars through their research projects, conferences and seminars. Secondly, through these interactions, think tanks have sought to inform conservative policy agendas. Importantly, think tanks do not operate alone but as part of a coalition of intellectual, material and partisan interests. Economic rationalism was not only espoused by the think tanks but also had a significant following within the Canberra bureaucracy – particularly in the Treasury, in government advisory bodies concerned with economic affairs (such as the IAC), backbench parliamentary groups such as the libertarian 'modest members' society, academics from the universities and other 'dries'. Think tanks, and others, were provided opportunities to entrench their discourse of economic liberalism as the dominant policy paradigm from the 1970s onwards as decision-makers sought new interpretative frameworks to comprehend the recessionary conditions and economic malaise of the Australian economy and as the federal Labor government of 1983–96 sought to distance itself from the problematic legacy of the Whitlam government era.

The 'enlightenment' model of understanding think tank influence does not adequately address the political dimensions of how these organizations attempt to create the intellectual conditions for problem solving by weakening prevailing policy orthodoxy. Think tanks have not relied on the inherent persuasiveness of ideas but enhanced ideational appeal through advocacy, outreach and dissemination of analyses. Networking has been a key component in opinion mobilization. The New Right think tanks have long-standing informal links with Coalition members as well as some ALP party figures, and have cultivated relations with and between conservative business leaders and academics. The Evatt Foundation is building a constituency based on the labour movement but also extending to other groups. WETtank draws its base from the women's movement. Individual scholars associated with think tanks also build their own more specialized networks around their research interests. By contrast, the AIIA is not concerned with political mobilization as its Charter prevents it from expressing a political view point. It would appear to be restricted to an enlightenment function.

The new think tanks have been far more successful in gaining political attention and media coverage as a consequence of their advocacy of specific and ideologically informed policy agendas. The self-styled 'progressive' Evatt Research Centre, for example, aims to support 'the goals and aspirations of the labour movement'. The market–liberal think tanks – the CIS, IPA, Tasman and Sydney Institutes – were less engaged in enlightenment than in persuasion and popularizing a market liberal policy agenda. They have a clear set of principles which inform their analysis and guide their policy recommendations. 'Enlightenment' presumes that knowledge trickles incrementally into public understanding. However, think tanks can hasten this process as policy entrepreneurs within policy networks. In seeking to entrench the discourse of the market within policy frameworks, think tank knowledge and intellectual activity is politicized. Furthermore, although direct support for political parties or legislation is eschewed by think tanks, the language employed and the frameworks of analysis often lead to conclusions that are of partisan advantage. For the new breed of Australian institutes to be educational and apolitical in the style of the AIIA is contradictory since the investigation of policy and recommendation of a course of action or series of options is intrinsically political. As the Director of CIS declared during an interview on the occasion of CIS's twentieth anniversary, 'it was not a matter of just putting [ideas] in the paper and feeling confident that your brilliant statement would win the day'. Instead, it is necessary 'to make the case' (Lindsay, 1996: 19–20).

The enlightenment model does not give adequate attention to the characteristics of the policy process which give some ideas more influence than others. For example, think tanks attempt to mould public opinion and set agendas by using the media and opinion-formers to amplify their discourses. Journalists are more frequently approaching think tanks for information and as a source of expert opinion. Some think tanks have been able to capitalize on this interest. John Hyde has had a column in *The Australian* for many years, while Gerard Henderson, director of the Sydney Institute, has had a

column in the *Sydney Morning Herald* and is a recognized political com-
mentator. Many other think tank fellows regularly feature in the newspapers
as a source of commentary. Peter Botsman, a former Director of the Evatt
Foundation, claims that 'the Right has become institutionalised in the media'
(Hughes, 1992). Certainly, the free-market think tanks treat the media as an
important channel to public opinion whilst journalists have a fruitful relationship in acquiring easy access to information and informed commentary.
Yet, occasionally, journalists have exposed feuding behind the scenes of what
appears to be the united front of the free-market think tanks, particularly as
'pressures for profile and funding fuel rivalry' (Lyons, 1991, Dusevic; 1990).
While links with the media are necessary, the extent of interaction varies
considerably from institute to institute. CEDA keeps an arm's-length distance with journalists and does not care for punditry. Similarly, the AIIA
cannot provide the polemical point of view often sought by journalists.

Although economic rationalists have been influential in entrenching a new
language of policy debate, these circumstances do not help explain the role
of other think tanks with less ideological sway. WETtank articulates a feminist policy discourse that does not have wide acceptance in policy circles.
Despite its unorthodox positions, WETtank is not ineffectual or hopelessly
marginalized. Instead, this institute represents a source of resistance for
patriarchal assumptions in policy and provides intellectual support for feminist redefinition of the role of women in society and the economy. Notwithstanding its minuscule resources, WETtank made the front page of *The
Australian* (14 April 1993) voicing criticism of one trade union's promotion
of child care policies that would keep women at home. It acts very effectively
as a 'ginger group'. More recently, the AustralAsia Centre looks primed to
counter the isolationist tendencies of the newly formed One Nation political party and promote a positive image of Australia in Asia.

Furthermore, influence need not be construed only in terms of the policy
impact of think tanks. Some Australian think tanks are not primarily policy-
focused. The AIIA, for example, is more concerned to promote wider understanding of international affairs in the community and serve its membership.
The St James Centre is not unlike the Institute for Business Ethics in Britain,
hoping to change attitudes both in private and public sectors concerning ethical conduct in business and professional life. The Tasman Institute has a
formal affiliation with Melbourne University and the Director of Tasman
teaches in the Economics Department. CIS has brought to Australia a
number of renowned international scholars, such as James Buchanan and
Milton Friedman, for its public lecture series. The Sydney Institute regularly
holds public lectures on Australian literature and the arts. These organizations perform a more subtle social and cultural role such as, for example,
contributing to the body of knowledge of and about Australia that does not
have direct policy relevance.

Despite the differential impact of individual think tanks, it is important to consider the collective impact of think tanks. In the past if individuals wished to contribute to decision-making on the basis of their expertise, they would have done so through government channels in a relatively uncoordinated fashion or through the political parties. That is, it would have been necessary to enter politics, seek appointment to Commissions of Inquiry or quangos, or make submissions to parliamentary committees and taskforces. The formal structures of power prevailed in determining advisory routes to decision-makers. Think tanks have been able to demonstrate the viability and validity of policy discussions generated outside government. In other words, the institutional focus for the co-ordination and direction of policy engaged experts who eschew direct partisan attachment, whether they be market–liberal or progressive in persuasion, has shifted, in small degree, outside government to organizations such as think tanks and lobby groups as well as commercial organizations like Access Economics. The process of formulating 'reform agendas' is pursued outside formal governmental institutions in other organizations where an initial consensus on goals and priorities is easier to fashion, from where other allies can be co-opted and galvanized, and a united front created (Fischer, 1991: 342). Furthermore, the very presence of think tanks is sufficiently noticeable to register with those who are politically cognizant. Over a period of time, think tanks collectively have been able to convince most of their targeted audiences, if not of their essentiality to policy debate, then of their ability to make critical contributions.

The final claim regarding the role of think tanks in the policy process is that they provide alternative points of view and are a 'manifestation of pluralism at work in a modern information society' (Parsons, 1995: 167). Institutes highlight the educational and professional credentials of staff and adjunct scholars, their experience in government, business or academe, institute peer review processes and a competence based on technical expertise to distinguish them from other sources of advice such as profit-motivated consultants. Their research and analysis is juxtaposed with that of government research agencies which are portrayed as captured and vulnerable to political pressures, and that of pressure groups pursuing vested interest. Think tank research reputations, political independence and commitment to 'open enquiry' are grounds from which they claim they are often better equipped than other groups to inform policy. Providing alternative analysis, they potentially act as a counter-balance to the dominance of bureaucratic advice.

Yet this only occurs if political and bureaucratic audiences are willing to listen to alternative perspectives. There is some evidence of this occurring in an *ad hoc* manner. Politicians and bureaucrats have attended conferences, been members of, and made speeches at the functions of, bodies such as the AIIA, CIS, Evatt, the Sydney and Tasman Institutes and the IPA. At the establishment of a new think tank such as the AustralAsia Centre, or opening of new premises, politicians cluster to applaud think tank contributions to public debate, or at the very least, to take advantage of a photo-opportunity. Think tanks often act as service organizations for government – organizing conferences or seminars and lectures by visiting international speakers. For example, the AIIA occasionally plays an unofficial role in the informal diplomacy of the Department of Foreign Affairs and Trade (Stone, 1996b). CEDA plays a quasi-public role in collecting and passing on information to decision-makers, responds to requests for information for business opinion on policy options, and helps explain public policy decisions to its members (see CEDA, n.d., in context of Bell, 1995: 27). The Tasman Institute undertakes contract research for the Victorian state government. In short, governments and politicians 'use' think tanks. This does not necessarily entail politicization of think tanks by government. Australian governments have not pressured these bodies to conform to a political line although it is possible (and not unknown) for think tank reports or analyses to be used to legitimate political or bureaucratic decisions. Political independence is declared by all Australian institutes. The influence they seek is that of an outsider. Indeed, a few institutes – WETtank, IPA and CIS – refuse to accept or apply for government grants.

A common feature evident in the promotional rhetoric of most institutes is that their independent status and alternative policy advice enhances the democratic functioning of society. The Tasman Institute's stance is indicative.

> Government institutions can also suffer from narrowness of focus, from absorption in the minutiae of administration. They often systematically lack important information and perspectives. It is thus vital for the health of democracy and freedom that governments not monopolise public policy debate. (1995)

CIS argues that 'competition in ideas' promotes better public policy by supporting 'the foundations of a free society' (CIS, n.d.). John Hyde has said, 'The free market think tanks are independent sources of ideas crucial for a liberal democracy. Their role is to set the political agenda by argument alone' (*Australian Financial Review*, 3 March, 1989). These statements reflect a pluralist argument that diverse, non-governmental voices highlight new ideas and present possible policy alternatives to decision-makers who might not otherwise receive full information. Policy research institutes provide a democratic fillip in broadening the agenda. Similarly, think tanks perform a useful 'watchdog' role in observing government, watching for instances of waste, inefficiency, corruption or poor policy implementation.

However, such a role is limited. Most policy institutes are run by an intellectual elite, speak to a small, politically educated audience, and have small membership bodies or none at all. Yet, they often claim to act in the public interest. It could be argued that the Australian citizenry is further marginal-

ized from policy debate by think tanks. The majority of the citizenry is a passive recipient of pronouncements that trickle down from experts in think
tanks via the media. As one journalist observed, 'each of these privately
funded research centres has a guiding philosophy, a set of beliefs it wishes to
foist on the community' (Dusevic, 1990). The participation of the individual citizen is further undermined in the absence of participatory structures
within think tanks. The pluralist 'market place of ideas' is not one of open
competition. In claiming superior input to public debate on the basis of the
knowledge they encompass, the expertise and credentials of their staff and
the exclusivity and elitism promoted by the use of technical and theoretical
language, think tanks can mystify policy debate and make it inaccessible to
the ordinary person who lacks professional standing (Jones, 1993: 267). The
'cult of the expert' can undermine the educative and critical functions often
presumed to be the *raison d'être* of think tanks. Think tanks do not necessarily represent a democratization of opinion but can further entrench the
position of intellectual elites.

Conclusion

In the broad scheme of Australian politics, think tanks are small and relatively unimportant organizations. Australian think tanks have not consolidated as a strong policy advice industry to become a recognized part of the
institutional scene as in the USA. They are on the margins not only of
bureaucracy but also of the political parties. To gain greater political, policy
and intellectual credibility, Australian think tanks need to be larger and more
prosperous with regularized channels of access to decision-makers. This is
unlikely with existing institutional constraints – a restrictive taxation system,
minimal corporate philanthropy, the strength of party political policy advice
and the structural dominance of (quasi-) bureaucratic analysis for which
there appears to be a political preference. These factors represent significant
institutional constraints on Australian think tanks and structure the environment in which they operate.

Nevertheless, a number of think tanks are acting strategically as policy
entrepreneurs to spread new ideas and ways of thinking about policy problems. At one level, think tanks target decision-makers and attempt to educate actors within policy networks. At another broader level, they are
engaged in the longer-term enterprise of societal influence on the climate of
opinion via mediums such as the media, educational establishments and
interest groups. In terms of their ability to shape the contours of public
debate and influence agenda setting, the coterie of economic rationalist
think tanks has been important in articulating the policy discourse of the
market that superseded the Keynesian policy paradigm from the mid-1970s

onwards. It has provoked the emergence of other institutes such as Evatt, WETtank and the Australia Institute in an attempt to counteract the influence of economic rationalism. Australian think tanks are sufficiently numerous to represent a new institutional dimension to policy debates. They are also worthy of attention in that their policy entrepreneurship, networking and discursive strategies are designed to distribute policy advice and intellectual arguments within the political system in such a way as to give some actors – who favour a particular world-view or policy paradigm – more power and intellectual credibility than others.

References

Over the period 1990–93, a number of interviews were conducted with executives of Australian think tanks to whom many thanks are extended. They include Peter Botsman, Eva Cox, John Hyde, Greg Lindsay, Alan Moran and Peter Gray. Andrew Norton at CIS and Clive Hamilton at the Australia Institute have also been of considerable assistance in reading earlier versions of this paper. Research for this paper was supported by the Economic and Social Research Council of the UK (Ref. No.: H52427008094).

Argall, Dennis (1990) 'The Role of the Parliamentary Research Service in Advising Members of the Australian Parliament', paper presented to the Conference of the Australasian Political Studies Association, Hobart, 24 September.

Bell, Stephen (1995) 'Between Market and State: the Role of Australian Business Associations in Public Policy', *Comparative Politics*, 28(1): 25–53.

Carey, Alex (1987) 'Conspiracy or Ground Swell', in K. Coghill (ed.), *The New Right's Australian Fantasy*, Ringwood, Victoria, McPhee Gribble/Penguin Books.

CCH Australia Ltd (1992) *1992 Australian Master Tax Guide*, New South Wales, CCH Australia Ltd.

Centre for Independent Studies (n.d.) *The Centre for Independent Studies in brief …* , Sydney, CIS, information and subscription pamphlet.

Committee for the Economic Development of Australia (n.d., *c.* 1995) 'CEDA and Public Policy Formulation', CEDA, mimeo.

Connell, R. W. and Irving, T. H. (1980) *Class Structure in Australian History*, Melbourne, Longman Cheshire.

Dror, Y. (1984) 'Required Breakthroughs in Think Tanks', *Policy Sciences*, 16: 199–225.

Dumais, Max (1995) 'Philanthropic Organizations and Corporate Philanthropy', in Tadashi Yamamoto (ed.), *Emerging Civil Society in the Asia Pacific Community*, Singapore, Japan Center for International Exchange and the Institute for Southeast Asian Studies.

Dusevic, Tom (1990) 'The Idea Factories', *Australian Financial Review*, 25 May, 1–3.

Evatt Foundation (n.d.) *Advancing the Ideals of the Labour Movement*, membership brochure, Sydney, Evatt Foundation.

Fischer, Frank (1991) 'American Think Tanks: Policy Elites and the Politicization of Expertise', *Governance*, 4(3): 332–53.

Hajer, Maarten A. (1993) 'Discourse Coalitions and the Institutionalization of Practice: The Case of Acid Rain in Great Britain', in F. Fischer and J. Forester (eds), *The Argumentative Turn in Policy Analysis and Planning*, London, UCL Press.

Hamilton, Clive (1996) Personal correspondence with Executive Director of the Australia Institute, 30 January 1996.

Hay, J. R. (1982) 'The Institute of Public Affairs and Social Policy in World War Two', *Historical Studies*, 20(79): 198–216.

Hughes, G. (1992) 'The Minds That Shape Australia', *Weekend Australian Review*, 4–5 July, 3.

Jarman, Alan and Kouzmin, Alexander (1993) 'Public Sector Think Tanks in Inter-Agency Policy Making: Designing Enhanced Governance Capacity', *Canadian Public Administration*, 36(4): 499–529.

Jones, Evan (1993) 'Economic Language, Propaganda and Dissent', in S. Rees, G. Rodley and F. Stilwell (eds), *Beyond the Market: Alternatives to Economic Rationalism*, Sydney, Pluto Press.

Kay, J. A. (1989) 'Research and Policy: The IFS Experience', *Policy Studies*, 9(3): 20–6.

Kemp, D. (1988) 'Liberalism and Conservatism in Australia since 1944', in B. Head and J. Walter (eds), *Intellectual Movements and Australian Society*, Melbourne, Oxford University Press.

Lindsay, Greg, interviewed by Greg Norton (1996) 'The CIS at Twenty', *Policy*, 12(2): 16–21.

Lyons, John (1991) 'Think-Tank Commanders', *Sydney Morning Herald*, 9 March, 43.

Marks, Bernard (1988) 'Corporate Finance and Taxation Aspects of Private Funding of Higher Education in Australia', in D. R. Jones, V. L. Meek and J. Anwyl (eds), *Alternative Funding Strategies for Australia's Universities and Colleges*, Melbourne, Centre for the Study of Higher Education.

Marsh, Ian (1980) *An Australian Think Tank?* Sydney, New South Wales University Press Ltd.

Marsh, Ian (1995) 'The Development and Impact of Australia's "Think tanks"', CEDA Information Paper No. 43, February, Melbourne and Sydney, CEDA.

Mathews, Race (1993) *Australia's First Fabians: Middle Class Radicals, Labour Activists and the Early Labour Movement*, Cambridge, Cambridge University Press.

Mead, Margaret (1985) 'A Perspective on Australian Economic Policy – CEDA's Contribution in the Past Twenty-Five Years Through Its Public Education "Communications Bridge" Conferences', in *Problems and Progress: A Book To Mark the 25th Anniversary Founding of CEDA*, Sydney and Melbourne, CEDA.

Millar, T. B. (1976) 'The Role of the Institute', *Australian Outlook*, 30(1): 1–15.

Oliver, Susan (1993) 'Lobby Groups, Think Tanks, the Universities and Media', *Canberra Bulletin of Public Administration*, 75 (December): 134–7.

Parsons, Wayne (1995) *Public Policy: An Introduction to the Theory and Practice of Policy Analysis*, Aldershot, Edward Elgar.

Pusey, Michael (1991) *Economic Rationalism in Canberra: A Nation Building State Changes Its Mind*, Melbourne, Cambridge University Press.

Sawer, Marian (1990) *Public Perceptions of Multiculturalism*, Canberra, Centre for Immigration and Multicultural Studies, Research School of Social Sciences, Australian National University.

Self, Peter (1993) *Government by the Market? The Politics of Public Choice*, London, Macmillan.

Stokes, Geoff (1994) 'Australian Political Thought: Editorial Introduction', in Geoff Stokes (ed.), *Australian Political Ideas*, Sydney, New South Wales University Press Ltd.

Stone, Diane (1996a) *Capturing the Political Imagination: Think Tanks and the Policy Process*, London, Frank Cass.

Stone, Diane (1996b) 'A Think Tank in Evolution or Decline?: The Australian Institute of International Affairs in Comparative Perspective', *The Australian Journal of International Affairs*, 50(2): 117–36.

Tasman Institute (1995) *Annual Review*, Melbourne, Tasman Institute.

Walter, J. (1988) 'Intellectuals and the Political Culture', in B. Head and J. Walter, (eds), *Intellectual Movements and Australian Society*, Melbourne, Oxford University Press.

Weiss, Carol H. (1990) 'The Uneasy Partnership Endures: Social Science and Government', in S. Brooks and A.-G. Gagnon (eds), *Social Scientists, Policy and the State*, New York, Praeger.

Think tanks and intellectual participation in Malaysian discourses of development

Introduction

Malaysian think tanks are a relatively recent phenomenon compared with their Western counterparts, having become a noticeable part of the Malaysian intellectual landscape only since the 1980s. Malaysia's continuing path of accelerated modernization has provided fertile ground for their growth and development. The reforms of the 1980s – embodied by the 'Malaysia Incorporated' slogan – enhanced links between government and industry, providing opportunities for policy entrepreneurs to bridge the public and corporate sectors. This trend has continued with the 'Vision 2020' policy of the 1990s which envisages not only a fully industrialized but also socially and spiritually developed country by the year 2020, thus creating opportunities to elaborate broader areas of social and cultural policy. The economic success of Malaysia and the Asian Pacific region has also furnished Malaysian think tanks with the challenge of building a new national and regional identity which looks towards a leading role in the future global order. The major unanswered question is: do they represent powerful dominant vested interests or are they merely an inevitable but benign consequence of the drive towards progress? By investigating their varying intellectual roles as technocrats, partisans or visionaries, this chapter takes a critical approach to Malaysian think tanks and interprets their emergence in the context of the ongoing struggle to define the agenda for Malaysian national development.

Malaysian think tanks

Malaysian and other East Asian think tanks differ from Western think tanks with respect to the question of organizational independence. The state is far more dominant in East Asia, making direct contact between think tanks and ruling governments a necessary condition for influence. Although all think tanks have to bridge the gap between knowledge and influence, think tank–government connections may be more transparent in East Asia, placing them in a grey area which lies between the private and public sectors.[1] Another difference is that some Malaysian think tanks have strong Islamic orientations and may combine Islamic ideas with secular ones, employing different concepts and terms of reference (Noda, 1995). Malaysian think tanks are active in articulating varieties of the 'Asian Values' discourse, together with 'reverse Orientalist' discourses which run parallel with it. These discourses construct the West as an oppositional category to 'Asia' (Sum, 1996). Asia is seen as the source of intellectual and economic leadership, led by Japan and the other newly industrialized Asian economies. The 'Asian Values' discourse stresses Malaysia's cultural affinity with other East Asian countries. While the exact formulations differ, these commonly include deference to authority, conservative 'family values' and consensualism expressed through a 'polite' discursive culture which avoids open conflict and contradiction. Some include 'respect for learning' and 'hard work' as part of these values.

Ethnicity is a major organizing principle in the Malaysian political system. However, ethnic positions are rarely phrased in an explicit manner, and an uneasy tension exists between support for multi-ethnic pluralism and recognition of Malay–Muslim dominance. Malaysia's ruling political coalition, Barisan Nasional (BN), reflects the dominance of ethnic politics, the main constituent parties being the hegemonic United Malays Nationalist Organisation (UMNO) and its junior partners the Malaysian Chinese Association (MCA) and the Malayan Indian Congress (MIC). These component parties of the ruling coalition have established think tanks to support their particular ethnic agendas, while opposition parties have tended to support non-governmental organizations. The MCA established the Institute of Strategic Analysis and Planning (INSAP) in 1989 to capitalize on the possibility of reforming post-1990 policy, while the MIC announced plans to form a similar think tank in 1995 to address issues relevant to its Indian constituency (*The Sun*, 29 January 1995).

With the exception of the Centre for Policy Research (CPR), Malaysian think tanks fall roughly into two phases of development. In the 1980s, think tanks arose as a response to the economic reforms of 'Malaysia Incorporated'. Malaysian think tanks began to mushroom with a second wave in the 1990s, a phenomenon which is explained by some as the direct result of the policy demands of 'Vision 2020', which combines the technocratic and strategic needs of accelerated industrialization with attempts to build a wider social consensus (Noda, 1995: 410). In 1993 it was estimated that there were 26 institutions pretending to the title of 'think tank' (*Asiaweek*, 15 September 1993). This chapter examines only a proportion of the institutions which are engaged in the production of policy, ideology and plans, and which have some degree of organizational independence. The Malaysian think tanks examined here are elite organizations which derive their influence from their connections with government, political parties, or political figures. University institutions are not included, with the exception of the CPR at the University of Science, Malaysia.

Set up in the 1980s, the Institute of Strategic and International Studies (ISIS), the Malaysian Institute of Economic Research (MIER) and the Institute of Development Studies (IDS), Sabah, are the more established think tanks employing a substantial core of full-time policy researchers (see Table 8.1). The others are smaller, although the Institut Kajian Dasar (IKD), Institute for Policy Studies and the Malaysian Strategic Research Centre (MSRC) have recently become highly visible as players on the national conference circuit. To some extent, a 'revolving door' exists between these larger think tanks, bureaucratic planning agencies and academia. Think tank staff move relatively easily into *ad hoc* committees and panels which are an important site of innovation within the central policy-making machinery, and staff may be seconded from one institution to another.

ISIS is the dominant think tank in Malaysia for several reasons. It is considered to be the most prestigious think tank, being the best funded and with the highest political connections. ISIS covers the widest policy area and it has served as both an organizational model and a training ground for emerging think tanks, thus earning itself the title of 'grandfather of think tanks in Malaysia' (*The Sun*, 30 March 1995). Policy entrepreneurs in Malaysia have learned from ISIS experience, recruiting ex-ISIS staff and learning the ISIS model through placements and fellowships offered by ISIS. Malaysian think tanks have adopted the ISIS model in establishing themselves as independent, non-profit companies, limited by guarantee. Establishment under company law allows think tanks to enjoy greater freedom than under the alternative legislation, the Societies Act (1966, amended 1983).

ISIS, MIER, IDS and the Institut Kefahaman Islam Malaysia (IKIM, Institute for Islamic Understanding) are partly government-funded through endowments of varying sizes. ISIS received RM$ 20 million, while the MIER's endowment from the Treasury was RM$ 2 million.[2] IKIM also received an endowment from the central government, while IDS is funded by the Sabah state government. Unlike ISIS, over half of MIER's endowment came from the private sector. Most of the larger think tanks depend on commissioned research and project-based grants for a major proportion of their funding, but MIER is unique in deriving significant revenue from membership fees and the sale of information to members. Other institutes are funded in a less transparent manner and smaller institutes such as IKD or the Institute of Mind Analysis (INMIND) are likely to depend on politically connected private sector benefactors. All think tanks also depend on funding

Table 8.1 Malaysian think tanks

Institution	Est.	By	Staff	Location	Main funding sources	Policy focus
Centre for Policy Research (CPR)	1974	University of Science	13	Penang	University Research and Development funds, contract research	Social policy, rural and regional development
Institute for Strategic and International Studies (ISIS)	1983	Mahathir Cabinet	50	Kuala Lumpur	Govt endowment, contract research, international organizations	All areas of national development policy. Second track diplomacy
Institute of Development Studies, Sabah (IDS)	1985	Sabah state govt	100	Kota Kinabalu	State govt grants, contract research, international organizations	State development policy, rural and regional development
Institute for Policy Studies (Institut Kajian Dasar, IKD)	1985	Anwar Ibrahim	20	Kuala Lumpur	Private sector sponsorship, seminars and conferences, international organizations	Social policy: culture, labour and youth affairs, Islamic development
Malaysian Institute of Economic research (MIER)	1986	COMIT	32	Kuala Lumpur	Govt endowment, private sector endowment, contract research, membership, international organizations	Economic research and forecasting
Institute of Strategic Analysis and Planning (INSAP)	1989	Malaysian Chinese Association	20	Kuala Lumpur	MCA Secretariat	Post-1990 policy liberalization, MCA strategy
Institute of Islamic Understanding (Institut Kefahaman Islam, IKIM)	1992	Mahathir Cabinet	49	Kuala Lumpur	Govt endowment, contract research	Islamic affairs
Malaysian Strategic Research Centre (MSRC)	1993	Najib Razak	8	Kuala Lumpur	Razak Foundation, international organizations	Strategic issues: defence, labour
Institute of Mind Analysis (INMIND)	1994	Selangor Chief Minister	7	Kuala Lumpur	Private sector benefactors, conferences	State economic strategy, information technology, financial and human resource planning, Islamic issues
Sarawak Development Institute (SDI)	1995	Sarawak State govt	n.a.	Kuching	State govt grant	State development issues

from international bodies for specific projects, notably the Canadian International Development Agency (CIDA) and German foundations such as the Konrad Adenauer Foundation.

INMIND, IDS and the Sarawak Development Institute (SDI) are state-based think tanks. While these think tanks can be viewed simply as providers of intellectual resources to individual states in competition with other states and the federal government, they also reflect the central role of Chief Ministers as power-dispensers in each of Malaysia's 13 states. INMIND is closely connected to the current Chief Minister of the state of Selangor, Muhammad Muhammed Taib, who took over a small non-governmental organization (NGO) involved in community welfare development and relaunched it as a think tank in 1994 'to channel and provide inputs towards achieving the objectives of Vision 2020 … for the State of Selangor' (INMIND press pack, n.d.). The Chief Ministers of Johor and Penang announced plans to set up think tanks in 1995, while the shadow chief minister of Kelantan also announced plans to set up a 'research panel' to improve the ruling BN coalition's position against the Parti Islam Se-Malaysia (PAS) in the only opposition-controlled state in Malaysia (*New Straits Times*, 2 May and 21 December, 1995).

Changes in leadership and policy direction have provided different opportunities and constraints for think tanks in their varying intellectual roles as technocrats, partisans or visionaries. The next section locates think tanks within the context of national development thinking, reflecting changing political leadership and the fluctuating balance of power at local, national and regional levels. To understand these complex dynamics, it is helpful to divide the historical background to think tanks into three phases, beginning with the New Economic Policy (NEP) of the 1970s, and followed by the era of Mahathirism in the 1980s. The 1990s represent a shift in political culture, a widened development agenda and, to some extent, a new and more hegemonic role for Malaysian think tanks.

The New Economic Policy and the preconditions for think tanks

A number of factors predating the rise of Malaysian think tanks contributed to their later development. The first of these factors was the New Economic Policy (NEP). Following ethnic riots in 1969, the Malaysian government introduced measures to meet Malay political demands. Multilateral political consultation came to be largely replaced with a closed system based on the judgement of the Prime Minister. The legitimacy of the government began to depend on legal measures restricting civil liberties and 'government processes became cloaked with obsessive secrecy' (Means, 1991: 112).

A State of Emergency was declared following the 1969 riots, enabling policy decisions to be made behind closed doors by a National Consultative Council which was appointed by the Prime Minister, Tun Abdul Razak (Means, 1991). In addition, Razak also began to draw upon informal advice from sources outside the government (*The Sun*, 30 March 1995). The Constitution was amended in 1971 to restrict the open debate of 'sensitive issues', and stringent laws were employed to regulate freedom of speech and public participation in the political process.[3] Intellectual participation in universities, a key site of public mobilization in the late 1960s and early 1970s, was also curbed by a draconian new law, the University and University Colleges Act (1971, amended 1975) (Means, 1991; Kahn and Loh, 1992). Key features of public policy, including the system of preferences for ethnic Malays, were thus removed from public discussion and an atmosphere of censorship and self-censorship prevailed.

The NEP era brought wide-ranging economic and social initiatives by the state, with two policy 'prongs' of (1) eradicating poverty and (2) restructuring patterns of education, employment and ownership of capital. It also involved increasing Malay ownership and control in the economy and the creation of a Malay middle class of professionals and entrepreneurs. Another important feature of NEP intervention was the rise of 'money politics' with the convergence of business and politics, a phenomenon characteristic of the 'developmental state' (Jesudason, 1989; Jomo, 1988). In order to realize the aims of the NEP, the Malay economic nationalists of the Razak government established semi-autonomous public enterprises or 'trust agencies'. Political and economic objectives were intertwined in the operation of these corporations and their affiliated companies, reflecting the twin aims of the NEP, which were to transfer corporate equity to *bumiputera* ownership (Malays and other indigenous people); and to provide training and employment for the new cohort of *bumiputera* technocrats. Political parties also became directly involved in corporate business, ostensibly on behalf of the ethnic communities they claimed to represent, paving the way for the present political-corporate complex in Malaysia. Mehmet (1988) and Gomez (1990) have shown that the deployment of trust agencies and the direct involvement of the ruling political parties in business led to the dominance of money politics and further concentration of corporate power in the hands of small cliques of politically connected elites. Business and political competition have converged with intra-party struggles and leadership contests, particularly within UMNO.

The analytical distinction between government and an autonomous private sector is thus problematic in the Malaysian case. The corporate sector is dominated by politically connected oligopolies, and power is best understood as lying within politically linked 'distributional coalitions', which are 'small, powerful and influential groups, organized as cartels, seeking rewards

through collusion, transaction costs and other forms of non-competitive bar-
gains' (Mehmet, 1988: 135). These distributional coalitions cannot be
directly equated with the discourse coalitions in which think tanks are key
players, but it is relevant to attempt to establish the degree to which these
two formations concur and overlap.

The Centre for Policy Research

Given the context of tightening security and greater restrictions on intellectual freedom, it was not surprising that few new organizations were formal-
ized in the 1970s. However, in 1974 CPR was established at the University
of Science, Malaysia. CPR was an academic institution aimed exclusively at
policy-oriented research to service the needs of local and national government agencies, which were undergoing expansion to meet the requirements
of the NEP. The CPR research programme was more oriented towards the
first NEP policy prong of 'eradicating poverty' by targeting poor and marginalized groups. CPR produced seminal research on poverty and income
distribution, giving special emphasis to agrarian regions and issues. A major
impetus behind the establishment of CPR was the concern that local expertise should be developed and employed, as development policy and planning
had up to the early 1970s relied heavily on foreign expertise.[4] On a more
general level, limited primary research had been conducted at the time, and
policy planning was relatively undeveloped. As the 1970s progressed, planning and policy divisions proliferated within the government and competition and replication began to characterize government policy-making. CPR's
research priorities fitted the 1970s development agenda under Razak's premiership, which was dominated by the discourses of redistribution and rural
development. By the 1980s, CPR's research strengths had become over-
shadowed by new concerns of strategic industrialization and growth, and a
new generation of policy entrepreneurs – the Mahathirist think tanks –
arose.

Mahathirist transformations

The Mahathir administration which took over the government in 1982 consolidated the political-corporate complex of the 1970s, but also ushered in
significant changes. The trend towards authoritarianism continued, while
the independent administrative role of the bureaucracy was increasingly
replaced by the corporate agendas of a heavily politicized private sector.
Jomo (1990) and Khoo (1995) note that more than any previous leader,
Mahathir drove policy-making with his own personal vision of transforming
Malaysia into a newly industrialized economy. He called for the country to

'Look East' and used the slogan 'Malaysia Incorporated' to mark greater complementarity between government and the private sector. Thus Almeida and Wong (1991: 7) observe:

> Think tanks were shaped by the new thinking in the country in the first half of the 1980s. The Mahathir Administration came into office in 1982 and not long after introduced a programme of 'radical' reforms. Among them are three which, we argue, directly influence the thinking about think tanks. These are a wider role for the private sector; the need for a smaller, more efficient civil service; and the additional need for a close working relationship between the private and public sectors. [the concept of 'Malaysia Inc.'] (1991: 7)

The think tanks of the 1980s embodied and contributed towards the 'Malaysia Incorporated' discourse, which promoted the open alliance of political power and corporate capital, and shifted the emphasis from the public to the private sector as the main motive force. The phenomenon of politics in business also entered a more active phase as Mahathir continued to advocate the development of Malay capitalism through political patronage channelled to key individual compradors and their associates. The reformist and deregulating role of think tanks have thus also to be seen in the Malaysian context of the neo-liberal 'Malaysia Inc.' formations and the ever-present 'distributional coalitions' in which government, corporate and individual interests have converged.

This is not to say that Malaysian think tanks only represent concerted and self-interested actions by the political-business elites. All think tanks subscribe to the idea of public-spiritedness, which is in itself a major distinguishing feature of think tanks (Stone, 1996: 15). The policy, ideology and plans produced by Malaysian think tanks may be public-spirited and, if implemented, result in progressive changes. Individual think tank directors and staff may be motivated by a wish to change the country for the better by 'reforming from within'. Nevertheless, the contention here is that the Mahathirist Malaysian think tanks such as ISIS, MIER, IKIM and post-1994 IDS have formed an important part of the machinery propagating the ideological hegemony of capitalism (for comparison see Alpert and Markusen, 1980: 174), but capitalism in a heavily politicized local form.

Islamic discourses entered the national mainstream in the 1980s. Recognizing that Islam had begun to emerge as a powerful potential force for political opposition, Mahathir successfully reclaimed the moral high ground for the Barisan government in 1982 by co-opting the charismatic leader of the ABIM, the Muslim Youth Movement (Angkatan Belia Islam Malaysia), Anwar Ibrahim, into his government. Mahathir and Anwar subsequently embarked on a massive Islamization drive, creating a powerful source of Islamic discourse at the national level. This entailed the expansion and centralization of Islamic affairs departments within the bureaucracy, and building prestigious institutions such as the International Islamic University and Lembaga Urusan Tabung Haji (LUTH Islamic Bank and Pilgrims Savings Fund) to support a moderate, reformist and pro-capitalist Islamic identity. However, the 'mainstreaming' of Islam appears to have been a two-way process. While Mahathir has built a governmental Islamic agenda through the co-option of Anwar and the 'assimilation' of Islamic ideas, that very co-option has led to the introduction of new ideas which have subtly, but profoundly, 'Islamized' the discourse of modernization in Malaysia.

The Institute of Strategic and International Studies: bypassing the bureaucracy

Mahathir's desire to bypass and downsize the bureaucracy was a major reason underlying the founding of ISIS.[5] It is no secret that Mahathir disliked the bureaucracy and was actively seeking ways to short-circuit the bureaucratic chain of command and to employ alternatives (Khoo, 1995: 129–30). Following a decade of bureaucratic expansion and vastly increased government spending under the NEP, the inefficiency of the Malaysian public sector had become an increasing burden by the 1980s, exacerbated by the dual problems of plummeting commodity prices and growing foreign debt. The major influence behind Mahathir's economic reforms was Daim Zainuddin. Daim was Finance Minister between 1984 and 1991, and was strongly associated with reforms which aimed to run Malaysia less like a government and more like a corporation. Daim initiated ISIS's first commission to come up with measures to slim down the civil service, thus bypassing the vested interests of the bureaucracy itself. An independent policy institute provided more flexibility for the Mahathir administration, providing opportunities to consider innovative inputs from 'outside', while allowing the key players (effectively the Prime Minister and his close associates) to retain complete autonomy over decision-making (Almeida and Wong, 1991: 17).

The institutional structure of ISIS clearly reflects a government-oriented, but independent, position. Mahathir was responsible for instigating ISIS, and appointed its first Chairman and half of its Board of Directors. The seniority of the appointed members demonstrates ISIS's influential position: these include the head of the military and holders of key cabinet positions: the Minister of Finance, the heads of the Prime Minister's research department and the Implementation and Co-ordination Unit, and the Ministers of Home and Foreign Affairs. However, despite these strong governmental linkages, ISIS derives a degree of independence from its funding and organizational structure, and from the seniority and intellectual standing of its Director-General, Noordin Sopiee. ISIS staff feel freer to make independent recommendations in comparison to civil servants or academics. Noordin maintains that intellectual independence is an important factor and considers ISIS to be 'revolutionary ... beyond the clutches of the civil service' and 'independent of civil service intrigue', having 'tremendous independence to come up with ideas':[6] 'We believe that our duty demands that we be objective and independent. We serve no function and we do not serve the country if we merely declaim the accepted conventional wisdoms and parrot the current orthodoxy' (*New Straits Times*, 19 January 1996).

ISIS research agenda rests largely with Noordin, who plays a strong personal role and works closely with the Prime Minister to develop policy positions, platforms and speeches. At a more devolved level, ISIS research staff work in a number of different bureaux, carrying out commissioned research which is less directly political and more technocratic. Domestically, ISIS has been a source of policy innovation through the promotion of ideas such as 'Caring Society' and especially the 'Vision 2020' agenda which has become the ubiquitous reference point for all official and unofficial policy discussion since Mahathir's launch of the concept in 1991.[7] Furthermore, it is likely that Noordin has influenced Malaysia's move towards a more conspicuous role in the Commonwealth. ISIS played a key role in persuading Mahathir not to withdraw Malaysia from the Commonwealth in 1987, and in Malaysia's subsequent positioning in the international community as a 'middle power' leader of small Southern nations. ISIS also functions as a kind of secretariat for the World Bank, co-ordinating and hosting World Bank seminars and workshops.

In the regional context of the Association of Southeast Asian Nations (ASEAN), regional integration has traditionally relied on tripartite bodies of business leaders, academics and public servants. ISIS has clearly established itself as the key national body engaged in this second track diplomacy (Camroux, 1994: 423). ISIS co-ordinates the major regional think tank network uniting the ASEAN think tanks – ASEAN-ISIS – which hosts the largest annual regional dialogue event, the Asia-Pacific Roundtable. ISIS also acted as the secretariat for the Council for Security Co-operation in Asia-Pacific (CSCAP) and Noordin has been the key Malaysian player involved in the articulation of the EAEG/EAEC concept (East Asian Economic Grouping/East Asian Economic Caucus). He has also been active in the drive to create and promote the Asia-consciousness which now informs the thinking of regional policy elites. He was the Convenor of the Commission for a New Asia, an elite group of 16 visionaries with the mission of creating a manifesto for an Asian Renaissance, a kind of '2020 Vision for Asia'.

The Malaysian Institute of Economic Research: an expression of 'Malaysia Incorporated'

MIER was formed in 1986 by the government and the private sector together, following an idea first mooted by the Prime Minister's Economic

Panel and later promoted by the Council on Malaysian Invisible Trade. Established by the former Vice-Chancellor of the University of Science, Dr Kamal Salih, MIER is a technocratic institution which embodies the discourse of 'Malaysia Incorporated'. MIER's policy role reflects the devolution of economic policy to the corporate sector, as the 'engine of growth'. MIER's sources of influence are bureaucratic and technocratic, rather than political. Its links to influence lie with the Treasury and the Central Bank (Bank Negara). Indeed, it is housed in the same building as the latter. It effectively demonstrates what its present Executive Director and former Ministry of Finance official, Dr Sulaiman Mahbob, calls a 'bridging role', connecting business, academic and governmental sectors through its research programme, seminars, conferences and publications, while providing an independent source of analysis and information.

MIER appears to play an economically strategic rather than politically visionary role. In this regard, MIER resembles the Taiwanese governmental research institute, the Taiwan Institute of Economic Research (TIER), which had in turn copied the Japanese model of combining the resources of business, government and academia to solve national economic problems (Anon, 1991: 30–5). MIER openly acknowledges the duality of the Institute's private and public sector constituencies, but integrated in its purpose in the sense of 'Malaysia Incorporated'. It sees its role in terms of facilitating harmonization between the state, the corporate sector and the public interest. The companies represented in MIER's private sector-government nexus are the large companies and conglomerates which are able to employ macroeconomic information and forecasting to their strategic advantage. MIER runs an independent 'Malaysian Economic Database' and produces economic forecast reports, surveys of business conditions and consumer sentiment and monthly economic bulletins. This information is provided to individual and corporate members on a commercial subscription basis. MIER is perhaps the premier provider of independent data and analysis on economic conditions and trends. Its activities show that 'Malaysia Inc.' may lead to greater interdependence between government and the private sector (see, for comparison, Weiss, 1995), but may also conversely provide greater independence for large corporations. Its output is both complementary and an alternative to governmental policy, providing information at shorter intervals than official sources (quarterly and annually, whereas the government's Economic Planning Unit produces figures every two-and-a half to five years). It demonstrates independence in its analysis and forecasts, which may vary from the official figures and opinions. Notable divergences have been MIER's preference for lower growth rates than current governmental policy and its concern with inflation; it may have influenced the governmental campaign since 1995 for 'zero inflation'.

The Institute of Development Studies, Sabah: state struggles with federal hegemony

IDS serves the state of Sabah in East Malaysia. The history of IDS is illustrative not only of the link between think tanks and power in Malaysia but also of Sabah's problematic position in the Malaysian federation which has resulted in changing agendas for IDS. IDS was established in 1985 as the Institute for Public Policy and Analysis by Jeffrey Kitingan, brother of Pairin Kitingan, then Chief Minister of Sabah. Renamed IDS in 1986, the think tank functioned from 1987 to 1994 as part of a wider initiative to restructure state government and state policy following the take-over of the state by the Parti Bersatu Sabah (PBS, United Sabah Party), with the aim of increasing state autonomy.

The inclusion of Sabah into the Federation of Malaysia in 1963 incurred considerable opposition from non-Malay elites who supported the idea of self-rule for the state. Federation was secured by an informal agreement, according Sabah a greater level of autonomy within the federation. However, from the 1960s until 1985, this notional autonomy was largely eroded by the efforts of the federal government to 'integrate' Sabah into the federation (Loh, 1992: 225). In the 1985 state elections, the opposition PBS won a surprise victory over the federal government. PBS sought to restructure the Sabah Foundation, a powerful quasi-governmental organization conceived as a non-political and non-profit instrument to channel the fruits of development to indigenous Sabahans, but which had in reality become a powerful, state-level body brokering money politics (Ansari, 1977). In 1987, Jeffrey Kitingan spearheaded the restructuring of the foundation and by 1988 it had been transformed into an organization promoting an alternative development programme called 'People Development' (Kitingan, 1987). This programme was rooted in a popular and charismatic social movement which emphasized self-reliant, human resource-based and participative models of rural development.

Despite the PBS joining the ruling BN coalition in 1986, federal–state relations remained chilly (Loh, 1996). The PBS attempts to retrieve greater autonomy and fiscal independence for Sabah were seen as a threat by federal authorities. The PBS leadership was denounced for 'fanning parochial sentiments' and being 'anti-federal'. The PBS incurred the full ire of the Mahathir government when it withdrew from the BN ruling coalition to join the challenging Gagasan Rakyat coalition in the 1990 election. In 1991, Jeffrey Kitingan was detained by the federal government on charges of inciting secessionism; his successor at IDS, Dr Maximus Ongkili, another PBS stalwart, was also subsequently arrested. Kitingan's orientation appears to have changed during his detention and he began to diverge from the PBS stance led by his brother, Pairin, moving instead to develop the 'New Sabah' (Sabah

Baru) concept. The 'New Sabah' policy discourse represented an integrationist view of Sabah–Federal government relations and an abandonment of the principle of Sabahan autonomy. By 1991, the federal government was bypassing the state government in allocating development funds, effectively starving the PBS administration of development funds (Loh, 1996). Hence, through a combination of carrot and stick manoeuvres, the federal authorities were able to undermine PBS support and build up an alternative federalist power base.

The PBS lost its hold on Sabah in 1994. The new federalist BN rule ushered in 'New Sabah' as the dominant policy paradigm with the promise of economic rejuvenation and a special development allocation of RM$ 500 million for the state. Since the change of government, the agenda of the IDS has changed from supporting the PBS to supporting the BN. Its role has shifted towards the promotion of integration and to introduce a 'paradigm shift' for Sabah state development. IDS has jointly produced the strategic planning document, the 'Outline Perspective Plan Sabah 1995–2010', together with the State Department for Development. This is to bring Sabah into line with the mainstream Peninsular model of economic development, aiming to push the state along a development trajectory of rapid economic expansion in accordance with the national strategy mapped out by 'Vision 2020'.

However, IDS remains different from the mainstream Mahathirist think tanks in one sense. It continues to engage in advocacy work for poor and marginalized groups in the mould of 'people development'. Its present head, Dr Yaakub Johari, maintains a continuity between the 'old' and 'new' paradigms of development and the institute continues to build expertise in fields of development communication and applied rural development. IDS continues to network effectively with non-governmental organizations (NGOs) involved in participatory development, including the Commonwealth Association for Local Action and Economic Development, a Commonwealth-wide NGO umbrella which supports local organizations involved in people-centred development. It plays an active role as a member of the Association for Development Research and Training Institutes for the Asia-Pacific (ADIPA), and maintains links with the Asia-Pacific Development Centre, a joint-venture set up by Asian-Pacific governments and NGOs. This network of activities essentially represents quite a different view of 'development from below'.

The MCA Task Force and the Institute of Strategic Analysis and Planning

INSAP is a party think tank established in 1989 by the leading Chinese component of the ruling BN coalition, the MCA. INSAP developed out of the

MCA Special Task Force, which was formed around 1988, pending the expiry of the NEP in 1990. INSAP has no permanent staff, relying on honorary members, mainly corporate figures, politicians and academics. In 1988, a wider consultative body, the National Economic Consultative Committee (NECC), had been formed to put forward policy proposals for the post-NEP era. The NECC committee brought together over 150 political, academic and non-governmental representatives from all ethnic groups to produce a 461-page report. As representatives of the MCA within NECC consultations, the MCA Special Task Force reflected the broad objectives of the MCA: to influence post-NEP policy towards greater ethnic as well as economic liberalization and to represent MCA-led Chinese business interests. The Special Task Force, and later INSAP, were headed by Yong Poh Kon, a successful Chinese entrepreneur. The Special Task Force produced a report which broadly reflected middle-class, non-Malay frustrations with the NEP, though it tactfully restricted itself to criticisms about implementation, rather than questioning the legitimacy of the NEP itself, and suggested that greater emphasis should be given to growth rather than redistribution.

The NECC report largely echoed the MCA Special Task Force. Both expressed views that were already present in mainstream policies since the mid-1980s, and the NECC report should have represented the major consultative document leading towards post-1990 policy. However, it was largely ignored by Mahathir. Yet, Jomo (1994) suggests that it may have influenced the Vision 2020 agenda which was subsequently developed with the help of ISIS and launched in 1991 to become the keynote for Malaysian development in the 1990s. INSAP, like the MCA Special Task Force which preceded it, is unable to gain much influence outside the MCA. It was also criticized for basing its advice on 'feel' rather than on empirical research.[8] As a party, the MCA is constrained by its junior position in the Barisan coalition and the political necessity of avoiding UMNO's displeasure. While Mahathir agreed to the NECC as a 'sop' to the MCA, he may have never meant to take it seriously (Jomo, 1994: 29). INSAP's influence thus reflects the limitations of the MCA leadership which, in turn, depends largely on the degree to which UMNO leaders are prepared to compromise.

The 1990s

The involvement between think tanks and politicians has become more apparent in the 1990s as leadership contests and more sophisticated campaigning methods have emerged. Since the 1980s, there has been a shift from inter-party competition towards intra-party struggles for leadership positions within the ruling party, UMNO (Means, 1991). Power has also continued to move upwards, concentrating in key officers in the dominant

UMNO, and especially in the person of the Prime Minister. Thus many 1990s think tanks need to be understood in relation to leadership contests between candidates for top posts in UMNO. For example, IKD is linked with the Deputy Prime Minister, Anwar Ibrahim, while MSRC is connected to the present Education Minister and contender for Deputy Prime Ministership, Najib Razak.

The 1990s represent a different policy environment from the Malaysia of the 1980s. Consistent economic growth of over 7 per cent per annum since 1987 and a highly appealing platform built on Mahathir's 'Vision 2020' have boosted the legitimacy and popularity of the Mahathir government, which returned to power in 1995 with a landslide victory, winning 85 per cent of the seats and 65 per cent of the vote (*New Straits Times*, 27 April 1996). In economic terms, the policy changes of the 1990s are simply a consolidation of Mahathir's reforms since the mid-1980s. In other ways, the 1990s have signalled a shift towards a more subtle form of hegemony building based on positive messages and the populist 'Vision 2020'. Strategic economic development is equated with the new project of nation-building which is expressed in positive and optimistic terms.[9]

It is within this context that new discourses such as 'New Asia', 'Asian Renaissance' and 'Pacific Century' have emerged. Think tanks have been instrumental in popularizing these new frames of reference for Malaysian development. In general, Malaysian think tanks have been key actors promoting the ideas of 'new Asian intellectuals' within the regional and international policy community. Malaysian political discourse in the mid-1990s reflects a more liberal tone, referring to 'civil society' and a 'new era in politics', as embodied by a new generation of younger, media-aware politicians with a less local-ethnic and more global outlook. A media boom has also taken place, with broadcast and print media playing a major role in constructing new state hegemonies, and information technology seems set to join in the articulation of the new modernist and technocratic, but distinctively 'Asian', vision which refers to both Islamic and East Asian culture.

The Institute for Islamic Understanding: the modernist Islamic platform

Influenced by, and responding to, the policy direction set by the '2020 Vision', the think tanks of the 1990s have been created not only to influence policy insiders, but also to mould and shape public opinion on a larger scale. Mahathir's Islamization drive has reached a new level in the 1990s with the establishment of IKIM. IKIM was established to influence public opinion through highly visible public platforms and the mass media. IKIM promotes a Malaysian identity which is at once modern, technocratic and multicultural, yet asserting the dominant position of Islam in a moderate fashion.

IKIM places a major emphasis on the 'image correction of Islam' (*Asiaweek*, 15 September 1995). It does not see itself as an 'Islamic institute based on religious knowledge', but as 'a policy-oriented group, looking at policy from an Islamic point of view'.[10] The academic research at the IKIM thus seeks to promote the idea of Islam's compatibility with the Mahathirist vision of accelerated industrialization.

IKIM reaches two distinct audiences: an international audience of intellectuals, academics and opinion-makers, and the Malaysian general public. IKIM's international role appears to be part of a wider move by Malaysia to position itself as a key player in the global Islamic discourse, promoting a reformist and 'positive Islamic world-view' whilst propagating Islam as part of a nation-building agenda. IKIM is putting itself forward for a future international role, anticipating a global shift in the centre of Islamic thought away from the Middle East and towards Southeast Asia. IKIM's scholarly network includes links with other international organizations like the International Institute of Islamic Thought in Washington DC, and similar institutions in Britain, Turkey, Australia and Japan. IKIM's moderate and pluralist approach emphasizes 'interface dialogues' and it has taken part in international interfaith events such as the 'Seminar of Christians and Muslims in Southeast Asia' and the 1994 'Parliament of World Religions' in Chicago. IKIM has had some success in its quest to become an authority on Islamic issues for the West, as it has been approached by European Union and Scandinavian governments for advice on Muslim minorities and the promotion of religious tolerance.

On the domestic front, IKIM makes extensive use of the local print and broadcast media in order to promote its local Malaysian Islamic agenda. It aims to garner greater acceptance of Islam from Malaysia's non-Muslims (who form 45 per cent of the population), and to show that Muslims are 'good role models'. IKIM attempts to educate and influence the public through regular columns in the Malaysian press: weekly in *The Star*, and fortnightly in the *New Straits Times* (the two leading English dailies), a translated article in the Chinese-language *Shin-min Daily News* and weekly columns in the Malay *Utusan Melayu* and *Berita Mingguan*. On television, it has a monthly programme on a government channel, RTM1, and a weekly appearance on the morning magazine programme *Selamat Pagi Malaysia* on the independent but UMNO-linked channel TV3. IKIM is an impressive manifestation of the Mahathir administration's efforts to domesticate and modernize the forces of Islam, and an illustration of the intellectual positioning that is afforded by Malaysia's economic growth. The patronage of both Mahathir and Anwar ensures a high profile, while its plush premises emphasize the resources available to develop Islamic ideas which are strategic to the mainstream vision of national development.

The Institute of Policy Studies: the Anwarist agenda

IKD represents a different intellectual heritage, a different agenda and different focus from the mainstream think tanks of the Mahathirist regime.
Until Anwar's rise to power in 1993, IKD employed an alternative conception and strategy of intellectual participation; one based on Islamic activism
rather than the agendas of the state-led elite policy networks. Established by
Anwar Ibrahim in 1985, and chaired by Anwar's political secretary and
speechwriter, Kamaruddin Jaafar, IKD was conceived as an activist institute
to conduct training programmes for youth and workers. It is instructive to
look at the other Islamic reformist institutions that have been set up under
Anwar's leadership, as IKD was part of this network: ABIM, the private
charitable educational foundation Yayasan Anda, and Islamic business co-
operatives. Their intellectual tradition reflected a concern with the inade-
quacies of existing models of development and a desire to elaborate a
modernist Islamic model. Islamic modernism emphasizes human development (*pembinaan insan*), giving importance to 'spiritual, moral and ethical
considerations, on which religious belief and the principles of development
are based' (IKD, 1995). A key feature of IKD and the Anwarist agenda was
the emphasis given to knowledge through the concept of *budaya ilmu*, or
'knowledge culture'. This approach to intellectual participation is more
'organically' intellectual than top-down technocratic. In line with the participative NGO ethos, it aims to widen intellectual participation, targeting
not only policy elites, but also middle-level public servants, junior managers,
shop-floor workers and students in higher education.

IKD's profile has changed since Anwar's ascendancy as heir apparent to
the Prime Ministership in 1993. By 1994–95, IKD had raised its public profile to become a mainstream and elite think tank by re-presenting itself as 'a
respectable research organization'.[11] In this respect it has begun to both compete and co-operate with other major think tanks. IKD has begun to employ
research staff to develop policy research programmes in the areas of social
and cultural policy. However, it is on the national seminar circuit that it has
gained most visibility. In 1995, IKD organized a major national seminar on
the theme of voluntarism in conjunction with the Ministry for Youth and
Sports, and a flamboyant seminar on the Filipino nationalist Jose Rizal as
part of the wider theme of 'Asian Renaissance'. Attended by heads of state,
diplomats, academics and politicians, they indicated a new, higher level of
official participation and co-operation at the national and regional levels.
The event also reflected the introduction of the 'Asian Renaissance' idea as a
theme in Anwar Ibrahim's personal political platform, through a public
event largely sponsored by private business.

IKD now reflects a mode of intellectual participation which is part academic, part political mainstream and part non-mainstream activism. Its activist

legacy connects it to youth organizations, especially the major national umbrella organization, the Malaysian Youth Council (Majlis Belia Malaysia) which represents some 2,410 organizations. It also reaches a wide section of mainly Malay civil society through its youth training programmes. The IKD position is structurally similar to that of IDS, linking the dominant policy mainstream with alternative paradigms of development. IKD and IDS continue to provide links between two spheres of participation: the NGO-grassroots constellation and the technocratic mainstream which is allied to dominant political figures and to state power. Both institutions have also shifted into the mainstream of political power, whereas their sphere of influence previously lay outside it. Finally, both institutions are networked to wider national and regional non-governmental organizations and maintain an involvement with grassroots activities.

Conclusion: Malaysian think tanks and the New Asia

There are two distinct intellectual trends underlying think tank activity in contemporary Malaysia. The first of these trends is towards the dominance of conservative mainstream agendas of deregulation and strategic economic development, represented by Malaysia's reforms of the 1980s. The role of Malaysian think tanks reflects a global consensus-building along neo-liberal lines, albeit an Asian variant that supports semi-authoritarian government control. The Malaysian mainstream conceives of development as being the convergence of economic and political goals along the lines of 'Malaysia Incorporated'. Malaysian think tanks are involved in creating a general climate of opinion through the propagation of ideas about 'New Asia' and 'Asian Renaissance'. They have joined other Asian think tanks to articulate a distinctly 'Asian' discourse within broader regional and global policy networks. The broad characteristic of this discourse is an elite-driven, conservative interpretation of democracy which strongly privileges collective priorities over individual freedoms, emphasizing 'family values' and enforcing respect for authority. Consensus is valued in decision-making, but this is clearly consensus with an authoritarian cast.

Think tanks such as ISIS, MIER and IKIM have emerged to service both the political and the technocratic needs of the central Mahathir administration, but other institutes have also represented internal power struggles and alternative or challenging positions to the Mahathir regime. However, the current consolidation of hegemony for the Mahathir/Anwar regime has meant that intellectual alternatives such as Islamic development and 'People Development' tend to be 'mainstreamed' or co-opted. On the whole, Malaysian think tanks help to preserve the political success of the present administration, together with the economic success of its compradors.

Despite this, think tanks such as IKD and IDS have retained elements of their distinctive alternative intellectual traditions, which may be boosted by the current boom in NGO activity (Yamamoto, 1995).

Second, leadership succession is likely to provide the greatest source of immediate change for think tanks, as already demonstrated by the transformation of IDS and IKD. Hence, the subtle differences between the new discourses of 'New Asia' and 'Asian Renaissance' can be seen in a different light when they are linked to different think tanks and the changing positions of their political 'owners'. There is a contrast between Mahathir's open authoritarianism and his likely heir Anwar's more populist approach to 'civil society'. Anwar's background in NGO movements and his support for civil society concerns may ensure the survival of alternative trends of 'people development'. The rise of another new generation in politics embodied by Anwar and his cadres may allow non-elite elements to enter the mainstream, giving national development a more populist twist. Concern with issues of rural development, poverty and participation may yet be harmonized with dominant goals of growth and industrialization. While influential think tanks with genuinely visionary leaders such as ISIS play the key role in the envisioning exercise, think tanks such as IDS and IKD may be best placed to build genuine synergies between government, the non-governmental sector and the people who are ostensibly the objects of development. This is because they have been straddling, perhaps with some difficulty, elite and non-elite conceptions of development policy and practice. Without efforts to recognize and build synergies between these two development constituencies, it is likely that the majority of people will continue to be excluded from genuine participation in the development process.

From a technocratic perspective, the demand for expertise and strategic planning is likely to continue to grow rapidly, especially in the 'new' areas identified by Malaysia's medium- and long-range development plans: human resource development, future-oriented industrialization, information and technology development, sustainable development, and the new 'social' agenda addressing problems of quality of life and moral and ethical development. As these new policy concerns develop, think tanks may be expected to play the roles not only of experts, but also of partisans. They may be involved in building policy platforms into discourses to suit existing distributional coalitions, or in facilitating the consolidation of new distributional coalitions associated with specific policy areas. Malaysian think tanks are also likely to continue playing a leading role in regional strategic and economic development. While ISIS has maintained a dominant position in the field of second track diplomacy, we can expect that institutions such as MSRC will find more specific policy niches as their research capabilities mature and they achieve a balance between collaboration and competition vis-à-vis other think tanks. At present, collaboration is evident in exchange programmes and the role that more established institutions play in training staff for newer think tanks. However, the finite quantity of policy niches and the realities of resourcing and political competition will also mean that new and emerging institutions will find it hard to compete with their well-resourced and better-established peers.

Notes

I would like to thank the think tank directors and staff who generously gave not only their time, but also hospitality to me during the period of fieldwork. Special thanks also to Patrick Pillai, Bunn Nagara, Roisin Kelly, Liam O'Dowd and Diane Stone, for helping me develop and clarify my ideas, and to the Department of Education, Northern Ireland, for providing the funding and support which has made the research for this chapter possible.

1 Interview with ISIS senior analyst, 24 March 1995.
2 £1 sterling = approximately RM$4 at current rates.
3 The legal measures included the use of the Internal Security Act (1966, amended 1972 and 1975) to detain persons without trial; the Official Secrets Act (1972, amended 1983 and 1986), the Printing Presses and Publications Act (1958) and the Sedition Act (1958, amended 1970) to limit free speech and the media and ban public rallies; and the Societies Act (1966) to control societies.
4 Interview with K. J. Ratnam, former Director of CPR, 19 June 1995.
5 Interview with Mohamed Noordin Sopiee, Director-General of ISIS, 10 April 1995.
6 *Ibid.*
7 Centre for Economic Research and Services, Malaysian Business Council (1991), 'Malaysia: The Way Forward'. Text of speech given by Prime Minister Mahathir Mohamed to the Malaysian Business Council, 28 February 1991.
8 Personal communication with INSAP member, 14 June 1995.
9 *Ibid.*
10 Interview with Ismail Haji Ibrahim, Director-General of IKIM, 22 March 1995.
11 *Ibid.*

References

Almeida, Pauline and Wong, Stephen C. M. (1991) 'Globalization, Governance and Think Tanks: Malaysia's Experience Thus Far', in John W. Langford and K. Lorne Brownsey (eds), *Think Tanks and Governance in the Asia-Pacific Region*, Halifax, Nova Scotia, Institute for Research on Public Policy.

Alpert, I. and Markusen, A. (1980) 'Think Tanks and Capitalist Policy', in G. W. Domhoff (ed.), *Power Structure Research*, Beverley Hills and London, Sage Publications.

Anon (1991) 'Think Tanks', *Free China Review*, 14(2): 30–5.

Ansari, Abdullah Ali (1977) 'The Legal Structure and Attendant Problems of the Sabah Foundation', Kuala Lumpur, unpublished paper submitted to the University of Malaya.

Asiaweek (1993) 'Making the Vision Work', 15 September.

Camroux, David (1994) 'The Asia-Pacific Policy Community in Malaysia', *The Pacific Review*, 7(4): 421–33.

Centre for Policy Research (1980) *Centre for Policy Research Handbook*, Penang, Centre for Policy Research.

Commission for a New Asia (1994) *Towards a New Asia: A Report of the Commission for a New Asia*.

Crouch, Harold (1993) 'Malaysia: Neither Authoritarian nor Democratic', in Kevin Hewison, Richard Robison and Garry Rodan (eds), *Southeast Asia in the 1990s: Authoritarianism, Democracy and Capitalism*, New South Wales, Allen and Unwin.

Gomez, Edmund Terence (1990) *Politics In Business: UMNO's Corporate Investments*, Kuala Lumpur, Forum.

Gomez, Edmund Terence (1994) *Political Business: Corporate Involvement of Malaysian Political Parties*, Townsville, James Cook University of North Queensland.

INMIND (n.d.) press pack.

Institute of Development Studies (1993) *Annual Report*, Kota Kinabalu, IDS.

Institut Kajian Dasar (1995) *Bulletin IKD*, 2(1).

Jesudason, James (1989) *Ethnicity and the Economy: The State, Chinese Business and Multinationals in Malaysia*, Singapore, Oxford University Press.

Jomo, K. S. (1988) *A Question of Class: Capital, the State and Uneven Development in Malaysia*, Singapore, Singapore University Press.

Jomo, K. S. (1990) *Growth and Structural Change in the Malaysian Economy*, London, Macmillan.

Jomo, K. S. (1994) *U-Turn: Malaysian Economic Development Policies After 1990*, Townsville, James Cook University of North Queensland.

Kahn, Joel and Loh, F. (eds) (1992) *Fragmented Vision: Culture and Politics in Contemporary Malaysia*, Sydney, Allen and Unwin.

Khoo Boo Teik (1995) *Paradoxes of Mahathirism*, Kuala Lumpur, Oxford University Press.

Kitingan, Jeffrey G. (1987) *People Development: A New Direction*, Sabah Foundation Policy Paper No. 1/87, Kota Kinabalu, The Sabah Foundation.

Loh Kok Wah, Francis (1992) 'Modernisation, Cultural Revival and Counter-hegemony: The Kadazans of Sabah in the 1980s', in J. Kahn and F. Loh (eds), *Fragmented Vision: Culture and Politics in Contemporary Malaysia*, Sydney, Allen and Unwin, 237–40.

Loh Kok Wah, Francis (1996) 'A "New Sabah" and the Spell of Development: Resolving Federal–State Relations in Malaysia', *South East Asia Research* 4(1): 63–83.

Malaysian Institute for Economic Research (1994) *Annual Report*, Kuala Lumpur, MIER.

Masahide, Shibusawa, Ahmad, Zaharia and Bridges, Brian (1992) *Pacific Asia in the 1990s*, London, Routledge.

Means, Gordon (1991) *Malaysian Politics: The Second Generation*, Singapore,

Oxford University Press.

Mehmet, Oza (1988) *Development in Malaysia: Poverty, Wealth and Trusteeship*, Kuala Lumpur, INSAN, (the Institute of Social Analysis).

Mohamed Ariff (1991) 'Managing Trade and Industry Reforms in Malaysia', in Sylvia Ostry (ed.), *Authority and Academic Scribblers: The Role of Research in East Asian Policy Reform*, International Centre For Economic Growth/National Centre for Development Studies of Australian National University/Economic Development Institute of the World Bank, 23–44.

Mohamed Noordin Sopiee (1991) 'Policy Research in Malaysia, 1983–1988: An Overview', *Ilmu Masyarakat*, 19: 21–37.

Noda, Makito (1995) 'Research Institutions in Malaysia', in Tadashi Yamamoto (ed.), *Emerging Civil Society in the Asia-Pacific Community*, Singapore and Toyko, Institute of Southeast Asian Studies/Japan Centre for International Exchange.

Smith, James Allen (1991) *The Idea Brokers: Think Tanks and the Rise of the New Policy Elite*, New York, The Free Press.

Stone, Diane (1996) *Capturing the Political Imagination: Think Tanks and the Policy Process*, London and Portland, Frank Cass.

Sum, Ngai-Ling (1996) 'Three Kinds of New Orientalism and Global Capitalism: Trade Competitiveness–Development Discourses and the Politics of Difference', unpublished paper presented to the British Sociological Association Annual Conference, 1–4 April.

Weiss, Linda (1995) 'Governed Interdependence: Rethinking the Government–Business Relationship in East Asia', *The Pacific Review* 8(4): 589–616.

Yamamoto, Tadashi (ed.) (1995) *Emerging Civil Society in the Asia-Pacific Community*, Singapore and Tokyo, Institute of Southeast Asian Studies/ Japan Centre for International Exchange.

Think tanks in Japan: towards a more democratic society

Introduction

Strong democracies require two major ingredients: citizens and political leaders eager to pursue democratic ideals and principles (such as pluralism of expression and public monitoring of government) and built-in social systems and institutions outside government such as public interest groups and policy research organizations that help implement these principles. Japan lacks both ingredients.

Japan is a democracy more in form than substance. The nation holds elections for its legislative branch leaders and has a parliament and an independent judiciary. However, while leaders are elected, public policy decisions affecting the daily lives of citizens are generally made by bureaucrats behind closed doors. Japan's opaque decision-making process is a cultural and historical legacy reflecting the Japanese people's long-standing trust in government. But the world is swiftly changing, and that trust is being undermined by events that have uncovered weaknesses in the closed policy-making process. Japan's political system and the governmental institutions that have maintained it served the nation well in spawning economic prosperity after World War Two; they are insufficient, however, for meeting the challenges of the twenty-first century.

These challenges include slower economic growth and the pressures of an ageing population. Japan's 'bubble economy' of the 1980s left its citizens with a mountain of debt. In 1996 the government used US$6.3 billion (685 billion yen) of taxpayers' money to bail out seven failed housing loan companies – a debacle similar in scope to the savings and loans crisis in the United States. In addition, debts accrued by the now defunct Japan National Railways will cost the Japanese public more than US$185 billion (20 trillion yen), saddling individual taxpayers with almost 30 times the burden of the housing loan bail-out. And this is only the beginning of the financial problems facing the nation. Japan's social security spending could also rise significantly, as its elderly population is projected to grow at a faster rate than in other developed countries; analysts believe that public pension premia would need to double between now and 2020 under current promises to Japan's elderly.

Beyond economic debt and changing demographics, which are having an impact on all major industrialized nations, Japan is also facing an unprecedented erosion of faith among its people in government. The leadership's perceived poor performance in responding to the devastating 1995 Kobe earthquake and, more recently, the scandal uncovering the Health Ministry's failure to recall HIV-tainted blood products from the market in the 1980s have led many Japanese citizens to rethink their centuries-old confidence in government. As a result, the traditional distrust of alternative views emanating from outside government is beginning to dissolve among the Japanese public, which is becoming more favourably disposed toward new ideas. The contribution that private groups have made to earthquake relief efforts and to public health crises are starting to open people's eyes to the positive 'independent' function that institutions separate from government might play in Japan.

Despite the nascent acknowledgement of the contributions that groups outside government can make to solving public problems, independent, objective policy research conducted outside the bounds of corporate or government sponsorship remains virtually non-existent in Japan. Public debate over national policy is an unfamiliar concept to the Japanese people.

The absence of infrastructure and aptitude for policy analysis does not make fertile ground for autonomous think tanks. Yet such institutions and a non-profit sector outside industry or government in which they might exist could play a key role in moving Japan towards a more pluralistic democracy. Better informed policy-making based on empirical research has the potential to enhance the quality of life in Japan and create a fuller presence for Japan in the international arena.

The balance of this chapter discusses the limits of political democracy as practised in Japan, particularly in light of the cultural and historical legacies that militate against a fully fledged American-style democracy; legal, economic, and cultural obstacles to the creation of autonomous think tanks; Japan's current think tank industry including specific think tank-like institutions; and steps that might be taken to construct an environment in which non-aligned think tanks might eventually thrive.

The limits of democracy in Japan

Japan is for the most part a homogeneous society that is inclined to reject diversity. Its strong sense of national identity, cultivated during a centuries-long seclusion from the outside world, creates a psychological barrier to the Japanese perceiving themselves as part of an international community (Reischauer, Naya and Kobayashi, 1989). Throughout history, the desire for harmony and maintenance of the *status quo* has dominated Japanese political and social relations. During the period before Japan's opening to the West in the mid-nineteenth century and as a defence against exposure to new ideas from the outside, the Japanese came to value highly their 'purity' and unified value system. Today, dissent and individual variation from the norm continue to be sacrificed for the greater good of consensus within Japanese society. The Nobel Prize-winning writer Kenzanburo Oe (1995) suggests that the Japanese respect for 'purity' has enabled it to survive the onslaught of outside influences without viewing them as contradictory to the Japanese 'essence'. Japanese culture, in fact, which finds beauty in ambiguity, harbours a profound resistance to Western empirical methods and logical thinking. This allows the Japanese to remain 'Japanese' while adopting technological know-how and fashion fads from the West.

Japan's democratic foundation, imposed on it by the United States after World War Two, did not and could not entirely displace the previous imperial institutional structure. Many Japanese implicitly still value certain elements of that structure, which was based on the paternalistic authority of the emperor and helps define Japan's national identity. One effect of this faith in an all-powerful though beneficent father figure was a failure to develop critical analysis on a national or individual level.

One example of Japan's difficulty in divorcing itself from its imperial past is reflected in its nationalists, who believe in the rectitude of the war and the authoritarian imperial system and who continue to wield influence in current affairs. In July 1996, for the first time in 11 years, Japan's Prime Minister visited the Yasukuni Shrine, erected in 1869 to glorify war heroes. The memorial is controversial because of its symbolism as well as the fact that many of Japan's World War Two criminals rest among the dead buried there. Prime Minister Ryutaro Hashimoto visited to express his nationalism and thereby win over a sizeable constituency still loyal to the war cause.

Another sign of Japan's lingering ties to its past is the quiet reintroduction a few years ago of its national anthem, which blesses the emperor's eternal sovereignty and was phased out after 1945. It is now the official anthem at ceremonial occasions such as Olympic sporting events and public school gatherings. Japan also remains linked to its past through the national flag and its official calendar system, which reckons years based on emperors' reigns.

Taking a public stand against these remnants of the Japanese imperial system is, to say the least, controversial and even dangerous. Some local leaders and educators who have resisted these affirmative links to the war and the emperor have received death threats and even been shot at by ultra-nationalists. Such a highly charged atmosphere makes it extremely difficult for any politician or party to state openly opinions about issues linked to Japan's past such as the constitution and security and defence matters – and thus to forge new paths to the future.

Japan's reluctance to break from its past is often justified by the nation's post-war economic success, which is much admired around the world. According to economist Yukio Noguchi (1995) of Hitotsubashi University, the nation's economic success is due less to the political reforms imposed on it by the US occupation forces after the war than to the continuity of a unique wartime structure that was put in place from the late 1930s and early 1940s until the end of World War Two. This structure aimed to strengthen Japan's national economy on the basis of three premises: production comes first, co-operation is necessary for the sake of the national interest, and competition is denied. But the same system that has served Japan's economy so well and efficiently in the post-war era may well be a yoke on economic success in the future.

An economic system that values production over consumption, consensus over pluralistic expression of ideas, and monopolization over free competition puts Japan at a disadvantage economically in a global economy that is becoming more heavily based on services and information. It also discourages the kind of open *political* debate and public involvement in national policy inherent to a true democracy. In Japan, decisions affecting the public interest have been confined exclusively to government bureaucrats and the Liberal Democratic Party, which ruled Japan uninterrupted from 1955 to 1994. Citizens nominally vote for their leaders, but public policies are made without voter participation, through *ad hoc* compromises reached in a process sealed off from public scrutiny. Decision-making has been largely turned over to government ministries; democratically elected law-makers do not advocate or legislate except for the sake of particular vested interests. Japanese politicians are better known for addressing the needs of very narrow constituencies such as the agricultural or construction industries rather than those of a larger public.

Obstacles to the emergence of think tanks in Japan

Stemming from the broader cultural and historical context are several practical obstacles to the emergence of independent policy research institutions in Japan. These include legal barriers, the public's limited access to information, Japan's education system, and the lack of a market for policy research.

Legal barriers

Japanese law does not permit an independent, non-governmental, non-profit sector. The lack of organizational and tax laws for non-profit organizations makes setting up such entities difficult. The only Japanese equivalent of US private, non-profit organizations that carry out public benefit activities are 'public non-profit corporations' (*koeki hojin*), established under the 1896 civil code. These entities are not independent because they are created solely at the discretion of government ministries or prefectural governments. In reality, Japan's public non-profits are extensions of the ministries that approved their formation. While the law does not specify the degree of supervision these authorities have over non-profits, the ministries provide fiscal, personnel and other control over them. As a result, non-profits' agendas are limited to the interests of the relevant bureaucracy, undermining these organizations' independence and flexibility. Efforts are now underway to revise current law, but reform will come slowly. Too many government bureaucrats benefit from the *status quo*, and Japanese people are traditionally suspicious of 'independent' groups operating outside government.

Japanese tax laws are another obstacle to the emergence of autonomous think tanks. Because Japan, unlike the United States, does not have a tax policy that favours private contributions to non-profit organizations, philanthropic funds to support independent research are limited. Furthermore, the granting of tax-exempt status, so central to the US non-profit sector, remains at the whim of the Japanese government and is not subject to precise policy or procedure. And tax exemption status by no means implies independence; tax-exempt organizations remain dependent on the government ministry that granted them this status. Certain revisions in the law that allow tax-exempt contributions indicate some change, but a major overhaul of the law is needed.

Limited access to information

Japan has not enacted a freedom of information law and Japanese government bureaucracy is rigidly structured, creating obstacles to independent groups and individuals wishing to access information. These impediments are especially difficult to overcome in ministries that regulate practically all areas of domestic policy and that jealously guard information. Yet think tanks and public interest groups of all kinds need information, especially data and statistics collected by government agencies.

Japan's education structure

Japanese intellectuals, from whom independent viewpoints might be expected, generally engage in self-censorship when commenting on government policies, hampering their ability to articulate an alternative public agenda. Japanese academics tend to view policy research as political or ideological, rather than academic, and therefore avoid it. This is due in large part to the education system from which they come. Education in Japan is a government matter. The Ministry of Education (MOE), which also handles cultural affairs, is one of Japan's oldest, largest and most wide-reaching public agencies. Parallel to the strong central control that the Ministry of Finance wields over Japan's economy, the MOE has regulated the educational system since 1871. After World War Two, the US occupation introduced democratic structural reforms to the education system. Nonetheless, the school system, educational administration system, school creation, curricula, teacher training and enrolment, course content, textbook content, and building standards and codes all fall under MOE jurisdiction. Public schools constitute 98 per cent of all schools in Japan. The private schools that do exist are also subject to the MOE's approval and regulations.

Japan's most prestigious universities are funded by the state and all university staff are employees of the national government. These national universities have always been the major supply source of government officials. In 1996, 80 per cent of those who passed the entrance exam for career government bureaucrats graduated from one of these institutions (a quarter alone were from the University of Tokyo). The MOE also controls the purse strings for research funds in Japan and is the exclusive source of grants for social science research. Granting of research funds is heavily skewed towards scholars and researchers in the national universities.

The absence of a market for policy research and a critical media

Few Japanese people have a clear understanding of the meaning of public policy and policy analysis. Post-war politics in Japan have been played out in the absence of policy debate, mainly because one party – the Liberal Democratic Party – dominated the national scene. The Japanese public is not, for the most part, interested in policy issues. Candidates for political office are selected not for their ability to create policy, which is handled by entrenched ministry bureaucrats, but, rather, for their personalities or relationship with the electorate. Outside of the bureaucrats who create and implement public policy, there is no audience for programme evaluations or policy findings.

Social values and attitudes are beginning to change in Japan, and the unprecedented rejection of the Liberal Democratic Party in 1994 unleashed a frenzied realignment among political parties as well as the hasty creation of new parties. But government has been extremely slow in responding to the changing attitudes of the electorate and, despite a broader recognition of

the need for open policy debate, few political leaders have come up with
innovative ideas. Serious discussion of public policy remains limited (Takenaka, 1996).

Perpetuating this disinterest in policy matters is the mass media. Exercising self-censorship in a similar way to Japanese academics, journalists – with
rare exceptions – have not traditionally monitored government policy, disseminated policy information to the public, or provided critical, objective
analysis of government policies. (It should be noted that the media are beginning to debate more openly the idea of governmental reform but that such
discussion is not informed by empirical research on what kinds of reform are
desirable or feasible.) Political reporters are assigned to a specific politician
or specific party for a certain period. Because of this, solid overviews on
policy and politics are missing in Japanese newspapers. Both newspapers and
television tend to focus on the sensational and give short shrift or no space
at all to in-depth, broad political analysis. Thus, Japanese citizens cannot
rely on the media to 'educate' them on policy issues and even publications
that do cover political and policy issues in more depth than the newspapers
do not have a large readership. The lack of an audience for objective,
thoughtful policy research is thus a major impediment to setting up
autonomous think tanks in Japan (Suzuki and Ueno, 1993).

Japan is not without its autonomous citizens' organizations that strive to
make their voices heard by government. Examples include groups of human
rights activists, consumers, environmentalists and lobbyists for international
aid. But their disagreement with the government line prevents them from
gaining ministry approval to incorporate, and thus to become a viable economic unit. Such groups have great difficulty in mobilizing a public that is
not inclined to organize for political ends and generally operate with minimal staff. They often disappear within the course of only a few years.

Japan's current think tank industry

The concept of 'American think tanks' became very popular in Japan over
two decades ago (Itonaga *et al.*, 1993; Ishida, 1996). The first think tank
boom began in 1970, when a government committee recommended the creation of a Japanese think tank. At that time, the Japanese concept of a 'think
tank' was modelled on American policy research institutions such as the
RAND Corporation (which was engaged in contract research for the US government) and the Battelle Memorial and Stanford Research Institutes (which
were engaged in contract research and development for government and
industry). Other US think tanks including the Brookings Institution, the
Council on Foreign Relations, and the Hoover Institution on War, Revolution and Peace were also introduced to Japan by scholars who had spent time

in the USA, though differences among these in terms of relative independence from government were neither understood nor appreciated (Ishida, 1996).

Japan was most interested in forming a think tank to research and develop technology and economic policy for the policy-making arms of government and industry. Many private and public institutions devoted to these ends were founded in the late 1960s and early 1970s. The Nomura Research Institute, established in 1965, and the Mitsubishi Research Institute, founded in 1970, are private, for-profit institutions modelled on the Battelle Memorial and Stanford Research Institutes respectively. In 1974 the government set up a quasi-public institution under the umbrella of the Economic Planning Agency called the National Institute for Research Advancement (NIRA). The 1970s saw the emergence of several public non-profit corporations that intended to conduct policy research but were unable to do so because of the constraints of their quasi-public status and the lack of money for autonomous research.

The second think tank boom, which occurred in the late 1980s, focused on helping Japanese industries understand and respond to global economic change but again produced few institutions devoted to critical public policy research. These institutions focused on economic forecasts and were mainly funded by large banks and financial institutions that had profited from the economic growth of the 1980s. None of these institutions predicted Japan's current financial crisis, perhaps because of their tendency to examine trends rather than causes and their resistance to studying issues that might shed negative light on particular industries.

A 1994 survey undertaken by NIRA profiled 225 Japanese research institutions comprising 95 for-profit corporations, 129 of what Japan considers 'public non-profit corporations' and one ('co-operative organization') that defies categorization (NIRA, 1994). The statistics resulting from the survey reveal how intimately tied to government and business Japan's research industry is relative to that in other industrialized nations, particularly the United States.

According to NIRA's *Shinku Tanku Nenpo* (Think Tank Almanac) of 1994, the 225 institutions profiled employ about 6,800 researchers. Two-thirds of these researchers work for for-profit institutions. Half of the institutions surveyed employ fewer than nine researchers, and three-quarters employ fewer than 19. The ten institutions that employ more than 100 researchers are for-profit corporations. Most institutions engage in activities other than research because they cannot sustain themselves through research projects alone; only 5 per cent of the institutions surveyed conduct research without engaging in other activities such as management consultancy, computer software services and market research.

Ninety per cent of think tanks surveyed engage in contract research commissioned by public agencies or private companies. In 1994, half of the money that went towards research in the institutions surveyed came from public agencies and half from private industry. Many of these think tanks receive grants and research personnel from their 'mother' agency or company that formed them. In 1994, the total revenue of these 225 institutions was reported to be about US$4.2 billion, roughly one-quarter of which was generated from research. Japan's top ten think tanks had revenue of $642 million in 1994 (see Table 9.1).

Most Japanese think tanks have been formed to promote national and regional infrastructure and economic development. Thus, their main topics of research are development and land-use planning, and economic and financial forecasting and policies, in that order. Policy research is not a priority. Research results are targetted at the government or industry 'client' that sponsored the research and are rarely made accessible to the public. This is true for for-profit think tanks as well as non-profits supported by public agencies. Of the 11,000 research reports produced by the institutions surveyed by NIRA in 1994, only 28 per cent were made accessible to the public. Nearly all think tanks engaging in more than ten research projects in 1994 produced research results that were not made accessible to the public. The larger the institution, the higher the proportion of research which was 'closed to the public' (kokai-fuka).

Because of their government or corporate sponsorship, it is not surprising that the research conducted by Japanese think tanks is typically funded and designed to address a government agency's or private company's interests rather than the interests of the broader public. In the words of Hajime Ishida (1996), director of NIRA's Center for Policy Research Information, 'Japanese think tanks are small-scale enterprises that work for the client's interest, conduct research with scarce time and money, and produce products that are never visible to society.' Two examples of Japanese think tanks, one chartered by government, one begun by private industry, help to illustrate the nature of the think tank industry in Japan.

The National Institute for Research Advancement

NIRA was authorized by the government through the National Institute for Research Advancement Act of 1974, which resulted from the government committee's recommendation to create think tanks through the combined initiatives of the government, business, academics, and labour communities. NIRA operates on income from an endowment comprising capital contributions and donations from both the public and private sectors. NIRA has three principal functions: to provide policy-makers with relevant and unbiased research information, to promote research development that contributes to the solution of various issues confronting contemporary society

Table 9.1 *Japanese think tank reference guide*

Name of institution	Establishment (approved by)	Location	Staff size (researchers)	Revenue (million yen)
Center for Financial Industry Information System	1984 (MOF)	Tokyo	61 (53)	Budget: 540
Chugoku Regional Research Center	1962 (NLA)	Hiroshima	28 (22)	Budget: 518
Engineering Consulting Firms Association	1990 (MITI, MC)	Tokyo	31 (19)	Budget: 320 assets: 500
Institute for Future Technology	1971 (STA)	Tokyo	59 (52)	Budget: 740 assets: 525
Institute for International Policy Studies	1988 (PMO, MITI, DA, MOF, MOFA, EPA)	Tokyo	36 (23)	Budget: 500 assets: 4,500
Institute for Policy Studies	1971 (MOF, MITI)	Tokyo	28 (25)	Budget: 300 assets: 500
Institute for Science of Labor	1921 (MOE)	Kawasaki	47 (25)	Budget: 549 assets: 305
Institute of Developing Economies*	1960 (MITI)	Tokyo	271 (184)	Budget: 5,380
Institute of Energy Economics	1966 (MITI)	Tokyo	167 (157)	Assets: 1,370
Institute of Research and Innovation	1959 (MITI)	Tokyo	75 (55)	Budget: 2,700 assets: 100
International Development Center of Japan	1971 (MOF, MOFA, etc.)	Tokyo	65 (34)	Budget: 1,400 assets: 1,600
Japan Center for Economic Research	1963 (MOF, MOE)	Tokyo	52 (18)	Budget: 698 assets: 972
Japan Economic Research Center	1946 (MOE, MITI)	Tokyo	48 (30)	Assets: 360
Japan Institute of Labor	1958 (by law)	Tokyo	144 (66)	Budget: 6,400 assets: 6,600
Japan Research Institute	1970 (EPA, MITI)	Tokyo	33 (27)	Budget: 741 assets: 586
Japanese Institute of Middle Eastern Economies	1974 (EPA, MITI)	Tokyo	34 (29)	Budget: 600 assets: 1,340
Kansai Institute of Information Systems	1970 (MITI)	Osaka	52 (34)	Budget: 1,380 assets: 550
Kyushu Economic Research Center	1946 (MOE)	Fukuoka	56 (37)	Budget: 520 assets: 1,230
National institute for Research Advancement	1974 (by law)	Tokyo	94 (46)	Budget: 1,600 assets: 32,700
Nippon Research Institute	1977 (EPA, MITI)	Tokyo	22 (20)	Budget: 546 assets: 1,080
Research Institute of Telecom-Policies and Economics	1967 (MPT)	Tokyo	38 (30)	Assets: 909
System Research & Development Institute of Japan	1969 (MOF)	Tokyo	82 (72)	Budget:3,200 assets: 68

Sources: NIRA's World Directory of Think Tanks,1996 and Shinku Tanku Nenpo, 1994.
Key: MOF= Ministry of Finance, MOE= Ministry of Education, MITI= Ministry of International Trade and Industry, PMO=Prime Minister's Office, DA=Defence Agency, NLA= National Land Agency, EPA= Economic Planning Agency, MPT= Ministry of Posts and Telecommunications, MOFA= Ministry of Foreign Affairs, STA= Science and Technology Agency.
* special corporation (*tokushu-hojin*)

and the economy and to undertake multi-disciplinary research by summoning expertise from the social sciences and technical fields.

NIRA conducts in-house studies, commissions research and provides funding for research projects conducted by other organizations and autonomous citizen groups. The institute has a staff of 94 including 46 research and 48 administrative staff (NIRA, 1996). NIRA's president, board members and staff come from the private sector and from several ministries, particularly the Economic Planning Agency, which authorized NIRA's creation. Most of the research staff are on temporary (about two- to three-year) loan from public (national and local) agencies and private companies. Staff conduct some in-house research, but major studies are handled by outside scholars who engage in *ad hoc* research projects for which NIRA provides financial support.

NIRA is Japan's foremost institution that cultivates public policy research and publicly disseminates all of its research results. NIRA also helps to foster the think tank industry in Japan. It publishes elaborate almanacs and a directory of think tanks around the world. The institution rarely engages in analysis and evaluation of government policies and programmes. Like other organizations that depend on endowment funds, NIRA has been suffering from Japan's recent recession and low interest rates.

The Mitsubishi Research Institute

One of Japan's most prominent institutes claiming (according to its literature) to be an 'independent, nonpartisan think tank' is the Mitsubishi Research Institute (MRI), founded in 1970. MRI was created by the Mitsubishi Corporation and its group of companies 'to further the progress of technology, industry, and the economy of the world'. Over 80 per cent of MRI's activities comprise market research, consultancy work and systems development for public and private sector clients. The remainder involves data processing and information services. Most of MRI's 680 professional staff are engineering specialists including urban/regional planners and civil and nuclear engineers. About 14 per cent of professional staff specialize in economics, business administration, political science and public administration. Annual revenue in 1993 was over $200 million, 52 per cent of which was from central and local government, 16 per cent from Mitsubishi-owned companies, and 32 per cent from other companies. The institute does not engage in research into, or critical analysis of, public policy.

Signs of change

Despite resistance to the idea of institutions existing outside of government or business, the prolonged recession, political instability, and events such as the Kobe earthquake, the banking crisis, and the HIV-tainted blood scandal have strongly shaken public faith in government, especially in the ministry bureaucracies. The reform of government administration, particularly that of the powerful Ministry of Finance, has been a major topic of debate within the media. These recent crises and calls for reform have created a climate more conducive to change.

There is evidence that the environment for autonomous institutions in Japan may gradually become more favourable. For example, politicians now realize that they need to put forward their own policy ideas to counter the bureaucrats' policy-making powers. Legislators are beginning to propose legislation to the Diet in their own language. Despite the confusion about Japanese political party goals and platforms, in the next two or three elections it is likely that voters will have a clearer understanding of the policies that politicians and political parties represent. Firmer policy stands on the part of politicians will make the legislative branch function in a healthier fashion and provide a balance to the executive branch of government.

During the July 1996 session of the Diet, legislators from the recently formed opposition party, the New Frontier Party or *Shinshin-to*, submitted 'Citizens' Public Corporation Incorporation Legislation'. This non-profit corporation law would allow private citizens' groups to incorporate legally with the sole permission of a local prefecture and *without* the approval of a national ministry. The law would also allow groups to form with less initial financial backing than currently required, making it easier for citizens to launch non-profits.

While the proposal is a cautious, limited step toward establishing non-profit independent organizations engaging in public interest activities, its very introduction was a revolutionary act for the Japanese Diet. The legislation was finally enacted in March 1998. It steers far from granting tax-exempt status to non-profits, but has helped set the debate for the future (Ichimura, 1996).

A further indication of a more receptive climate for the emergence of autonomous think tanks is the growing interest on the part of academe, the public and the media in 'independent' research. Individuals from these communities are now talking about making research institutes that are currently under the control of government agencies or businesses more independent. While the degree of freedom such institutions will probably obtain remains limited, public use of the term 'independent' is an astonishing development that has only occurred during the last five years.

With respect to policy research in universities, initiatives are starting to take hold in Japan. Beginning in 1990, primarily Western-trained faculties in five universities have set up new 'policy science' or 'comprehensive policy studies' departments and graduate schools. These are gaining a strong reputation among students and the general public. Japanese scholars are not only translating English-language textbooks on policy research, they are also starting to write their own books on policy analysis. Several books published over the last two years will contribute significantly to understanding the role and function of policy research and analysis in democratic societies (Miyakawa, 1995; 1996).

Public policy-related professional associations and academic societies are also being formed. The idea that policy research and analysis and government administration and management are legitimate areas of concern to social scientists is slowly gaining ground within the academic community. Interest in policy research and the idea of independent think tanks has grown among young college students and even among conservative university professors. Finally, Japan's foundations, which had previously shown no interest in policy research, are starting to discuss the idea of supporting public policy research.

Conclusion

Japan is not about to change its laws overnight, but over time it may well be possible to cultivate a climate in which independent research is more feasible. This is a lesson learned from a project initiated in 1991 by the present author with support from the Sasakawa Peace Foundation (Struyk, Ueno and Suzuki, 1993; Telgarsky and Ueno, 1996). The goal of this initiative was to introduce to the Japanese people the benefits of autonomous think tanks to society and to provide a model of the kind of institution that might be established on Japanese soil. Five years later, it has become clear that Japan is not yet equipped to accommodate an independent policy research institution. It now appears that a more realistic goal, and one that seems promising in light of current political uncertainty in Japan, is to take the incremental steps necessary to change the institutional, legal, and social environments for free-thinking research.

One fundamental step in this direction would be to establish a freedom of information law, giving individuals and groups outside government access to data for independent policy analysis. Another step would be to strengthen the legislative branch of government, creating a policy research institution under the jurisdiction of the Diet. The current legislative branch is too weak to oppose and check the initiatives of the executive branch, and lacks the capacity to form its own policy ideas.

Fostering a stronger and more genuine democracy in Japan will require that the nation cut itself off from the authoritarian aspect of its past imperial political structures in a cleaner way than it has to date. This will involve a certain amount of political and social dissension and polarization which, due to the Japanese proclivity for harmony, are not welcomed and will not come naturally or swiftly. Further democratization and the emergence of autonomous research institutions in Japan to lend assistance to this process will undoubtedly contribute to the nation's future well-being. Policies that are well-conceived, clearly articulated, and backed up by rigorous social science research will help the Japanese government both to continue to live up to its citizens' high expectations and to play a more substantive role in world affairs.

References

Ichimura, Kouichiro (1996) 'NPO Reports from the Front Line', *Keizai Semina*, nos. 494–501: March–October.

Ishida, Hajime (1996) 'Seido no minaoshi to jouhou kokai wo isoge', *This is Yomiuri*, August.

Itonaga, Sayoko, Ishida, Hajime, Iwamatsu, Jun, and Kobayashi, Akio (1993) *An Overview of Think Tank Trends*, Tokyo, Center for Policy Research Information, National Institute for Research Advancement.

Miyakawa, Tadao (1995) *Seisaku-kagaku no Kiso*, Tokyo, Toyo-Keizai-Shimposha.

Miyakawa, Tadao (1996) *Seisaku-kagaku Nyumon*, Tokyo, Toyo-Keizai-Shimposha.

Noguchi, Yukio (1995) *1940nen Taisei*, Tokyo, Toyo-Keizai-Shimposha.

NIRA (1994) *Sinku Tanku Nenpo 1994*, Tokyo, NIRA.

NIRA (1996) *NIRA's World Directory of Think Tanks*, 2nd edn, Tokyo, Simul International, Inc.

Oe, Kenzaburo (1995) *Japan, the Ambiguous, and Myself*, Tokyo, Kodansha International.

Reischauer, Edwin O., Naya, Yuji and Kobayashi, Hiromi (1989) *Internationalization of Japan: A Dialogue with Dr. Reischauer*, Tokyo, Bungei-Shunju-sha.

Struyk, Raymond, Ueno, Makiko and Suzuki, Takahiro (eds) (1993) *A Japanese Think Tank: Exploring Alternative Models*, Washington DC, The Urban Institute.

Suzuki, Takahiro and Ueno, Makiko (1993) *Sekai no Sinku Tanku*, Tokyo, The Simul Press.

Takenaka, Heizo (1996) 'Seisaku no Hikidashi ga karappoda', *This is Yomiuri*, August.

Telgarsky, Jeffrey and Ueno, Makiko (eds) (1996) *Think Tanks in A Democratic Society: An Alternative Voice*, Washington DC, The Urban Institute.

Russian think tanks, 1956–1996

Introduction

The period between 1956 and 1996 saw a series of momentous changes in the relationship between knowledge and power in Soviet and post-Soviet Russia. Increasingly, scholars are turning their attention to the role played by ideas and knowledge in the shift from political and ideological monism to political and ideological pluralism. To date, however, relatively little attention has been paid to the activities of think tanks in this process. A variety of structural and ideological constraints – including, in particular, an 'official' ideology, the dominance of the party–state bureaucracy and a shifting configuration of political forces – hindered their growth and activities before the collapse of Communism in 1991. Despite this environment, a number of research institutes came to occupy a prominent role in the policy-making process and indeed are a notable feature of the present Russian political scene.

The structure of this chapter reflects the momentous changes in the Russian political landscape during this period. It focuses primarily on the interaction between the institutional configuration of the state, the correlation of political forces within the party–state bureaucracy and the activities and ideas of think tanks. The growth and development of think tanks, and their role in the process of policy-making, can be divided into three sub-periods: 1956–82, 1982–91 and 1991–96. In the first period, the role and impact of think tanks remained subject to the political and ideological controls exercised by the Soviet Communist Party (CPSU). In the second, the CPSU gradually relaxed its control over the process of ideological production and dissemination and the policy process became more open and accessible to influence from outside the bureaucracy. In contemporary Russia, the intellectual milieu has seen a proliferation of policy research centres, as new organizations have sprung up, and old ones have withered and declined.

Think tanks in Soviet Russia, 1956–1991

The structure of intellectual life: the politico-ideological complex

One of the most difficult issues surrounding the analysis of think tanks in Russia concerns the way in which to define a 'think tank'. Studies of think tanks in the non-Communist world have tended to focus upon organizations which are (relatively) independent of government, political parties and the state, engaged in public policy research on a non-profit basis. The question of profit is not an issue in the Soviet context. The question of independence and autonomy, however, clearly is. The structure of intellectual life in Soviet Russia prior to 1988 precluded the emergence of independent policy research institutes, and calls into question the validity of applying the word 'autonomous'.

Intellectual life in the USSR was dominated by a vast politico-ideological complex. This was a conglomerate of departments, agencies and organizations which undertook the production, dissemination and control of ideas. Control of ideological work rested with the party secretariat and its apparatus, the vast bureaucratic apparatus of departments staffed by full-time paid officials and functionaries (Hough and Fainsod, 1979: ch. 11).

The Central Committee (CC) of the CPSU had three departments engaged in the production, dissemination and control of ideology, as well as a CC Secretary with overall responsibility for ideology. These departments were:

- CC Department of Propaganda and Agitation;
- CC Department of Culture;
- CC Department of Science and Education.[1]

Each department was sub-divided into a number of different sections, and was responsible for the oversight of different ministries, agencies and committees of the state structure. In general terms, the function of these departments and agencies was to control communications (Waller, 1988: 35–40). Control extended across both the media and the education system. Taken together, these various agencies and organizations formed a vast institutional network within the political hierarchy, exercising a widespread influence over the whole life of the country. In effect, there was a fusion of the worlds of knowledge and power. In this sense, there was no clear 'space' within the politico-ideological hierarchy in which an institute could emerge and develop independently of the state. All institutes were funded by the state, all *instituteniki* were employees of the state (although not necessarily members of the CPSU) and there was only one 'official' belief-system.

Within this framework of ideological and political monism, however, the period after 1956 saw a gradual loosening of intellectual constraints, as the party increasingly sought to draw 'expert' knowledge into the policy-making process. It was at this level – policy-making – that institutes were able to develop a degree of autonomy from the state and, in doing so, to attempt to exert a degree of influence over the policy-making process. If the broad contours of Marxism-Leninism were not open to discussion, the practical tasks of policy formulation were. In the process of discussing policy alternatives after the death of Stalin in areas such as economic policy, foreign affairs, welfare, housing and legal reform, it became possible for institutes outside the party–state hierarchy to develop a degree of autonomy. These institutes were mainly located in the Academy of Sciences[2] – a network of research institutes which encompassed the whole field of human knowledge. In institutional terms, the Academy was located between the party–state hierarchy, on the one hand, and the academic world of the universities, on the other. This institutional 'space' allowed institutes to develop a degree of autonomy in their work, even if this was always heavily dependent upon the correlation of political forces within the wider political system. These institutes form the basis for the following analysis; the contingent nature of their 'autonomy' should, however, be stressed at the outset.

The emergence and impact of think tanks, 1956–1967

The year 1956 is widely perceived as a key moment in the emergence of a set of autonomous policy research institutes within the Academy of Sciences. Around this period, many new institutes were created, and many existing ones began to display a greater degree of autonomy than previously. Many institutes remained conservative proponents of orthodoxy, however, and it would be misleading to suggest that the Academy of Sciences (comprising approximately 200 research institutes) had somehow become a vast and genuinely autonomous policy research conglomerate. The impetus was provided by the party and its bureaucratic apparatus who together began to create an environment which fostered the emergence of institutes geared towards policy research. Certain institutes went on to develop a more autonomous stance as a function of three separate factors: the broad field in which they were working; the attitude and outlook of the head of the institute and their relationship with key figures within the bureaucracy and the CPSU; and the degree of critical-mindedness and intellectual autonomy of the *instituteniki* themselves.

These institutes arose out of a context shaped by Khrushchev's 'Secret Speech' at the twentieth Congress of the CPSU, the process of 'de-Stalinization' and the cultural and intellectual 'thaw' which followed it. The intellectual atmosphere in Soviet society was far more conducive (albeit within selected areas) to the fostering of more innovative thinking and ideas. This atmosphere became institutionalized under Khrushchev, who began to draw groups of 'consultants' into the policy-making process from outside the party hierarchy (Hough and Fainsod, 1979: 422). The structure created by the participation of consultants in the policy-making process is of profound significance in understanding the reasons for the growth of Soviet think tanks, as it inaugurated the process of opening up the politico-ideological complex to influence from 'outside'. The initial stimulus came (somewhat ironically) in the field of ideological renewal. The ideological consequences of de-Stalinization opened the way for young intellectuals to be drawn into the politico-ideological hierarchy (Burlatsky, 1988; Arbatov, 1992: 62–70).

The need for ideological renewal led to the creation of intellectual or creative 'collectives', whose composition and work were largely determined by the personalities and beliefs of the lead-figures who headed them. The group drawing up the new philosophy textbook was headed by Otto Kuusinen – a key figure in selecting and sheltering young, reform-minded intellectuals. Initially, membership of the editorial collectives was determined by the Department of Propaganda. Kuusinen was dissatisfied with the people assigned to him, and began to search for a new, more dynamic team (Arbatov, 1992: 62–70).

The creation of these collectives set something of a precedent. A variety of institutes and groups were formed in the late 1950s, many of which quickly earned reputations as centres of innovative and creative thought (Arbatov, 1992: 62–90). The impulse behind their creation lay in the wider consequences of the process of de-Stalinization, of which two aspects in particular stand out. First, the need for economic reform meant that the leadership was forced to encourage innovative thinking amongst economists, in order to break the stranglehold of Stalinist orthodoxy and explore new ways of understanding the Soviet economy. Secondly, the acquisition of the socialist bloc led to the need to elaborate new approaches to the study of the socialist countries of Eastern Europe, and to the study of the capitalist countries. New analytical centres were formed, as the leadership sought more specialist knowledge of different regions and problems in the international arena. Perhaps the most important grouping was the consultant group set up by Iurii Andropov in 1961 as part of the CC Department for Relations with Communist and Workers' Parties of the Socialist Countries. This group of consultants was drawn into the ideological apparatus proper, having input into the discussions and policy formation and making contacts with party officials at all levels (Burlatsky, 1988: 40–65). This group cannot be classified as an autonomous research institute because it was located within the bureaucracy. However, the individuals within this group would later form the core of the policy coalition of political leaders, media figures, instituteniki and bureaucrats which emerged after 1985.

Two economic centres are worthy of note. Under Khrushchev, Akademgorodok (Academic City) just outside Novosibirsk in Siberia was created in

1957. This was a collection of 22 scientific institutes, concentrated in one area, and developed into something of a haven for younger, more radical and innovative scholars. The geographical position of Akademgorodok, far from Moscow and hence relatively free from direct party supervision, enabled scholars to exercise a degree of intellectual autonomy. The best-known members of this community of scholars were Abel Aganbegyan and Tatanya Zaslavskaya, who both joined the Institute of Economics and Indus-trial Organization (EKO) in the early 1960s (Cohen, 1989: 115–17). A second group was formed at the Institute of World Economy and Interna-tional Relations (IMEMO). This institute was created in the mid-1950s, under the directorship of A. A. Arzumanyan, and quickly became a place of progressive and innovative thinking. The removal of Khrushchev in 1964 did not, at first, prevent the emergence of new institutes or arrest the further growth and development of those recently created. Innovative new insti-tutes, such as the Central Economic and Mathematical Institute and the Institute for Concrete Social Research, were formed as the leadership con-tinued to search for new ways to rejuvenate the economy. In 1967, the Insti-tute for the Study of USA and Canada (ISKAN) was set up, institutes for the study of Africa, Latin America and the Far East emerged and an Institute of Sociological Studies (ISS) was created.

Although the size, structure and functions of these institutes varied some-what, they did possess a core of common features. First, they were financed wholly by the state, and the lifestyle of the *instituteniki* was a relatively priv-ileged one. Secondly, they were comparatively large, employing up to 700 research staff. Thirdly, they were highly specialized bodies. The institutes were designed to cover all aspects of the study of a particular topic or region, and within that individual scholars also specialized. Fourthly, there was little or no competition for these research institutes, who consequently enjoyed a monopoly of research expertise and information (Antonenko, 1996: 1).

In what ways did these institutes seek to influence the policy process during the period 1956–67? In terms of direct contact, the institutes who were 'outside' the bureaucratic apparatus generally responded to the initia-tives of the bureaucracy, usually in the form of research reports, proposals or analytical studies. Consultants had a more central role, as they were for-mally attached to the party bureaucracy, without being full 'insiders'. Their brief was to write documents, memoranda, speeches and to draft CC deci-sions, all of which were subject to subsequent revision and redrafting by *apparatchiki* or political leaders (Hough and Fainsod, 1979: 422; Arbatov, 1992: 82–90). The institutes and *instituteniki* also contributed to the wider political and intellectual climate by publishing ideas and proposals via a number of different outlets. Many institutes generated their own 'in-house' journals. Newspapers with editors sympathetic to the publication of more unorthodox ideas, or with contacts amongst members of the institutes, were another potential outlet. However, the continued existence of prior censor-ship set clear limits to the ability of institutes to extend the boundaries of dis-cussion and thereby contribute to the shaping of policy through shifting the parameters of the debate, developing new concepts and so on.

The extent and character of the influence exerted by institutes was also heavily constrained. The policy process was dominated by the party–state apparatus. Yet it became evident as early as the 1950s that the analytical capacity of this apparatus had dwindled substantially. The bureaucracy was dominated by careerists who avoided responsibility, were intellectually conformist, highly resistant to change and ill-equipped for the challenges of de-Stalinization (Arbatov, 1992: 142–8). The imperatives of economic mod-ernisation, the challenge of post-Stalinist social policy and the new interna-tional commitments in Eastern Europe required levels of analysis which the apparatus was unable to provide. The party elite initiated the process of soliciting 'expert' contributions in these areas, but without shifting control of policy outside the apparatus itself.

Interestingly, the size of the bureaucratic apparatus and the wide variety of bureaucratic agencies involved (divided according to geography as well as functional specialism) actually helped to foster the work of policy research centres at this time. The ISS is a good example of this. It was set up solely to undertake field research for the party in order to facilitate policy-making. The multiple access points within the apparatus afforded by the extent and reach of the bureaucracy meant that the Institute was able to create a Union-wide network of centres, commissioned by the party to do fieldwork on a variety of issues. Endorsement and funding by the party also ensured that, despite the overarching ideological constraints, conditions were conducive to specific field research. The best example was a study on 'Socialism and Youth' conducted in 1968 for the CC of the Komsomol (the Communist Youth League). The outcome of this research was questioned by the party, as it revealed a disparity between ideology and attitudes amongst the youth. Even so, at this point in time, the party was willing to accept this type of information.[3]

The receptivity of the party–state bureaucracy to the ideas and proposals generated from 'outside' was dependent upon a number of factors. Of these, the most important was arguably the extent to which the proposals corre-sponded to the goals of the party leadership at the time, or conformed to the latest ideological *diktat*. For example, Tatyana Zaslavskaya (who joined the Institute of Economics in Akademgorodok at Novosibirsk in 1957) related the following incident:

> In 1957 a colleague at the Institute and I were asked to compare labour pro-ductivity in the USA and the USSR. We researched for two years and wrote a one hundred page report. There was enormous interest in the subject, so about a hundred copies were sent to various institutes in Moscow, and a date was set

for the discussion of the report. At nine on that morning my colleague and I got urgent calls that the director of our institute wanted to see us immediately ... All morning his driver had been retrieving copies of the report from everybody who had received one. All the copies were locked in the institute's safe and classified, including even our personal copies. It turned out that Khrushchev had just announced that American productivity was three times greater than Soviet productivity, while our findings showed that it was more like four or five times greater ... our report never saw the light of day. (quoted in Cohen, 1989: 120)

Further constraints were provided by the wider political struggle within the party between reformers, who wished to extend the changes inaugurated by Khrushchev, and conservatives, who wished to maintain the Stalinist *status quo*, albeit without mass terror. The struggles of critical-minded, more intellectually creative individuals and institutes to exert influence in the face of a bureaucratic apparatus which was resistant to change and opposed to intellectual liberalization reflects the wider struggles in Soviet society between reformism and conservatism. In the field of economics, for instance, the radical and innovative sectors (the EKO or the Central Institute of Economics and Mathematics) were often most vehemently opposed by traditionalist academic institutions: the Economics Department of Moscow State University in particular (Arbatov, 1992: 158). The universities have throughout the Soviet period been subject to a higher degree of political control than the institutes of the Academy of Sciences, and consequently have remained much more conservative, conformist institutions within the system.

The role of key political figures in this process is also worthy of note. The surest way for an institute to guarantee its autonomous status, or for individuals to gain access to the policy-making process, was through the patronage of a leading political figure. At the same time, the opposition of conservative figures could see the closure or emasculation of whole institutes, or the isolation and ostracism of individuals. One of the central struggles of the 1960s was that between Andropov (who was to become General Secretary in 1982) and Mikhail Suslov. Andropov was the patron of a group of liberal intellectuals and party reformers and was keen to inject dynamism and creativity into the work of the party–state apparatus. Suslov (along with Sergei Trapeznikov) was the central guardian of ideological orthodoxy.

The era of consolidation and retrenchment, 1967–1982

The invasion of Czechoslovakia in 1968 marked a turning-point, as the regime reverted to a policy of re-Stalinization, and of ideological and political retrenchment. The (temporary) victory of the conservative tendency within the CPSU created a new climate which was much less conducive to critical thinking and new ideas. The sphere of autonomy which had been opened up between 1956 and 1967 began to narrow, as ideological dogmatism returned. Unorthodox thinking risked being labelled as 'dissident', with a consequent loss of position, status, income and possibly liberty. For example, the Andropov group of consultants was disbanded, and Andropov was sent to become head of the KGB.[4] The radical Institute of Methodology in the Department of History was disbanded (Markwick, 1994). All this had a profound effect on the research institutes.

A number of constraints were imposed on the work of the research institutes. At the ISS, researchers had to submit their proposals for validation, rather than submitting the outcomes. Many projects failed to get off the ground (Mansourov, 1996). The recruitment and promotion process was dominated by notions of political loyalty and reliability rather than professional competence. Heads of the ISS came from philosophy, economics and elsewhere. Many scholars were fired for publishing 'unorthodox' opinions. In the Soviet Writers Union, financial inducements were offered to those willing to write on state-approved topics, or produce panegyrics to Soviet achievements. Ostracism, exile and loss of earnings was the fate for those who refused (Garrard and Garrard, 1990: 184).

The research centres struggled on, however, adopting diverse strategies to survive during the period until 1982. The institutes at Akademgorodok benefited by their distance from Moscow and were able to survive re-Stalinization. The attitudes of those in charge of the centres were crucial: often they would 'shelter' critical-minded scholars, and would promote the dissemination of ideas and proposals through specialist departmental journals with a restricted readership. Scholars also developed particular styles of writing to facilitate the expression of their ideas. As Arbatov (1992: 145) has recalled: 'The pressure of censorship and the restrictions on the freedom of speech had one benefit. They forced you to become finely tuned, to write cleverly, to express important thoughts between lines – through innuendo, through omissions and through irony.'

The contrast between the stultifying conformism of 'official' public life, on the one hand, and the continued search for intellectual creativity and dynamism, on the other, was one of the enduring paradoxes of the 1970s. The leadership sought to understand the underlying causes of social and economic problems and to find new ways of interpreting developments in the international arena. All this drew the research centres into the consultation and policy-making process (Lewin, 1988: 85–95). Yet nothing could be officially published which contradicted the view put forward by the official ideology. The work of the ISS bears witness to this strange 'dual life'. As Mansourov (1996) later recalled:

> It was a very strange situation at that time. We were very popular at that time as sociologists. Every seminar, every meeting of lecturers, or political leaders of regional CC of communist parties, of ideological workers we were invited to … and they were very interested in the results of our research. But it was closed

information, only for them. It was prohibited to publish this information in the press.

A similar situation emerged in the sphere of economics. Attempts to reform the economy led the leadership to commission research from a wide variety of centres, both conservative and reformist. The relationship between the research centres, the political leadership and the bureaucratic apparatus was a complex one. Arbatov (1992: 159–60) outlines how the leadership sought out the research centres because of the sterility of the ideas coming from the bureaucracy and the universities:

> political leaders started to turn to those familiar with world economics – for example to Academician Inozemtsev and the experts at IMEMO, to my colleagues and myself at ISKAN … Gradually, an unofficial working group took shape … this group conterbalanced the old ways of thinking in economics and helped to generate and legitimise ideas that had long been considered seditious … The practical effect of our work … was a different matter altogether. Here, we were to be deeply disappointed. Speeches were made, documents were printed – and then nothing, absolutely nothing, happened. The attempts to breach the stout walls of the administrative–bureaucratic fortress were fruitless, despite the fact that we often managed to scale these walls by means of instructions, persuasions, and proposals coming from the top leadership itself.

The bureaucratic apparatus was not always an 'unbreachable fortress', however. At times, officials within the bureaucratic apparatus who were interested in the results of the empirical research were able to defend the ISS from the attacks of conservatives in order to maintain the flow of accurate information about the state of the country (Mansourov, 1996).

The arena in which the policy research centres enjoyed most autonomy was that of international relations/national security, as the conflicts between reformists and conservatives were mainly concerned with domestic developments. The roles of the IMEMO and ISKAN in the development of Soviet foreign and defence policy appear to have been fairly significant (Cobb, 1981). In personnel terms, many of its researchers were members of the *nomenklatura*,[5] or their families. Diplomats and bureaucrats from the Ministry of Foreign Affairs went there to study and gain a degree. Retired military officials often went to the ISKAN to work. Most importantly, however, the heads of the two bodies (Inozemtsev and Arbatov) were full members of the CC of the CPSU. This access to the political leadership, and the availability to it of classified material and Western information, enabled it to undertake expert research on a variety of topics (Cobb, 1981: 51–4).

The output ranged from 'policy analysis to dissemination of official lines both domestically and abroad' (Cobb, 1981: 54). The defence of Soviet policy and the criticism of the actions of capitalist powers reflected the political and ideological constraints, while the more specific policy proposals embodied the analytical policy research of the institute. This situation exemplifies the incredibly complex position that Soviet think tanks occupied up until Brezhnev's death in 1982. The policy research centres adopted a number of different strategies to enable them to survive, but also to attempt to exert influence. Their relationship with the political leadership and with the bureaucracy is very difficult to summarize accurately. The functional variables – broad political context, the relationship of individuals within the various bodies and the specific area of the research – shifted and changed across this latter period (1967–82). However, it does appear that the think tanks which were able to retain a degree of autonomy, and to have significant input into the policy process, were those which:

- were concerned with ideologically less sensitive areas (in particular, foreign affairs and social policy);
- enjoyed close links between its sector heads and the political leadership, and between its staff and members of the bureaucratic apparatus;
- were able to demonstrate ideological orthodoxy and analytical innovation simultaneously.

The death of Brezhnev brought a substantial shift in the ideological and political climate within which the analytical centres operated. As the following section will show, the eras of Andropov and Gorbachev saw the erosion and (eventually) the collapse of the politico-ideological complex, opening the way for a reconfiguration of the institutional architecture of the state. Gorbachev's call for 'new thinking' brought these autonomous research centres into the middle of political discourse and the policy-making process.

Think tanks in the era of *perestroika*, 1982–1991

The accession of Andropov saw the start of the shift in the configuration of power within the politico-ideological complex. Between 1982 and 1991, there was a gradual loosening of the ideological and political constraints on intellectual activity, combined with an overhaul of the personnel and the institutions engaged in the production of both ideology and policy. The hegemony of reformist thinking in the party leadership not only created a genuine sphere of autonomy for intellectuals and academics, but also fundamentally changed the relationship between the party, the bureaucracy and think tanks. The status of the latter changed, especially under Gorbachev, from 'outsiders' to 'insiders', as a clear policy coalition of party reformers and Academy of Sciences *instituteniki* emerged.

Under Andropov's tenure, greater encouragement was given to analytical research. The party expressed its dissatisfaction with the existing sources of information about the country and encouraged wide-ranging sociological

studies to rectify this problem (Mansourov, 1996). The so-called Novosibirsk Report was another example of the new climate. This report was a con-
fidential seminar paper organized by the economic departments of the CPSU
CC, the USSR Academy of Sciences and Gosplan (the state planning committee) and was held at the EKO (headed by Aganbegyan) in Novosibirsk. It
contained some (within the context of that era) radical reform proposals and
demonstrated the new willingness of the research centres to propose innovative policies (Cohen, 1989: 121–2). Andropov also began to shake up the
personnel within the politico-ideological complex. Trapeznikov was
replaced by Vadim Medvedev at the Department of Science and Education.
Aleksandr Yakovlev was appointed head of IMEMO in 1983.

It was not until Gorbachev came to power in 1985 that the trends which
Andropov had started were codified and institutionalized. The Gorbachev
leadership shifted the configuration of forces in three ways. First, the new
intellectual climate of *glasnost* (openness) and *novoe politicheskoe mishlenie*
(new political thinking). Secondly, a renewal of the personnel within both
the party and think tanks – and the creation of a variety of new institutions.
And thirdly, the establishment of a policy coalition comprising the party
leadership, selected think tanks, and sections of the media and the bureaucracy.

Glasnost did not set out to establish freedom of speech. Rather, it was
designed as an instrumental policy of selected openness to facilitate the
wider processes of economic reform. Yet the search for innovative ideas, creative and critical thought fostered a climate of greater tolerance for unorthodox ideas, and widened the sphere of acceptable topics for public discussion.
Although limits to discussion and publication still existed, the period after
1986 saw these gradually eroded, as Soviet society began to create a public
sphere marked by pluralism, dialogue, diversity and conflicts of opinion. It
was now possible for think tanks to use the media to disseminate their views
more widely. The activities of Soviet think tanks were profoundly affected
by this change in the external environment.

The renewal of the ideological establishment reflected the pro-reform orientation of the new leadership. The leadership began to replace the
'guardians of orthodoxy' with more reformist figures at all levels of the
Academy of Sciences, the party and the bureaucracy. The network of liberal
scholars and party reformers who had emerged under Khrushchev became
the central figures of the policy process during *perestroika*. Yakovlev and
Medvedev, who were the main ideological secretaries, had both been directors of institutes within the Academy of Sciences. *Instituteniki* were now able
to make more use of the media to amplify their ideas: Aleksandr Bovin
(*Izvestiya*) and Fyodor Burlatsky (*Literaturnaya Gazeta*) had close personal
links to members of the research institutes and key political figures.[6] Economists from different centres – Bogomolov (IMEMO), Aganbegyan and

Zaslavskaya (EKO), Abalkin (Institute of Economics) – became close advisors to the leadership. Personal aides to Gorbachev – Frolov and Shakhnazarov – were former *instituteniki*. New institutes were also created, reflecting the changing policy priorities of the leadership. Examples here (Shimotomai, 1990: 92–4) include:

- Institute of Europe;
- Institute of Peace Research;
- Institute for the Exchange of Experience of Socialist Construction;
- Centre for the Study of Public Opinion on Socio-Economic Problems;
- Centre for the Study of Politics.

However, the internal structure of the institutes – size, functional specialism, state funding – remained unchanged.

Arising out of the changes in the external environment and changes in personnel came a shift in the relationship between party, bureaucracy and think tanks. There were two slightly contradictory trends at work here. *Glasnost* created an environment in which think tanks could develop substantive intellectual autonomy, as the ideological and political monism of the system was eroded. At the same time, however, the policy process became increasingly dominated by a group of think tanks espousing the values and outlook of the new leadership. A new intellectual orthodoxy emerged, only this time including rather than excluding the think tanks. The research institutes were drawn directly into the policy-making process, shifting their position from essentially outsiders to insiders. This policy input ranged from drawing up practical recommendations in selected fields, to dynamic shifts in the worldview of the party. Examples of these coalitions include the collaborative efforts of the State Agricultural Committee (*Gosagroprom*) and the Agricultural Academy, and the creation of the National Committee for Economic Cooperation on Asia-Pacific Affairs (SOVNA-PECC) which comprised members of IMEMO and ISKAN, of the Ministry of Foreign Affairs, trading organizations and Far Eastern local authorities for Asia-Pacific and Siberian development (Shimotomai, 1990: 94).

Checkel has detailed the role of ideas, experts and institutions in the emergence of a new view of the international arena in Soviet foreign policy under Gorbachev (Checkel, 1993). His analysis demonstrates how the changed external environment brought about by *perestroika* created opportunities for participation in foreign policy debates and policy formulation amongst a variety of institutional actors. The key role played by IMEMO in this process was a function of three separate issues: the activities and abilities of the head of the institute in acting as a policy entrepreneur, the particular expertise of the institute and the access channels with the political leadership. As Checkel (1993: 287) argues:

[B]y late 1986 the largely deductive, Marxist-Leninist view of the international system that for so long had been a staple of Soviet leadership statements had been replaced by an empirical non-class vision – one based on an ideology of world politics championed by IMEMO for nearly 20 years. New ideas and specialist expertise – with a mighty assist [*sic*] from a very able entrepreneur and an open window – had triumphed over the kind of Leninist dogma upheld by *the* most powerful political institution: the Soviet Communist Party.

Reformist think tanks under *perestroika* enjoyed something of a golden era. Relative intellectual freedom, access to the policy process and to the political leadership, access to information from abroad and unrestricted funding brought them to the centre of the political process. Their experiences under Gorbachev demonstrate the importance of ideas and expertise in shaping policy, but also in fostering a set of values and norms among a key section of the policy-making elite. Before turning to examine the experiences of think tanks in the post-Soviet period, a brief analysis of the influence or impact of think tanks across the period 1956–91 is in order.

The impact of think tanks in Soviet Russia

Clearly, the institutional architecture of the Soviet state imposed serious constraints on the emergence and growth of autonomous policy research centres. The absence of a 'public sphere', the stratification of intellectual life through the dominance of the politico-ideological complex, and the control exercised over the policy-making process by the party–state bureaucracy all combined to make it exceptionally difficult for research institutes to carve out an autonomous position for themselves, and hence to exert influence over the policy process. The tangible dangers of unorthodox thinking – unemployment, exile, incarceration – tended to promote conservatism among many institutes and their personnel.

Yet this very architectural configuration also facilitated the growth of these institutes once the leadership had decided to create them, as the bureaucracy required increased levels of expertise in policy formation. Access to resources was not a problem. The functional and geographical divisions of the bureaucracy (including its nominally federal structure) afforded the research centres numerous access points. The analytical weakness of the Soviet bureaucracy – a function of the recruitment policy which rewarded political loyalty and obedience, conservatism and conformity – forced the leadership to turn to experts for input when the tasks of governing and reforming a modern industrial society became apparent after the death of Stalin.

The development and consolidation of think tanks in Soviet Russia was also closely linked to the wider correlation of political forces within the system. The close linkages between reformist political figures and institute

heads, and the use of institutes by reformers to 'push' innovative policy proposals, ties the development of think tanks to wider political developments.
The (temporary) hegemony of the conservative neo-Stalinists in the 1970s
was accompanied by the dominance of ideological orthodoxy and of the
bureaucratic apparatus. In intellectual terms, this constituted the marginalization of the think tanks. The victory of the reformers under Gorbachev
tilted the balance firmly in favour of the Academy of Sciences over the
party–state bureaucracy.

Given the constraints within which Soviet think tanks were operating,
questions about the influence or impact of think tanks are highly pertinent.
Two issues stand out. First, did the research institutes bring a greater degree
of 'rationality' to bear upon the decision-making process? (Dror, 1984).
Undoubtedly, Soviet think tanks did widen the scope of policy alternatives,
partly due to the analytic weakness of the bureaucracy, but also because the
party deliberately sought out this advice. Their input was courted precisely
to feed into the policy-making process. However, the important qualification to this is that the range of policy alternatives was extremely narrow. The
think tanks did provide alternative advice and analysis, but this was a very
limited selection of alternatives.

The second issue concerns the character of the influence which the think
tanks attempted to exert over the policy process. Did they have an educative
function, shaping the climate of public opinion? Or were they 'enlighteners'
in the form of setting the terms of discourse within which policies were formulated? (Weiss, 1990). In other words, did they produce a 'paradigm shift'
within the official ideology which eventually fed into the policy process?

The wider educative function – informing the public of policy issues and
so widening the scope of the debate – was not feasible given the controls on
the dissemination of information exercised by the party. It can be argued that
the think tanks did, however, perform a quasi-enlightenment function. Institutes often developed new ideas and concepts which overturned the existing
orthodoxy (the example of the radically different world-view espoused by
IMEMO is particularly apt). However, this shift only fed into the policy
process because of the correlation of political forces and due to the links
between the institutes and the key political figures. The think tanks provided
a reformist discourse, but this discourse only became embedded in the policy
process due to the wider political and institutional configuration of forces
under *perestroika*.

Think tanks in the era of post-Communism

The period since 1991 has seen a vast change in the political landscape. In
terms of the intellectual life of post-Soviet Russia, there has been a prolifer-

ation of new research centres. Alongside the old institutes from the Academy of Sciences – many of which are struggling to survive in the new political and financial climate – a bewildering variety of analytical research centres have blossomed. Contemporary Russia is a fertile area for think tank studies (see, for example, Antonenko, 1996; Bruckner, 1996; Yakubovsky, 1995).

The contemporary think tank scene: plus ça change ... ?

Of the old institutes which existed, the following are still active and influential in the new conditions:

- Institute for Ethnology and Anthropology;
- Institute of Oriental Studies;
- Institute of African Studies;
- Institute of Sociological Studies;
- Institute of Slavic and Balkan Studies;
- Institute of Europe;
- Institute of USA and Canada;
- Institute of Economy;
- IMEMO.

In terms of new institutes, the following are worthy of note:

- Centre for Political Technologies;
- Russian Public Policy Centre;
- Centre for Applied Political Studies;
- Russian Institute for Humanitarian and Political Studies;
- Centre for Economic and Political Studies;
- Russian–American University (RAU) Corporation;
- Centre for Ethnopolitical and Regional Studies;
- Humanitarian and Politological Centre 'Strategia';
- Working Centre for Economic Reforms;
- Institute of Economic Analysis;
- Institute of Economic Transition;
- Council on Foreign and Defence Policy;
- All-Russian Centre for Public Opinion Research;
- Gorbachev Foundation;
- Foundation for Parliamentary Development in Russia;
- Centre for Current Studies in Russian Politics;
- 'Experimental Creative Centre' Corporation;
- Centre for National Security and International Relations;
- Moscow School of Political Studies[7] (Antonenko, 1996; Day, 1993; World of Learning, 1994).

Why has there been such a proliferation? The collapse of Communism produced a massive institutional shake-up, which fractured many of the links and practices of the old policy process. The new system which has begun to emerge contains three distinctive elements which have led to the contemporary growth of research centres. First, there has been substantial fragmentation. The drastic reduction in funding for the Academy of Sciences led able researchers to create their own analytical centres, or to join new ones, which now co-exist alongside the old research institutes. Secondly, the previous situation of virtual 'monopolies' of expertise has given way to a more competitive environment. Thirdly, the modern political situation has prompted diversification. Multi-partyism and new political institutions have created new axes of differentiation. In addition to functional specialization, these conditions have also created differentiation along political and ideological lines (Bruckner, 1996: 1–3; Antonenko, 1996: 1).

The funding situation has provided a substantial obstacle to the think tanks developing autonomy from particular interests, be they political or business. Political parties, banks and Russian companies have all sought out research from the new centres, who are driven by economic necessity to seek work wherever they can. The embryonic state of the Russian political system, and the severe economic constraints within which they are working have made it almost impossible for any centre – new or old – to function satisfactorily and autonomously. Only time will tell whether the funding situation will enable the think tanks to become genuinely autonomous (Shubin, 1996; Bruckner, 1996: 2 4; Antonenko, 1996: 2–3) (see Table 10.1).

All these factors affected the internal structures of the new research centres. The centres are now much smaller, with a great deal more specific

Table 10.1   *Selected profile of Russian think tanks*

Institution	Founded	Location	Staff
Institute of European Studies	1988	Moscow	110 (57 researchers)
Institute of USA and Canada	1967	Moscow	200
Institute of World Economy and International Relations	1956	Moscow	300
Institute of Peace Research	1990	Moscow	7
Centre for Political Technologies	1993	Moscow	10 permanent
Centre for Applied Political Studies	1990	Moscow	12 permanent
Centre for Economic and Political Studies	1990	Moscow	18
Institute of Economic Transition	1990	Moscow	10
Russian Institute for Strategic Studies	1992	Moscow	70+
All-Russian Centre for Public Opinion Research (VTsIOM)	1988	Moscow	80
Centre for Ethnopolitical and Regional Studies	1991	Moscow	8 permanent

Sources: Day, 1993; Antonenko, 1996.

short-term contract work. Even the old institutes have shrunk substantially – IMEMO has seen its staff reduced from around 700 to approximately 300 by 1995 (Kislov, 1996) – and new centres average about 15–20 full-time staffers. Many of the former *instituteniki* now work in the new centres, although many are forced to seek alternative or additional employment because of funding problems. The centres now cover a broad range of policy issues, as opposed to the prior functional specialization. This is in the main due to the overriding need to generate income, leading to a diversification of activities. This, in turn, has led the new centres to employ researchers on short-term contract to undertake specific projects. The new centres have shifted their focus towards the use of the media to disseminate their ideas (Antonenko, 1996: 2). The context of their activities and their internal structures have shown radical changes from the think tanks under Communism. Are the changes as marked in the means by which post-Communist think tanks have sought to influence the policy process?

Influence over the policy process

The underdeveloped nature of the Russian political system means that it is unwise to make any definite observations about the impact and influence of think tanks in the post-Communist era. However, one or two observations about the emerging system can be made. One of the critical features of the current period is the relative strength of the Russian Presidential Administration vis-à-vis the parliament and the government. This makes access to the presidency critical to the development of channels of influence for the think tanks (Antonenko, 1996: 3–8). Interestingly, the old Soviet culture and practice of personal links between political figures and researchers appears to be being reproduced at present:

> At the Presidential level all 'in-house' analytical information is prepared in the Presidential Analytical Centre and by Presidential advisors. In most cases, members of the respective Presidential advisory groups were originally connected with one of the Academy of Sciences institutes (advisors were usually the directors of institutes). In their work for the Presidential Administration, official analysts therefore usually still refer to their old institutes, which have often been transformed into new centres, to provide intellectual support. (Antonenko, 1996: 4)

The arena in which they have been able to exert most influence is in the state Duma, which has the most undeveloped in-house analytical capabilities. Political parties have also used new centres extensively in their activities. In the interim it seems likely that the domination of decision-making by the presidency and the analytic strength of the Presidential Analytical centre are liable to restrict the opportunities for think tanks to become involved in the policy-making process, especially those without the necessary personal contacts (Antonenko, 1996: 5–8).

The issue of access/influence via personal contacts is the main continuity with the past. The impact of contemporary think tanks is mediated far more through the media and the corporate sector than in the past. The destruction of the party–state politico-ideological complex has removed the huge bureaucratic apparatus as the main access point into the policy-making process. Consequently, Russian think tanks are seeking influence through a wider variety of means than before, whilst struggling for survival (Bruckner, 1996: 2–3).

Conclusion: think tanks, democratization and the transition debates

Quigley (1995: 84) has argued that think tanks:

> have a key role in fostering competition that is essential to any democracy; they develop alternative policy approaches that compete with those of the government and various political interests. They are a vehicle for extending citizen engagement in the political process, and are an essential intermediating institution between the state and the individual … By enhancing civic skills and extending citizen participation, think tanks help protect citizens from abuses by the state. Thus think tanks perform an essential democracy building function.

There are two themes here. First, that think tanks enhance pluralism in society by providing a range of alternative perspectives (Parsons, 1996). Secondly, that think tanks contribute to the process of building and consolidating democracy. Does the case of Russia support these assertions?

In terms of pluralism, the Russian case is an interesting one. The growth and activities of think tanks in the Soviet period contributed to the gradual erosion of political and ideological monism, through the extension of participation outside of the party–state bureaucracy. Certain think tanks in particular – IMEMO, ISKAN – had access to the policy-making process which enabled them to make a significant contribution to the shaping of policy, or the reframing of discourse within a particular field. They were central to the creation of public sphere of dialogue and to the belief in the acceptability and utility of alternative ideas and policies. In this sense the think tanks between 1956 and 1991 promoted the demonopolization of party–state control over the policy process.

But how 'pluralist' was this? Not only was there a highly restricted number of institutions, but these operated within a fairly narrow ideological paradigm: 'reform communism'. The institutes and their staff which were drawn into a coalition with the party elite and the bureaucracy under Gorbachev represented a narrow section of opinion. They were a group of 'liberal' intellectuals, who shared a number of common attitudes: a positive view of the West, concern with humanistic and civic values, greater openness and individual autonomy, greater emphasis upon the consumer and private initiative in the economy. In effect they were 'liberalizers' and 'Westernizers', rather than 'democratizers', preferring to graft Western civic and economic practices onto a more tolerant and participatory Soviet political system.

Demonopolization is not necessarily synonymous with democratization. Think tanks in the Soviet system rendered the system more pluralistic whilst simultaneously restricting the extent of this pluralism. There is some evidence to suggest that the hegemony enjoyed by a number of institutes after 1985 excluded voices and ideas from the policy process, restricting debate. What emerged was an elite of experts and intellectuals within the party and the institutes who shared a common set of norms and values, but who could not stem the tide of popular pressure for change unleashed during 1989. The think tanks in Soviet Russia did contribute to the process of democratization, but only in an indirect sense by promoting the end of the political and ideological monopolies of the CPSU and Marxism-Leninism. In the sphere of policy-making, they became forces for elitism and exclusion, marginalizing the citizenry and restricting the scope of debate.

In the post-Soviet period, while it is a little early to draw more than tentative conclusions, the same reservations must be applied. The old institutes and new research centres also seem to be institutionalizing these same tendencies of exclusion, elitism and expertism, as a coalition of business elites, analytical centres and key political figures emerges. The limitations on the political discourse of the transition process provided by this new coalition threatens to sustain one of the enduring divides in Russian history, between the rulers and the ruled, the elite and the *narod* (masses). The evolution of think tanks in Russia will undoubtedly play an important role in shaping the nature of Russian democracy.

Notes

The interviews conducted in Moscow in 1996 were funded by the School of Humanities, De Montfort University. Thanks also to Ed, for much advice and support.

1 The Department of Propaganda and Agitation had responsibility for the propagation of Marxism-Leninism in all spheres of life, as well as for the training and organization of all the propaganda and agitation workers in the party. The main function of the Department of Culture was to oversee and control the cultural institutes of the state apparatus. The main function of the Department of Science and Education was to control and supervise the scientific and educational institutions, and to place and train cadres.

2 The Academy of Sciences had a long history of relative autonomy under communism. It was the direct descendant of the Tsarist 'Russian Academy of Sciences',
   and was the only cultural organization which did not come under the direct control of the Commissariat of Enlightenment after the revolution (see Vucinich,
   1984: 91–122).
3 The information on the ISS came from an interview conducted with Valerie Mansourov, Deputy Director of the Institute in Moscow on 9 July 1996.
4 Conservative figures were appointed to head the three main sections of the CC
   Department of Ideology which exercised oversight of the work of the Academy of
   Sciences (via censorship, recruitment, funding and so on). The Science and Education department was headed by Trapeznikov, the Department of Culture by V.
   F. Shauro. The Propaganda Department remained without a Director until 1972
   when Alexander Yakovlev was appointed. He was removed on spurious grounds,
   and the department also became a Stalinist stronghold.
5 The *nomenklatura* was the ruling elite in the USSR. It was a system of two lists:
   one list of all the important positions in the system, one of all the politically reli-
   able individuals eligible to fill these posts. Needless to say it carried great privileges with it.
6 Both Bovin and Burlatsky had been members of Andropov's consultant grouping,
   along with Arbatov, the head of ISKAN.
7 There are many others. This list is merely a snapshot at the time of writing
   (December 1996).

References

Antonenko, Oksana (1996) 'New Russian Analytical Centers and Their Role in Polit-
   ical Decision-Making', *Strengthening Democratic Institutions Project*, Cambridge,
   MA, Harvard University Press.
Arbatov, Georgii (1992) *The System*, New York, Times Books.
Bruckner, Scott (1996) 'Policy Research Centres in Russia: Tottering Towards an
   Uncertain Future', *NIRA Review*, Summer, www.edi.org, pp. 1–4.
Burlatsky, Fyodor (1988) 'Posle Stalina' [After Stalin], *Novyi Mir*, 10: pp. 5–80.
Checkel, Jeff (1993) 'Ideas, Institutions and the Gorbachev Foreign Policy Revolu-
   tion', *World Politics*, 45: 271–300.
Cobb, Tyrus W. (1981) 'National Security Perspectives of Soviet Think Tanks', *Prob-
   lems of Communism*, November–December: 51–9.
Cohen, Stephen and vanden Heuvel, Katrina (eds) (1989) *Voices of Glasnost': Inter-
   views with Gorbachev's Reformers*, New York, W. W. Norton.
Day, Alan J. (1993) *Think Tanks: An International Directory*, London, Longman.
Dror, Y. (1984) 'Required Breakthroughs in Think Tanks', *Policy Sciences*, 16:
   199–225.
Garrard, John and Garrard, Carol (1990) *Inside The Soviet Writers' Union*, New
   York, I. B. Tauris.
Hough, Jerry and Fainsod, Merle (1979) *How the Soviet Union is Governed*, Cam-
   bridge, MA, Harvard University Press.

Kislov, Aleksandr (1996) Interview at Institute of Peace Research/IMEMO, Moscow, July.

Lewin, Moshe (1988) *The Gorbachev Phenomenon*, London, Hutchinson Radius.

Mansourov, Valerie (1996) Interview in Institute of Sociological Studies, Moscow, July.

Markwick, Roger D. (1994) 'Catalyst of Historiography, Marxism and Dissidence: The Sector of Methodology of the Institute of History, Soviet Academy of Sciences, 1964–68', *Europe–Asia Studies*, 46(4): 579–96.

Parsons, Wayne (1996) *Public Policy: An Introduction to the Theory and Practice of Policy Analysis*, Aldershot, Edward Elgar.

Quigley, Kevin F. F. (1995) 'Think Tanks in Newly Democratic Eastern Europe', in Jeffrey Telgarsky and Makiko Ueno (eds), *Think Tanks in a Democratic Society: An Alternative Voice*, Washington DC, Urban Institute.

Remnick, David (1993) *Lenin's Tomb*, London, Penguin.

Shimotomai, Nobuo (1990) 'Perestroika, Glasnost' and Society' in Tsuyoshi Hasegawa and Alex Pravda (eds), *Perestroika: Soviet Domestic and Foreign Policies*, London, Sage Publications.

Shalpentokh, Vladimir (1990) *Soviet Intellectuals and Political Power*, London, I. B. Tauris.

Shubin, Vladimir (1996) Interview at Institute of African Studies, Moscow, July.

Vucinich, Alexander (1984) *Empire of Knowledge*, Berkeley, University of California Press.

Wallace, William (1994) 'Between Two Worlds. Think Tanks and Foreign Policy', in Christopher Hill and Pamela Benhoff (eds), *Two Worlds of International Relations: Academics, Practictioners and the Trade in Ideas*, London, Routledge and the London School of Economics.

Waller, Michael (1988) 'What Is to Count as Ideology in Soviet Politics?', in Stephen White and Alex Pravda (eds), *Ideology and Soviet Politics*, Basingstoke, Macmillan.

Weiss, Carol H. (1990) 'The Uneasy Partnership Endures: Social Science and Government', in S. Brooks and A.-G. Gagnon (eds), *Social Scientists, Policy and the State*, New York, Praeger.

World of Learning, The (1994) 'Russia and the Former States of the USSR', London, Europa Publications.

Yakubovsky, Vladimir B. (1995) 'A Short History of Russian Think Tanks', *NIRA Review*, Winter: 35–40.

Ideas and influence

Introduction

The more complex the problems which governments face, the more developed their societies and economies, the greater their need for advice and for intelligent criticism. The more uncertainty over policy choices, the greater the demand not only for information and analysis but also for alternative concepts and ideas. The growth of think tanks throughout the developed world since World War Two, which this volume has described, has paralleled a geometric increase in the scale and complexities of government, flowing from the transformation and internationalization of production; the continuing revolutions in technology and in communications; the expansion of the welfare functions of government and the consequent rise in the proportion of national income taken in taxation and redistributed through state expenditure; the shift in the demographic balance between young and old; the decline of rural commmunities and the growth of conurbations, and the decreasing ability of national governments to manage their domestic societies and economies without active co-operation with other public and private actors.

All government depends upon ideas as well as upon administration and the enforcement of order – as theorists from Adam Ferguson and Karl Marx to contemporary social scientists agree. Religious or secular governing ideologies, the intellectual hegemony of concepts and assumptions acceptable to the elite, the conventional wisdom of 'practical' policy-makers, all impose barriers to the introduction of new ideas onto the policy agenda. The traditional role of intellectuals was as priests and prophets: priests justifying and explaining the exercise of temporal power, prophets warning of the misuse of power or denouncing its abuse.

The modern role is not dissimilar, though more diverse. Think tanks perhaps best operate at the edge of the conventional wisdom, expressing their ideas in language sufficiently familiar to those in power to be acceptable but sufficiently novel to make them reconsider their working assumptions. But – as this book has made clear – there are established institutes which see their role as one primarily of reinforcing governing ideas, and others imbued with prophetic zeal to attack the intellectual hegemony of received opinion: to 'blow up the consensus' (as one of the intellectuals of the British New Right described their aims). Think tanks deal in 'soft power' (the term coined by Joseph Nye, though drawing on Gramsci and others before him): in shaping policy agendas, in challenging the language and terminology of public debate, in redefining the mental maps of policy-makers. These are all subtle processes, the workings of which are harder to trace than the direct impact of hard political bargaining, but which set the terms within which political bargaining is conducted in modern political systems.

Religion and ritual provided legitimating concepts for the simple order of pre-modern societies. Modernizing states manufactured more self-conscious ideologies: state religions communicated through state churches, national myths cultivated by licensed intellectuals. But they also needed to learn concepts and techniques from their competitors, and to teach them to their officials and entrepreneurs. Eighteenth-century Russia, late nineteenth-century Japan, both invested heavily in learning from more advanced economies and societies while attempting at the same time to filter out dangerous foreign ideas as their more acceptable elements were introduced to the domestic policy debate. Modernizing Asian societies such as Korea, Malaysia and China have attempted in different ways to follow the same pattern: licensing intellectuals to work within certain limits, while using such concepts as 'Asian values' to signal that there remained clear differences between the outer limits of acceptable conventional wisdom within their states and what might be acceptable ideas within other political systems.

Nineteenth-century Russia educated an elite to carry forward this process of modernization, only to experience the emergence of an 'intelligentsia' radically opposed to the orthodoxy of the regime. Post-revolutionary Soviet Russia struggled with similar contradictions, swinging in cycles from cautious encouragement of policy debate to purges of heretical intellectuals. Mark Sandle traces its ambivalent dependence from the 1950s onwards on the licensed intellectuals within the Academy of Sciences for informed ideas and alternative policies. Japan and Malaysia, as the chapters in this volume argue, have benefited from their more consensual traditional cultures in avoiding open antagonism between a Westernizing intelligentsia and a modernizing state, though at some cost also in avoiding open and informed debate about difficult policy choices.

The countries which led the way towards modernization and industrialization – above all Britain and the United States – followed a different path. Enlightenment Liberalism both promised social and economic progress through the application of reason to the problems of government and expounded a philosophy of government by civil society and free expression. The first generation of think tanks, and the university social science faculties which grew up alongside them, were firmly rooted within this liberal intellectual hegemony. The problems which the new industrial and urban societies faced at the end of the nineteenth century were to be tackled through the collection of statistics, the analysis of trends, and the application of critical intelligence informed by comparison with relevant foreign models. The Fabian Society and the founders of the London School of Economics shared this view, as did the Brookings Institution and the Woodrow Wilson School. Those who shaped these early think tanks, as the chapters on Britain and the USA show, believed in a liberal consensus: that reasonable and educated men (they *were*, with very few exceptions, all men) presented with reasoned arguments based on accumulated 'facts' would reach conclusions which differed only marginally from each other.

Enlightened men in France and Germany did not have the same luxury of limited government within a settled state, within which to develop a consensual view of the relationship between public intellectuals and government. The state, its relationship with society and economy, its boundaries and their defensibility, all remained open to challenge. The French intellectual tradition, from the Dreyfus affair to the 1970s, was marked by the split between those who supported and those who opposed the state. The experience of defeat in 1940 reinforced among those who set out to rebuild postwar France the Saint-Simonian idea that it was the duty of intellectuals to dedicate their skills and critical faculties to the task of modernizing the state. Max Weber delivered his classic lectures on the different vocations of intellectuals and politicians in the turbulent aftermath of the defeat of 1918. Those of his students and colleagues who attempted to follow his liberal prescription, as those around them committed themselves to competing ideologies, were able to apply them successfully only in exile in Britain or America after the Weimar Republic had collapsed.

Think tanks and political systems

It will be clear from this volume to every reader that the political structure and culture of different states plays a crucial role in shaping the relationship between intellectuals, intellectual institutions, and government. The strength or weakness of state structures, the primary or secondary role of political parties, the degree of public or private ownership of the economy, the openness – or resistance – of both government itself and of elites to new ideas, all set the context within which think tanks and related bodies operate. The distinctive patterns of interaction which mark the policy debate in different political systems, as the chapters above have noted, still bear the marks left by evolution or revolution over the past two hundred years or more.

It therefore makes little sense to define a 'think tank' too precisely. The functions which think tanks fulfil – research relevant to public policy, promotion of public debate, the questioning of the conventional wisdom, the formulation and dissemination of alternative concepts and policy agendas – can be fulfilled in many ways, under different constraints. The role of the CNRS in France, as a state-funded organization set up to examine social and economic trends in France and abroad from a longer-term and more detached perspective than responsible policy-makers themselves, is in some ways comparable to that of the Academy of Sciences in the pre-1989 Soviet Union. Both have operated within tighter limits of acceptable dissent from governmental orthodoxy than privately funded bodies. But so have such contract-research bodies as the RAND Corporation and the Hudson Institute, and the formally autonomous but publicly funded economic institutes which shape the debate on economic policy in Germany.

At the opposite end of this wide spectrum, partisan think tanks shade into campaigning groups and lobbies. Conference Boards research questions of interest to their business sponsors from a business perspective. Environmental institutes start from the premise that environmental issues deserve a much higher policy priority than governments have yet been willing to accept. Pressure groups in democratic systems establish 'policy institutes' to lend added weight to the arguments they wish to make – and in some countries to take advantage of differences in tax status between research and campaigning activities. Political parties similarly dignify their development of policy by working through formally autonomous centres and institutes, using them to float ideas which do not immediately commit the party leadership or to conduct internal debates among different tendencies. Contract research in turn shades into political consultancy, for governments (and business lobbies) which prefer to contract out long-term or expert studies rather than conduct them 'in-house'.

The evolution of think tanks and of the broader networks of policy intellectuals in different states is also affected by the particular domestic context: the strength or weakness of political parties and of their own policy-making machinery, the role and professional staffing of parliaments and their committees, the prestige and research ethos of universities. The chapters on France and the USA emphasize the link between the weakening of mass parties and of their ability to develop policy and the emergence of independent groups and institutes – often associated with particular leaders or tendencies within parties – to assume the agenda-setting role which mass parties once claimed to perform. In Germany, in contrast, the entrenchment of political parties in the political structure after World War Two, and the provision of generous state subsidies to the party foundations, gives parties themselves and their affiliated think tanks still a much larger role in the policy debate.

Agencies such as the Congressional Budget Office or the (British) National Audit Office are effectively autonomous of government, feeding expert analysis and informed criticism directly into the political debate. The strength of the US Congress within the American political system, the constant demand of its members, its committees and their substantial staffs for new ideas, offers an open market for the think tank world of Washington. The weakness of the Japanese Diet in debating policy choices leaves critical intellectuals there dependent on government agencies for access and influence. The weakness both of parliament and of parties in Fifth Republic France (together with the strength of the state and the weakness of the private sector) has left French politicians dependent upon the 'groupuscules' of political clubs which Fieschi and Gaffney have described.

Particular styles of national intellectual recruitment and advancement are also reflected in the different patterns of influence described in this volume. It is impossible to understand the peculiarities of the policy debate in France without taking into account the role of the Grandes Écoles in shaping the French elite. Those who are acknowledged as the brightest in the highly-competitive French educational system are recruited into the service of the state; those who find themselves as researchers within the Centre National de la Recherche Scientifique or teachers in the universities do not rise so high in this pyramid of educational achievement. The slow development of centres of expertise and advice outside the state, let alone outside Paris, needs little further explanation. Anglo-Saxon universities grew up alongside weaker states, as autonomous centres of prestige and expertise, from which intellectual advisors may circulate through think tanks into government and back as respected members of a broad elite. Italian professors – as Radaelli and Martini note – have had greater prestige than a corrupt political establishment, but lacked a strong enough basis for independent advice within overstretched universities; so lending their prestige to the development of think tanks committed to economic and social reform.

Waves of past think tank development – and for the future?

The luxuriant growth of think tanks in the United States allows the observer to identify all of these variants. The proliferation of private foundations, the ease with which charitable donations for public purposes can be set against tax, provide a firm financial base for intellectual diversity; availability of public funding from competing agencies within government and Congress widens opportunities further. The division of powers and the openness of policy negotiation within Washington which this promotes gives easy access to those who wish to influence the debate, while encouraging policy protagonists to look around for supporting arguments to help press their case. No other political system offers such an open and dispersed policy debate within which think tanks can operate, nor such diverse and generous sources of public and private finance. Perhaps only in Brussels, in the permanent negotiations within dispersed political institutions which characterize European policy-making, can we discern the development of a similar pattern: of policy research contracted out, of lobbies and political consultancies, and of the development of think tanks oriented to the European Union's policy agenda both in Brussels and in the different member states.

Cross-national influence in the evolution of think tanks has therefore flowed far more often from the USA to other countries than the reverse. The formation of the Council on Foreign Relations owed much to the initiative of British participants in the 1919 Versailles Peace Conference. The Centre for Strategic and International Studies in Washington, as Abelson notes, was partly modelled on the new Institute for Strategic Studies in London. The party foundations in Germany provided the model for the National Endowment for Democracy – though this American derivative operates primarily outside the USA in working with other political parties, rather than feeding ideas into the debate within Washington. But for the most part it is the American example which others seek to follow: debating the case for a 'British Brookings', setting up a Japanese National Institute for Research Advancement to encourage and sponsor comparable policy research, setting up national institutes of international affairs or economic development to feed into the transnational network of policy elites through which national governments attempt to influence each others' debates – and through which linked groups of intellectuals in different countries attempt to concert their efforts to influence the international agenda.

How far should we therefore assume that the waves of development of American think tanks described above provide a pattern which other countries are likely to follow? The country chapters, as we have noted, have underlined the significance of distinctive political cultures and institutions in shaping (or stunting) the growth of think tanks. Yet they have also identified the common pressures to which *all* modern and modernizing political systems – democratic, semi-democratic and authoritarian – respond.

In mid-nineteenth-century Britain, then the world's most advanced economy and society, the business of government remained simple enough for a minister to spend a long summer away from his office, and for an MP to gather the information he needed from the library of his club before he walked over to the House of Commons. By the end of the nineteenth century, the advance of technology and the involvement of the state in economic management and social reform required much more detailed knowledge to inform policy-making. The first wave of think tanks, along with the development of economics, statistics and the other social sciences in universities and the growth of official committees of enquiry and royal commissions, responded to this demand.

The second wave of think tanks grew out of the experience of the two world wars, in which governments successfully harnessed intellectual expertise to mobilize the resources of their societies. Optimism in the West, and orthodoxy in the East, carried this wave through the period of post-war reconstruction to the late 1950s and early 1960s, without stopping to question the models of economic and social development within which their prescriptions were formulated. The third wave of think tanks – both in the democratic West and in the authoritarian Soviet Union – swelled up as policy elites lost confidence in their underlying models, and intellectuals allied with counter-elites to challenge their conventional wisdom. The fourth wave has taken this process of dissensus further, with partisan advisors allied to political leaders fighting for intellectual hegemony.

In Soviet Russia, in Japan, in Malaysia, in France, powerful state authorities have attempted to license degrees of dissent without opening the door to uncontrolled free-thinking. In the Anglo-Saxon world – increasingly in Australia and Canada as well as in the USA and the UK – the diversity of think tank development is now well beyond the discreet limitations to acceptable ideas which elites in power would prefer to set. Japan in one sense provides a test case for future think tank development, as a society and economy which has successfully modernized without entirely abandoning the limits to intellectual dissent which marked traditional and modernizing systems.

Can the Japanese economy and the country's social and political structures successfully adapt to the shift from an industrial to a post-industrial society without opening its political elite to the stimulus of contending concepts which the third and fourth waves of think tanks have provided in Anglo-Saxon countries? Can developing states such as Malaysia – and Singapore, and behind them China – maintain the delicate balance between intellectual political orthodoxy and openness to expert criticism and new ideas which they have so far successfully managed? That will depend partly on how skilled their domestic think tanks are in speaking truth to power without bitterly offending those in power, partly on how much access those in power are willing to grant their licensed intellectuals.

The business of government at the end of the twentieth century continues to grow more complex. The over-burdened policy-maker, as he or she dashes from domestic bargaining to international negotiation, struggles to cope with the mass of information needed and the conceptual frameworks within which to analyse the information which flows in. The critic of government, in parliament, in business, in party hierarchy, pressure group or newspaper office, searches for informed criticism from a preferred alternative perspective. New issues crowd onto the public agenda, from global warming to genetic engineering, from medical ethics in public health provision to the utilization and control of information technology, on which generalist policy-makers must turn to the contending recommendations of expert advisors before they can grasp the choices to be made. The political demand for the services which think tanks can offer is thus likely to increase further, in all highly developed industrial and post-industrial societies. It is therefore likely that the supply of institutionalized expertise, packaged in different ways to fit the requirements of political debate and policy-makers will continue to grow in response.

Index

Academy of Sciences (Soviet Union) 204, 208, 211, 212, 215-17, 221, 224, 226
Access Economics 148, 160
ADELS 54, 55
advocacy coalitions 15, 60, 72-9, 83-4, 91, 92, 94-5, 98, 100, 102, 104, 157
advocacy tanks 24, 25, 113-14, 121
AEI 12, 24-5, 90, 108, 116, 119, 122, 123
AIIA 145, 146, 149, 150, 151, 153, 158, 160, 161
AILES 54, 55
AIPP 147, 148, 149
Andropov, I. 205, 208, 209, 211, 212
Anwar, Ibrahim 173–4, 182, 184
ASI 8, 22, 25, 32, 33, 35, 61, 94
Asia Society 148
Atlas Foundation 9, 147
Australia Institute 147, 149, 150
AustralAsia Centre 147, 159, 160

Bentham, Jeremy 27, 34
Blair, Tony 37
Brookings Institute 13, 24, 26, 30, 54, 59, 65, 90, 94, 108, 109, 110, 111, 113, 116, 119, 120, 122, 123, 128, 145, 194, 225

Caledon Institute 129, 130, 131
Canadian Centre for Policy Alternatives 131, 134, 139

Carnegie Endowment (and allied bodies) 4, 111, 113, 116, 119
Carter, Jimmy 114–15, 116
CATO Institute 94, 116, 117, 119, 120
CCSD 128, 129, 130, 131, 133, 134, 137, 141, 142
CCF 110
C. D. Howe Research Institute 128, 129, 130, 131, 134, 135, 137, 138, 148
CEDA 145, 146, 149, 151, 152, 156, 157, 158, 160, 161
Censis 59, 60, 61, 62, 63, 65, 66, 69, 76
Centro Einaudi 61
CER 59, 60, 65, 76, 77
CFR 110, 116, 119, 120
Chadwick, Edwin 27
Chatham House see RIIA
CIEP 129, 130, 131, 132, 134, 137
CIS 146, 147, 149, 150, 151, 152, 156, 157, 158, 160, 161
Club de l'Horage 54, 55–6
CNRS 53, 54, 226, 227
Cockett, Richard 32–4
COHA 123
Conference Board (Canada) 5, 128, 130, 131, 132, 133, 137, 139, 141, 142
contract research 24–5, 60, 112–13, 117, 133, 136, 142, 168, 226
CPR 167, 168, 169, 172

CPRN 129, 130, 131, 132, 137, 138, 139
CPRS 27, 31
CPS 8, 14, 22, 25, 26, 31, 32, 33, 35, 152
CSSP 29
CTF 128, 130, 131, 132, 133, 141
CWF 128, 131, 134, 137, 138, 139

Dahrendorf, Ralf 34
Delors, Jacques 48, 51
Demos 22, 35, 146
DGAP 84, 89, 97, 103
Dicey, A. V. 27, 33, 34
DIW 90, 97, 99

EAC 30
ECC 129, 137
economic liberalism 9, 10, 17, 21, 25, 27, 31, 33, 35, 36, 37, 55, 61, 85, 92, 94, 117, 129, 145, 146, 147, 150, 152, 155–9, 161, 173, 183, 224
EKO 206, 208, 212
elite theory 13–14, 155–62
ENA 44, 58
epistemic communities 15–16, 43
European Union 5, 62, 63, 69, 74, 76, 78, 228
Evatt Foundation 147, 148, 149, 150, 152, 153, 158, 159, 160, 163

Fabian Society 21, 22, 28, 29, 32, 34, 48, 145, 225
FES 93, 95, 98, 100
Feulner, Edwin 113–14, 122
FNS 94, 95, 98
Fondazione Agnelli 60, 65, 66, 76
Formez 65, 67
Frankfurter Institute 85, 94
Fraser Institute 129, 131, 133, 134, 135, 137

Gingrich, N. 114, 120
Gorbachev, M. 12, 211, 212, 213, 214
GRECE 54, 55–6

Green movements 50, 85, 91, 153

Hawke, Bob 147, 153
Hayek, Friedrich 32, 33
Heath, Edward 31
Heritage Foundation 12, 14, 15, 25, 59, 61, 65, 107, 113, 114, 117, 119, 120, 122, 148
Hoover Institution 4, 12, 14, 54, 108, 110, 111, 120, 122, 123, 194
H. R. Nicholls Society 147, 149, 156
Hudson Institute 112, 116, 226
Hume, Joseph 27
HWWA 90, 97, 99
Hyde, John 148, 158, 161

ICARE 55
IDS 168, 169, 170, 173, 177–8, 183, 184
IEA 22, 31, 32, 35, 94, 147
IFO 90, 97, 99
IFS 5, 25
IfW 90, 94, 99
IISS 9
IKD 168, 169, 180, 182, 183, 184
IKIM 168, 169, 173, 180–3, 184
IMEMO 206, 210, 212, 213, 214, 215, 216, 218, 219
IMF 62
INMIND 168, 169, 170
INSAP 167, 169, 178–9
INSEE 53
Institute for Contemporary Studies 117
Institute for Policy Studies (US) 25, 113, 115
Institute of Pacific Relations 146
Institute on Governance 129, 130, 131, 137, 139
Internet 120, 137
IPA 15, 145, 146, 147, 148, 149, 150, 152, 153, 156, 157, 158, 160, 161
IPPR 22, 35, 147
IRPP 128, 129, 131, 132, 134, 137, 138, 139, 140
IRS 60, 62, 64, 65, 66, 76
ISEAS 3, 4
ISIS 168, 169, 173, 174, 175, 184–5

ISKAN 206, 210, 213, 219
ISS 206, 207, 209
IW 86–7, 99, 100, 103
IWG 85, 92
IWH 90, 97

Jenkins, Roy 29
Joseph, Keith 33, 36

KAS 93, 98, 100
Keating, Paul 153
Keynes, John Maynard (and
    Keynesianism) 11, 32, 35, 155, 156,
    157, 162
Kruschev, N. 204, 205, 206, 208

Lloyd George, David 29
LSE 28, 34, 225

MacDonald, Ramsay 30
Macmillan, Harold 30
Mahathir, Mohamed 8, 170, 171–4,
    178, 179, 180, 181, 184
'Malaysia Incorporated' 166–7, 173,
    176, 183
marxism 13, 14, 15, 155, 156, 223
Mayntz, Renate 82–4
Menzies, Robert 152
MIER 168, 169, 171, 175–6, 184
Mitre Foundation 24
Mitsubishi Research Institute 195,
    198
Mitterand, F. 51–2, 57
Molesworth, Sir William 27
Mont Pelerin Society 9, 95
MSRC 168, 169, 180, 184

NBER 5, 13, 116
NCF 110
NEDC 29
'New Economic Policy' (Malaysia)
    170–2, 174
'New Right' see economic liberalism
Nicholson, E. Max 29
NIESR 22, 24, 29, 30, 37, 145, 148
NIRA 195–8, 228
Nomisma 59, 60, 63, 65, 66, 76

Nomura Research Institute 195

OECD 62
Oeko-Institute 85, 91, 102

PEP 22, 29, 32
'perestroika' 15, 211–14
Philosophic Radicals 27, 28, 33
Pirie, Madsen 32
Place, Francis 27
pluralism 1–2, 10, 14, 160–2, 181
Politeia (Italy) 61, 66
poll tax 33
PPI 14, 107, 120
pressure groups 3–4, 16, 25, 36, 41, 45,
    85–6, 113, 226
Progress and Freedom Association
    114–15, 116
PSI 22, 25, 29, 35, 37
Public Opinion 3, 17, 26–7, 30, 32, 33,
    34, 37, 69–70, 72, 90–1, 93, 100,
    108, 119, 120, 134, 139–40, 155,
    157, 162, 181, 193–4, 212, 215
Public Policy Forum 129, 130, 132, 137

RAND Corporation 4, 16, 23, 24, 88,
    111, 112, 113, 115, 122, 194, 226
Reagan, Ronald 121–3
Redwood, John 35
Ricci, David 23, 24, 26
RIIA 9, 22, 24, 29, 89, 145
Rothschild, Victor 27, 31
Round Table 146
Russell Sage Foundation 110
RWI 90, 97, 99

St James Ethics Centre 147–8, 149, 159
SAU 25
SDI 169, 170
SMF 22, 35–6
SWP 84, 86, 88–9, 96, 97, 99, 102,
    103
Sydney Institute 147, 149, 158, 159,
    160

Tasman Institute 147, 148, 149, 150,
    151, 156, 158, 160, 161

tax laws 6–7, 92, 114, 150–1, 192
Thatcher, Margaret 8, 14, 26, 31, 33,
    34, 35, 36, 152
Toynbee, Arnold 28
Trade Unions 8, 55, 86, 88, 89, 92, 94,
    96, 98–9, 129, 148, 159

'universities without students' 4, 24–5,
    31, 60, 84–9, 102, 104, 111
Urban Institute 24, 112, 113, 116

vanity tanks 36, 114–15
'Vision 2020' (Malaysia) 166–7, 170,

    175, 178, 179, 180, 181

Walter-Eucken Institute 85, 94
Wallace, William 31
Weaver, Kent 22, 25, 60, 108, 111, 117
Webb, Sydney 28, 34
WETtank 147, 149, 151, 158, 159,
    161, 163
Wiarda, Howard 121–2
Willetts, David 8, 35, 36
WRI 3
WSI 86, 94, 99, 100, 103
WZB 84